1 MONTH OF
FREE
READING

at
www.ForgottenBooks.com

By purchasing this book you are
eligible for one month membership to
ForgottenBooks.com, giving you
unlimited access to our entire
collection of over 1,000,000 titles via
our web site and mobile apps.

To claim your free month visit:
www.forgottenbooks.com/free186432

ISBN 978-0-484-79297-4
PIBN 10186432

LUTHER'S

EPISTLE SERMONS

EPIPHANY, EASTER AND PENTECOST

TRANSLATED WITH THE HELP OF OTHERS

BY

PROF. JOHN NICHOLAS LENKER, D. D.

AUTHOR OF "LUTHERANS IN ALL LANDS," TRANSLATOR OF
LUTHER'S WORKS INTO ENGLISH AND PRESIDENT OF
THE NATIONAL LUTHERAN LIBRARY ASSOCIATION

VOL. II.

(Volume VIII of Luther's Complete Works.)

THIRD THOUSAND

The Luther Press

MINNEAPOLIS, MINN., U. S. A.
1909.

Dedication

To All, Pastors and Laymen, who appreciate the true place of Luther's Writings in the Evangelization of Europe, and are interested in the Evangelization of the world, this volume of Easter and Pentecost Epistle Sermons of the English Luther is gratefully and prayerfully dedicated.

Foreword

The Evangelization of the World is being accomplished more rapidly than we think. Three mighty movements are constantly at work—Reformation, Heathen Missions and Emigration or Colonization. By the Reformation Europe was evangelized; by Heathen Missions Asia and Africa are being evangelized and by Emigration or Colonization North and South America and Australia have been to a large extent evangelized. In "Lutherans In All Lands," published in 1893, and in the introduction to the volume on St. Peter's Epistles of the English Luther, we emphasized the relation of the Evangelical-Lutheran church and of Luther's writings to the evangelization of the world through these three movements. In view of the recent marvelous growth in interest in Heathen Missions and the false ideas about Luther's relation to this theme, the following may be in place here in this volume of Easter and Pentecost sermons:

The Christian religion being preëminently missionary the Reformation of the Christian Church would necessarily be missionary. Protestant missions began with Protestantism.

Herzog's Encyclopedia says: "Luther himself already seizes every opportunity offered by a text of the Divine Word in order to remind believers of the distress of the Heathen and Turks and earnestly urges them to pray in their behalf, and to send out missionaries to them. In accord with him all the prominent theologians and preachers of his day, and of the succeeding period inculcated the missionary duty of the Church. Many also of the Evangelical princes cherished the work with Christian love and zeal."

Luther's interest in the work of true evangelization is seen in the name he designedly chose for the church of his followers. He did not call it Protestant nor Lutheran, but conscientiously insisted upon it being called the Evangelical, or in plain Anglo-Saxon, the Gospel church, the Evangelizing church. Because of Luther's emphasis on the word evangelical there are properly speaking no Lutheran, but only Evangelical-Lutheran churches. He is the evangelist of Protestantism in the true sense.

Of the library of 110 volumes of which Luther is the author, 85 of them treat of the Bible and expound its pure evangelical teachings in commentaries, sermons and catechetical writings. He popularized the word evangelical. With his tongue and pen he labored incessantly for the evangelization of Europe. That Europe is evangelized is due more to his labors and writings than to those of any other. What those writings did for Europe they may do, and we believe, will do, for the world in a greater or less degree.

3

The greatest evangelist of Europe has a God-given place in the evangelization of the world. His most evalgelical classics should be translated into all the dialects of earth as soon as the Bible is given to the people in their native tongue.

Dr. Warneck says: "By the Reformation the christianizing of a large part of Europe was first completed, and so far it may be said to have carried on a mission work at home on an extensive scale." Further he says: "The Reformation certainly did a great indirect service to the cause of missions to the heathen, as it not only restored the true substance of missionary preaching by its earnest proclamation of the Gospel, but also brought back the whole work of missions on Apostolic lines. Luther rightly combats, as Plitt insists, 'the secularizing of missionary work.'"

In explaining the 117th Psalm Luther says: "If all the heathen shall praise God, he must first be their God. Shall he be their God? Then they must know him and believe in him, and put away all idolatry, since God can not be praised with idolatrous lips or with unbelieving hearts. Shall they believe. Then they must first hear his Word and by it receive the Holy Spirit, who cleanses and enlightens their heart through faith. Are they to hear his Word? Then preachers must be sent who shall declare to them the Word of God." So in his familiar hymn, "Es wolle Gott uns gnaedig sein."

> "And Jesus Christ, His saving strength
> To Gentiles to make known,
> That thee, O God, may thank and praise
> The Gentiles everywhere."

In commenting on the words of the Second Psalm, "Ask of me and I will give thee the heathen for thine inheritance," Luther says: "Christ, therefore, being upon earth and appointed king upon Mount Zion, receives the Gentiles who were then promised unto him. The words "of me" are not spoken without a particular meaning. They are to show that this kingdom and this inheritance of the Gentiles are conferred on Christ, not by men, nor in any human way, but by God, that is, spiritually."

All who retain the good old custom of the fathers in reading Luther's Postil sermons on the Gospel and Epistle texts for each Sunday know what deep missionary thoughts are found in the sermons for Epiphany, Ascension Day and Pentecost.

In one sermon for Ascension Day on "Go ye into all the world and preach the Gospel to the whole creation," we read, "these words of the Sovereign Ruler commission these poor beggars to go forth and proclaim this new message, not in one city or country only, but in all the world."

For the history of the writing of these sermons the reader is referred to volumes 10, 11, 12 and 13 of the Gospel sermons of Luther's works in English.

The German text will be readily found in the 12th volume of the Walch and of the St. Louis Walch editions, and in the 8th volume of the Erlangen edition of Luther's works.

Due acknowledgment is hereby made of aid received from the translation of Pastor Ambrose Henkel, and published in 1869, at New Market, Virginia. Also to Pastor C. B. Gohdes, for comparing the manuscript from the Third Sunday before Lent with the German text and making valuable improvements.

J. N. LENKER.

Home for Young Women,
Minneapolis, Minn., March 22, 1909.
4

Contents

SUMMER PART OF THE EPISTLE POSTIL.

First Sunday After Epiphany

Text: Romans 12, 1-6.

1 I beseech you therefore, brethren, by the mercies of God, to present your bodies a living sacrifice, holy, acceptable to God, which is your spiritual service. 2 And be not fashioned according to this world: but be ye transformed by the renewing of your mind, that ye may prove what is the good and acceptable and perfect will of God. 3 For I say, through the grace that was given me, to every man that is among you, not to think of himself more highly than he ought to think; but so to think as to think soberly, according as God hath dealt to each man a measure of faith. 4 For even as we have many members in one body, and all the members have not the same office: 5 so we, who are many, are one body in Christ, and severally members one of another. And having gifts differing according to the grace that was given to us.

THE FRUITS OF FAITH.

1. In the preceding sermons I have treated sufficiently of faith and love; and of crosses and afflictions, the promoters of hope. Faith, love and affliction bound the Christian's life. It is unnecessary that I should further discourse on these topics. As they—or anything pertaining to the life of the Christian—present themselves, reference may be had to those former postils. It is my purpose now briefly to make plain that the sum of all divine doctrine is simply Jesus Christ, as we have often heard.

2. This epistle lesson treats not of faith, but of the fruits

of faith—love, unity, patience, self-denial, etc. Among these
fruits, the apostle considers first the discipline of the body—
the mortification of evil lusts. He handles the subject here
in a manner wholly unlike his method in other epistles. In
Galatians he speaks of crucifying the flesh with its lusts; in
Hebrews and Colossians, of putting off the old man and
mortifying the members on earth. Here he mentions presenting the body as a sacrifice; he dignifies it by the loftie*
and most sacred terms. Why does he so?

First, by making the terms glorious, he would the m*.
emphatically urge us to yield this fruit of faith. The whole
world regards the priest's office—his service and his dignity
—as representing the acme of nobility and exaltation; and
so it truly does. Now, if one would be a priest and exalted
before God, let him set about this work of offering up his
body to God; in other words, let him be humble, let him be
nothing in the eyes of the world.

3. I will let every man decide for himself the difference
between the outward priesthood of dazzling character and
the internal, spiritual priesthood. The first is confined to a
very few individuals; the second, Christians commonly
share. One was ordained of men, independently of the Word
of God; the other was established through the Word,
irrespective of human devices. In that, the skin is besmeared with material oil; in this, the heart is internally
anointed with the Holy Spirit. That applauds and extols
its works; this proclaims and magnifies the grace of God,
and his glory. That does not offer up the body with its
lusts, but rather fosters the evil desires of the flesh; this
sacrifices the body and mortifies its lusts. The former permits the offering up to itself of gold and property, of honor,
of idleness and pleasure, and of all manner of lust on earth;
the latter foregoes these things and accepts only the reverse
of homage. That again sacrifices Christ in its awful perver-
sions; this, satisfied with the atonement once made by
Christ, offers up itself with him and in him, by making
similar sacrifices. In fact, the two priesthoods accord about
as well as Christ and Barabbas, as light and darkness, as

God and the world. As little as smearing and shaving were factors in Christ's priesthood, so little will they thus procure for anyone the Christian priesthood. Yet Christ, with all his Christians, is priest. "Thou art a priest for ever after the order of Melchizedek." Ps 110, 4. The Christian priesthood will not admit of appointment. The priest is not made. He must be born a priest; must inherit his office. I refer to ˙ᴇ new birth—the birth of water and the Spirit. Thus all ⌐istians become priests, children of God and co-heirs with ‿ᴜist the Most High Priest.

Ꝑ4. Men universally consider the title of priest glorious and honorable; it is acceptable to everyone. But the duties and the sacrifice of the office are rarely accepted. Men seem to be averse to these latter. The Christian priesthood costs life, property, honor, friends and all worldly things. It cost Christ the same on the holy cross. No man readily chooses death instead of life, and accepts pain instead of pleasure, loss instead of gain, shame rather than honor, enemies rather than friends, according to the example Christ set for us on the cross. And further, all this is to be endured, not for profit to one's self, but for the benefit of his neighbor and for the honor and glory of God. For so Christ offered up his body. This priesthood is a glorious one.

5. As I have frequently stated, the suffering and work of Christ is to be viewed in two lights: First, as grace bestowed on us, as a blessing conferred, requiring the exercise of faith on our part and our acceptance of the salvation offered. Second, we are to regard it an example for us to follow; we are to offer up ourselves for our neighbors' benefit and for the honor of God. This offering is the exercise of our love—distributing our works for the benefit of our neighbors. He who so does is a Christian. He becomes one with Christ, and the offering of his body is identical with the offering of Christ's body. This is what Peter calls offering sacrifices acceptable to God by Christ. He describes priesthood and offering in these words: "Ye also, as living stones, are built up a spiritual house, to be a holy priesthood, to offer up spiritual sacrifices, acceptable to God

through Jesus Christ." 1 Pet 2, 5.

6. Peter says "spiritual sacrifices," but Paul says our bodies are to be offered up. While it is true that the body is not spirit, the offering of it is called a spiritual sacrifice because it is freely sacrificed through the Spirit, the Christian being uninfluenced by the constraints of the Law or the fear of hell. Such motives, however, sway the ecclesiasts, who have heaped tortures upon themselves by undergoing fasts, uncomfortable clothing, vigils, hard beds and other vain and difficult performances, and yet failed to attain to this spiritual sacrifice. Rather, they have wandered the farther from it because of their neglect to mortify their old Adam-like nature. They have but increased in presumption and wickedness, thinking by their works and merits to raise themselves in God's estimation. Their penances were not intended for the mortification of their bodies, but as works meriting for them superior seats in heaven. Properly, then, their efforts may be regarded a carnal sacrifice of their bodies, unacceptable to God and most acceptable to the devil.

7. But spiritual sacrifices, Peter tells us, are acceptable to God; and Paul teaches the same (Rom 8, 13): "If by the Spirit ye put to death the deeds of the body, ye shall live." Paul speaks of mortifying through the Spirit; Peter, of a spiritual sacrifice. The offering must first be slain. Paul's thought is: "If ye mortify the deeds of the body in your individual, chosen ways, unprompted by the Spirit or your own heart, simply through fear of punishment, that mortification—that sacrifice—will be carnal; and ye shall not live, but die a death the more awful." The Spirit must mortify your deeds—spiritually it must be done; that is, with real enjoyment, unmoved by fear of hell, voluntarily, without expectation of meriting honor or reward, either temporal or eternal. This, mark you, is a spiritual sacrifice. However outward, gross, physical and visible a deed may be, it is altogether spiritual when wrought by the Spirit. Even eating and drinking are spiritual works if done through the Spirit. On the other hand, whatsoever is wrought through the flesh is carnal, no matter to what ex-

tent it may be a secret desire of the soul. Paul (Gal 5, 20) terms idolatry and heresies works of the flesh, notwithstanding they are invisible impulses of the soul.

8. In addition to this spiritual sacrifice—the mortifying of the deeds of the body—Peter mentions another, later on in the same chapter: "But ye are . . . . a royal priesthood . . . . that ye may show forth the excellencies of him who called you out of darkness into his marvelous light." Here Peter touches upon the preaching office, the real sacrificial office, concerning which it is said (Ps 50, 23), "Whoso offereth the sacrifice of thanksgiving glorifieth me." Preaching extols the grace of God. It is the offering of praise and thanks. Paul boasts (Rom 15, 16) that he sanctifies and offers the Gospel. But it is not our purpose to consider here this sacrifice of praise; though praise in the congregation may be included in the spiritual sacrifice, as we shall see. For he who offers his body to God also offers his tongue and his lips as instruments to confess, preach and extol the grace of God. On this topic, however, we shall speak elsewhere. Let us now consider the words of the text.

OUR SPIRITUAL SERVICE.

"I beseech you therefore, brethren."

9. Paul does not say, "I command you." He is preaching to those already godly Christians through faith in the new man; to hearers who are not to be constrained by commandments, but to be admonished. For the object is to secure voluntary renunciation of their old, sinful, Adam-like nature. He who will not cheerfully respond to friendly admonition is no Christian. And he who attempts by the restraints of law to compel the unwilling to renunciation, is no Christian preacher or ruler; he is but a worldly jailer.

"By the mercies of God."

10. A teacher of the Law enforces his restraints through threats and punishments. A preacher of grace persuades and incites by calling attention to the goodness and mercy of God. The latter does not desire works prompted by an unwilling spirit, or service that is not the expression of a cheerful heart. He desires that a joyous, willing spirit shall

incite to the service of God. He who cannot, by the gracious and lovely message of God's mercy so lavishly bestowed upon us in Christ, be persuaded in a spirit of love and delight to contribute to the honor of God and the benefit of his neighbor, is worthless to Christianity, and all effort is lost on him. How can one whom the fire of heavenly love and grace cannot melt, be rendered cheerfully obedient by laws and threats? Not human mercy is offered us, but divine mercy, and Paul would have us perceive it and be moved thereby.

"To present your bodies."

11. Many and various were the sacrifices of the Old Testament. But all were typical of this one sacrifice of the body, offered by Christ and his Christians. And there is not, nor can be, any other sacrifice in the New Testament. What more would one, or could one, offer than himself, all he is and all he has? When the body is yielded a sacrifice, all belonging to the body is yielded also. Therefore, the Old Testament sacrifices, with the priests and all the splendor, have terminated. How does the offering of a penny compare with that of the body? Indeed, such fragmentary patchwork scarcely deserves recognition as a sacrifice when the bodies of Christ and of his followers are offered.

Consequently, Isaiah may truly say that in the New Testament such beggarly works are loathsome compared to real and great sacrifices: "He that killeth an ox is as he that slayeth a man; he that sacrificeth a lamb, as he that breaketh a dog's neck; he that offereth an oblation, as he that offereth swine's blood; he that burneth frankincense, as he that blesseth an idol." Is 66, 3. Similarly, also: "What unto me is the multitude of your sacrifices? saith Jehovah: I have had enough of the burnt-offerings of rams, and the fat of fed beasts; and I delight not in the blood of bullocks, or of lambs, or of he-goats." Is 1, 11. Thus, in plain words, Isaiah rejects all other sacrifices in view of this true one.

12. Our blind leaders, therefore, have most wretchedly deceived the world by their mass-offerings, for they have forgotten this one real sacrifice. The mass may be celebrated

and at the same time the soul be not benefited, but rather injured. But the body cannot be offered without benefiting the soul. Under the New Testament dispensation, then, the mass cannot be a sacrifice, even were it ever one. For all the works, all the sacrifices of the New Testament, must be true and soul-benefiting. Otherwise they are not New Testament sacrifices. It is said (Ps 25, 10), "All the paths of Jehovah are lovingkindness and truth."

"A living sacrifice, holy, acceptable to God."

13. Paul here makes use of the three words "living," "holy" and "acceptable," doubtless to teach that the sacrifices of the Old Testament are repealed and the entire priesthood abolished. The Old Testament sacrifices consisted of bullocks, sheep and goats. To these life was not spared. For the sacrifice they were slain, burned, consumed by the priests. But the New Testament sacrifice is a wonderful offering. Though slain, it still lives. Indeed, in proportion as it is slain and sacrificed, does it live in vigor. "If by the Spirit ye put to death the deeds of the body, ye shall live." Rom 8, 13. "For ye died, and your life is hid with Christ in God." Col 3, 3. "And they that are of Christ Jesus have crucified the flesh with the passions and the lusts thereof." Gal 5, 24.

14. The word "living," then, is to be spiritually understood—as having reference to the life before God and not to the temporal life. He who keeps his body under and mortifies its lusts does not live to the world; he does not lead the life of the world. The world lives in its lusts, and according to the flesh; it is powerless to live otherwise. True, the Christian is bodily in the world, yet he does not live after the flesh. As Paul says (2 Cor 10, 3), "Though we walk in the flesh, we do not war according to the flesh"; and again (Rom 8, 1), "Who walk not after the flesh." Such a life is, before God, eternal, and a true, living sacrifice. Such mortification of the body and of its lusts, whether effected by voluntary discipline or by persecution, is simply an exercise in and for the life eternal.

15. None of the Old Testament sacrifices were holy—

except in an external and temporal sense—until they were consumed. For the life of the animal was but temporal and external previous to the sacrifice. But the "living sacrifice" Paul mentions is righteous before God, and also externally holy. "Holy" implies simply, being designed for the service and the honor of God, and employed of God. Hence we must here understand the word "holy" as conveying the thought that we let God alone work in us and we be simply his holy instruments. As said in First Corinthians 6, 19-20, "Your body is the temple of the Holy Ghost . . . and ye are not your own . . . therefore glorify God in your body, and in your spirit, which are God's." Again (Gal 6, 17), "I bear branded on my body the marks of Jesus." Now, he who performs a work merely for his own pleasure and to his own honor, profanes his sacrifice. So also do they who by their works seek to merit reward from God, whether temporal or eternal. The point of error is, they are not yet a slain sacrifice. The sacrifice cannot be holy unless it first lives; that is, unless it is slain before God, and slain in its own consciousness, and thus does not seek its own honor and glory.

16. The Old Testament sacrifices were not in themselves acceptable to God. Nor did they render man acceptable. But in the estimation of the world—before men—they were pleasing, even regarded highly worthy. Men thought thereby to render themselves well-pleasing in God's sight. But the spiritual sacrifice is, in man's estimation, the most repugnant and unacceptable of all things. It condemns, mortifies and opposes whatever, in man's judgment, is good and well-pleasing. For, as before stated, nature cannot do otherwise than to live according to the flesh, particularly to follow its own works and inventions. It cannot admit that all its efforts and designs are vain and worthy of mortification and of death. The spiritual sacrifice is acceptable to God, Paul teaches, however unacceptable it may be to the world. They who render this living, holy sacrifice are happy and assured of their acceptance with God; they know God requires the death of the lusts and inventions of the flesh, and he alone desires to live and work in us.

17. Consequently, Paul's use of the word "body" includes more than outward, sensual vices and crimes, as gluttony, fornication, murder; it includes everything not of the new spiritual birth but belonging to the old Adam nature, even its best and noblest faculties, outer and inner; the deep depravity of self-will, for instance, and arrogance, human wisdom and reason, reliance on our own good works, on our own spiritual life and on the gifts wherewith God has endowed our nature.

To illustrate: Take the most spiritual and the wisest individuals on earth, and while it is true that a fraction of them are outwardly and physically chaste, their hearts, it will be found, are filled with haughtiness, presumption and self-will, while they delight in their own wisdom and peculiar conduct. No saint is wholly free from the deep depravity of the inner nature. Hence he must constantly offer himself up, mortifying his old deceitful self. Paul calls it sacrificing the body, because the individual, on becoming a Christian, lives more than half spiritually, and the evil propensities remaining to be mortified Paul attributes to the body as to the inferior, the less important, part of man; the part not as yet wholly under the Spirit's influence.

"Which is your spiritual (reasonable) service."

18. A clear distinction is here made between the services rendered God by Christians and those which the Jews rendered. The thought is: The Jews' service to God consisted in sacrifices of irrational beasts, but the service of Christians, in spiritual sacrifices—the sacrifice of their bodies, their very selves. The Jews offered gold and silver; they built an inanimate temple of wood and stone. Christians are a different people. Their sacrifices are not silver and gold. Their temple is not wood and stone; it is themselves. "Ye are a temple of God." 1 Cor 3, 16. Thus you observe the unfair treatment accorded Christians in ignoring their peculiar services and inducing the world to build churches, to erect altars and monasteries, and to manufacture bells, chalices and images by way of Christian service—works that would have been too burdensome for even the Jews.

19. In brief, this our reasonable service is rightly called a spiritual service of the heart, performed in the faith and the knowledge of God. Here Paul rejects all service not performed in faith as entirely unreasonable, even if rendered by the body and in outward act, and having the appearance of great holiness and spiritual life. Such have been the works, offerings, monkery and stringent life of the Papists, performed without the knowledge of God—having no command of God—and without spirit and heart. They have thought that so long as the works were performed they must be pleasing to God, independent of their faith. Such was also the service of the Jews in their works and offerings, and of all who knew not Christ and were without faith. Hence they were no better than the service and works of idolatrous and ignorant heathen.

"And be not fashioned according to this world: but be ye transformed by the renewing of your mind, that ye may prove what is the good and acceptable and perfect will of God."

20. As before said, the world cannot endure the sight or hearing of this living sacrifice; therefore it opposes it on every side. With its provocations and threats, its enticements and persecutions, it has every advantage, aided by the fact that our minds and spirits are not occupied with that spiritual sacrifice, but we give place to the dispositions and inclinations of the world. We must be careful, then, to follow neither the customs of the world nor our own reason or plausible theories. We must constantly subdue our dispositions and control our wills, not obeying the dictates of reason and desire. Always we are to conduct ourselves in a manner unlike the way of the world. So shall we be daily changed—renewed in our minds. That is, we come each day to place greater value on the things condemned by human reason—by the world. Daily we prefer to be poor, sick and despised, to be fools and sinners, until ultimately we regard death as better than life, foolishness as more precious than wisdom, shame nobler than honor, labor more blessed than wealth, and sin more glorious than human righteousness.

Such a mind the world does not possess. The mind of the world is altogether unlike the Christian's. It not only continues unchanged and unrenewed in its old disposition, but is obdurate and very old.

21. God's will is ever good and perfect, ever gracious; but it is not at all times so regarded of men. Indeed, human reason imagines it to be the evil, unfriendly, abominable will of the devil, because what reason esteems highest, best and holiest, God's will regards as nothing and worthy of death. Therefore, Christian experience must come to the rescue and decide. It must feel and prove, must test and ascertain, whether one is prompted by a sincere and gracious will. He who perseveres and learns in this way will go forward in his experience, finding God's will so gracious and pleasing he would not exchange it for all the world's wealth. He will discover that acceptance of God's will affords him more happiness, even in poverty, disgrace and adversity, than is the lot of any worldling in the midst of earthly honors and pleasures. He will finally arrive at a degree of perfection making him inclined to exchange life for death, and, with Paul, to desire to depart that sin may no more live in him, and that the will of God may be done perfectly in himself in every relation. In this respect he is wholly unlike the world; he conducts himself very differently from it. For the world never has enough of this life, while the experienced Christian is ready to be removed. What the world seeks, he avoids; what it avoids, he seeks.

22. Paul, you will observe, does not consider the Christian absolutely free from sin, since he beseeches us to be "transformed by the renewing of the mind." Where transformation and renewal are necessary, something of the old and sinful nature must yet remain. This sin is not imputed to Christians, because they daily endeavor to effect transformation and renovation. Sin exists in them against their will. Flesh and spirit are contrary to each other (Gal 5, 17), therefore we do not what we would. Rom 7, 15.

Paul makes particular mention of "the mind" here, by contrast making plainer what is intended by the "body"

which he beseeches them to sacrifice. The scriptural sense
of the word "mind" has already been sufficiently defined as
"belief," which is the source of either vice or virtue. For
what I value, I believe to be right. I observe what I value,
as do others. But when belief is wrong, conscience and
faith have not control. Where unity of mind among men
is lacking, love and peace cannot be present; and where
love and faith are not present, only the world and the devil
reign. Hence transformation by renewal of the mind is of
vital importance. Now follows:

SOBER THOUGHTS OF OURSELVES.

"For I say, through the grace that was given me, to
every man that is among you, not to think of himself
more highly than he ought to think; but so to think as
to think soberly, according as God hath dealt to every
man a measure of faith."

23. Paul, in all his epistles, is careful to give this instruction to Christians. His purpose is to preserve simplicity of
faith among them everywhere; to prevent sects and schisms
in Christian life, which have their origin in differing minds,
in diversity of belief. To make admonition the more forcible, he refers to his apostolic office; to the fact that he was,
by the grace of God, chosen and sent to teach the things he
advocates. His words here mean: "Ye possess many graces,
but let everyone take heed to confine his belief and opinions
to the limits of faith. Let him not esteem himself above
another, nor attach to the gifts conferred upon himself
greater value than he accords those conferred upon another.
Otherwise he will be inclined to despise the lesser gifts and
emphasize the more exalted ones, and to influence others to
the same practice." Where there is not such humility, re-
course is had to works and to the honoring of gifts, while
faith is neglected. Thus belief prompts to do as the world
does, to value what is exalted and to despise what is humble.

24. This principle cannot be better illustrated than by
the prevailing examples of our time. For instance, monks
and priests have established spiritual orders which they regard highly meritorious. In this respect they do not think

soberly, but extravagantly. They imagine ordinary Christians to be insignificant in comparison with them. But their orders represent neither faith nor love, and are not commanded by God. They are peculiar, something devised by the monks and priests themselves. Hence there is division. Because of the different beliefs, numerous sects exist, each striving for first place. Consequently, all the orders become unprofitable in God's sight. The love and faith and harmony which unite Christians are dissipated.

25. Paul teaches that, however varied the gifts and the outward works, none should, because of these, esteem himself good, nor regard himself better than others. Rather, every man should estimate his own goodness by his faith. Faith is something all Christians have, though not in equal measure, some possessing more and others less. However, in faith all have the same possession—Christ. The murderer upon the cross, through faith, had Christ in himself as truly as had Peter, Paul, Abraham, the mother of the Lord, and all saints; though his faith may not have been so strong. Therefore, though gifts be unequal, the precious faith is the same. Now, if we are to glory in the treasures of faith only, not in the gifts, every man should esteem another's gifts as highly as his own, and with his own gifts serve that other who in faith possesses equal treasure with him. Then will continue loving harmony and simple faith, and none will fall back upon his own works or merits. Of this "mind," or belief, you may read further in the preceding postils, especially in the epistle selection for the third Sunday in Advent. Further comment on this text will be left for the next epistle lesson, the two being closely connected.

Second Sunday After Epiphany

Text: Romans 12, 6-16.

6 And having gifts differing according to the grace that was given to us, whether prophecy, let us prophesy according to the proportion of our faith; 7 or ministry, let us give ourselves to our ministry; or he that teacheth, to his teaching; 8 or he that exhorteth, to his exhorting: he that giveth, let him do it with liberality; he that ruleth, with diligence; he that showeth mercy, with cheerfulness. 9 Let love be without hypocrisy. Abhor that which is evil; cleave to that which is good. 10 In love of the brethren be tenderly affectioned one to another; in honor preferring one another; 11 in diligence not slothful; fervent in spirit; serving the Lord; 12 rejoicing in hope; patient in tribulation; continuing stedfastly in prayer; 13 communicating to the necessities of the saints; given to hospitality. 14 Bless them that persecute you; bless, and curse not. 15 Rejoice with them that rejoice; weep with them that weep. 16 Be of the same mind one toward another. Set not your mind on high things, but condescend to things that are lowly.

GIFTS AND WORKS OF CHRIST'S MEMBERS.

1. This lesson begins in a way that would seem to call for a portion properly belonging to the epistle for the preceding Sunday, and terminates short of its full connection. Evidently it was arranged by some unlearned and thoughtless individual, with a view simply to making convenient reading in the churches and not to its explanation to the people. It will be necessary to a clear comprehension, therefore, to note its real connections.

2. In the epistle for last Sunday, the apostle teaches that as Christians we are to renew our minds by sacrificing our bodies, thus preserving the true character of faith; that we are not to regard ourselves as good or perfect without faith, if we would avoid the rise of sects and conflicting opinions among Christians; that each is to continue firm in the measure of faith God has given him, whether it be weak or strong; that he shall use his gifts to his neighbor's profit, and then they will not be regarded special favors by the less gifted, and the common faith will be generally prized as the highest and most precious treasure, the result being satisfaction for all men. Paul next adds the simile: "For even as we have many members in one body, and all the members have not the same office: so we, who are many, are one body in Christ, and severally members one of another." Then follows our selection for today, the connection being, "And having gifts differing according to the grace that was given to us," etc. Paul likens the various gifts to ourselves, the different members of the common body of Christ.

It is an apt and beautiful simile, one he makes use of frequently; for instance, 1 Cor 12, 12 and Eph 4, 16. It teaches directly and clearly the equality of all Christians; that one common faith should satisfy all; that gifts are not to be regarded as making one better, happier and more righteous than another, in the eyes of God. The latter idea is certainly erroneous, and destructive of faith, which alone avails with God.

WE ARE BORN MEMBERS OF CHRIST.

3. First, if we examine this simile, we shall find that all the members perform certain functions of the body because they are members of it; and no member has its place through its own efforts or its own merits. It was born a member, before the exercise of office was possible. It acts by virtue of being a member; it does not become a member by virtue of its action. It derives existence and all its powers from the body, regardless of its own exertions. The body, however, exercises its members as occasion requires.

The eye has not attained its place because of its power of seeing—not because it has merited its office as an organ of sight for the body. In the very beginning it derived its existence and its peculiar function of sight from the body. It cannot, therefore, boast in the slightest degree that by its independent power of seeing it has deserved its place as an eye. It has the honor and right of its position solely through its birth, not because of any effort on its part.

4. Similarly, no Christian can boast that his own efforts have made him a member of Christ, with other Christians, in the common faith. Nor can he by any work constitute himself a Christian. He performs good works by virtue of having become a Christian, in the new birth, through faith, regardless of any merit of his own. Clearly, then, good works do not make Christians, but Christians bring forth good works. The fruit does not make the tree, but the tree produces the fruit. Seeing does not make the eye, but the eye produces vision. In short, cause ever precedes effect; effect does not produce cause, but cause produces effect. Now, if good works do not make a Christian, do not secure the grace of God and blot out our sins, they do not merit heaven. No one but a Christian can enjoy heaven. One cannot secure it by his works, but by being a member of Christ; an experience effected through faith in the Word of God.

5. How, then, shall we regard those who teach us to exterminate our sins, to secure grace, to merit heaven, all by our own works; who represent their ecclesiastical orders as special highways to heaven? What is their theory? They teach, as you observe, that cause is produced by effect. Just as if mere muscular tissue that is not a tongue becomes a tongue by fluent speaking, or becomes mouth and throat by virtue of much drinking; as if running makes feet; keen hearing, an ear; smelling, a nose; nourishment at the mother's breast, a child; suspension from the apple-tree, an apple. Beautiful specimens, indeed, would these be—fine tongues, throats and ears, fine children, fine apples.

6. What sort of foolish, perverted individuals are they

who so teach? Well might you exclaim: "What impossible undertakings, what useless burdens and hardships, they assume!" Yes, what but burdens do they deserve who pervert God's truth into falsehood; who change the gifts God designed for man's benefit into acts of service rendered by man to God; who, unwilling to abide in the common faith, aspire to exalted and peculiar place as priests and beings superior to other Christians? They deserve to be overwhelmed in astonishing folly and madness, and to be burdened with useless labors and hardships in their attempts to do impossible things. They cheat the world of its blessings while they fill themselves. It is said of them (Ps 14, 4-5): "Have all the workers of iniquity no knowledge, who eat up my people as they eat bread, and call not upon Jehovah?"—that is, they live not in faith. And continuing— "There were they in great fear"; meaning that here and there they make that a matter of conscience which is not, because they cling to works and not to faith.

EACH MEMBER CONTENT WITH ITS OWN POWERS.

7. In the second place, the simile teaches that each member of the body is content with the other members, and rejoices in its powers, not being solicitous as to whether any be superior to itself. For instance, the nose is inferior in office to the eye, yet in the relation they sustain to each other the former is not envious of the latter; rather, it rejoices in the superior function the eye performs. On the other hand, the eye does not despise the nose; it rejoices in all the powers of the other members. As Paul says elsewhere (1 Cor 12, 23): "Those parts of the body, which we think to be less honorable, upon these we bestow more abundant honor." Thus we see that hand and eye, regardless of their superior office, labor carefully to clothe and adorn the less honorable members. They make the best use of their own distinction to remove the dishonor and shame of the inferior members.

8. However unequal the capacities and distinction of the individual members of the body, they are equal in that they are all parts of the same body. The eye cannot claim any

better right to a place in the body than the least distinguished member has. Nor can it boast greater authority
over the body than any other member enjoys. And thus
it does not essay to do. It grants all members equal participation in the body. Likewise, all Christians, whether
strong in faith or weak, perfect or defective, share equally
in Christ and are equal in Christendom. Each may appropriate the whole Christ unto himself. I may boast as much
in Christ as Peter or the mother of God may boast. Nor do
I envy Peter because he is a more distinguished member of
the Christian Church than I. I am glad of it. On the other
hand, he does not despise me for being a less honored member. I am a part of the same body to which he belongs, and
I possess Christ as well as he does.

9. The self-righteous are unable to concede this equality. They must stir up sects and distinctions among Christians. Priests aspire to be better than laymen; monks better than priests; virgins than wives. The diligent, in praying and fasting, would be better than the laborer; and they
who lead austere lives, more righteous than they of ordinary
life. This is the work of the devil, and productive of every
form of evil. Opposed to it is Christ's doctrine in our text.
Under such conditions as mentioned, faith and love are sub-
verted. The unlearned are deluded, and led away from faith
to works and orders. Inequality is everywhere. The ecclesiasts desire to sit in high places, to receive all honor, to have
their feet kissed, and will honor and respect none but themselves. Indeed, they would ultimately intercede for poor
Christians, would be mediators between them and God, attaching no importance whatever to the stations in life occupied by these. They proceed as if they alone were members
of Christ, and as if their relation to him could not be closer.
Then they presume by their works to constitute others members of Christ, being careful, however, to demand adequate
financial return for the service. They are members of the
devil; not of Christ.

EACH MEMBER SERVES ALL THE OTHERS.

10. In the third place, according to the simile each mem-

ber of the body conducts itself in a manner to profit the others—the whole body. The eye prepares the way for hand and foot. The foot, in its carriage of the body, safeguards the eye. Each member ever cares for and serves the others. More beautiful figures of love and good works are not to be found than those derived from the body with its members. In the members we daily bear about with us, and with which we are continually familiar, God has described the law of love in a living and forcible manner. Upon the principle there illustrated, the Christian should act, conducting himself in a way to profit not himself but others, and having a . sincere interest in them. Under such conditions, schisms and sects could not spring up among us.

11. But we are blind; we neither see nor read the beautiful lesson taught us in our own bodies. We proceed to invent good works as a means of improving our condition and bringing ourselves into a saved state. This error is attributable to our lack of faith and of heart knowledge of Christ. Hence we are restless in soul, seeking to be liberated from sin and to become righteous. The heart in its ignorance of the sufficiency of common faith, engages in these abnormal, special works. There is where foolish individuals begin to disregard faith and love, imagining such works true ways to heaven. One takes up one thing, and another something else, and so it goes, until there is nothing but sects. One sect condemns and rejects the other. Each, exalting itself beyond measure, claims superiority.

EACH MEMBER SUFFERS AND REJOICES WITH ALL.

12. In the fourth place, "whether one member suffereth, all the members suffer with it; or one member is honored, all the members rejoice with it," as Paul says. 1 Cor 12, 26. In short, no member lives and acts for itself; all obey and serve one another, and the more honored members serve most. Each seems to say: "I desire not to be otherwise than as I am. I am satisfied to be a member of the same body with the others, and to have equal rights and honors therein. It is unnecessary for me to exert myself to share in that body, for I am already a member of it, and content. My

efforts I direct to serving the body—all the members, my beloved brothers and partners. I assume no peculiarities. I would not cause discord and conflict."

13. Observe, this is the way all true, righteous Christians do, as we have frequently said. They who conduct themselves otherwise cannot be true Christians; they are worse—more pernicious—than heathen. They cannot refrain from instigating sects; from assuming some peculiarity, some special doctrine, wherein they proudly exalt themselves above other men. Thus they lure to themselves the hearts of the unlearned. Against this class Paul here, as everywhere, faithfully warns us.

14. See, then, that you become a member of Christ. This is to be accomplished through faith alone, regardless of works. And having become a member, if God has appointed you a duty according to your capacity, abide in it. Let no one allure you away from it. Esteem not yourself better than others, but serve them, rejoicing in their works and their offices as you do in your own, even if they are less important. Faith renders you equal with others, and others equal with you, and so on.

CHRISTIAN EQUALITY AND CHRISTIAN GIFTS.

Paul's design in this epistle is to teach equality. He would have no one "think of himself more highly than he ought to think; but so to think as to think soberly, according as God hath dealt to each man a measure of faith." Or, to express it differently: "Let each one regard that his work for which he has a gift, and let him perform it. But he is not consequently to esteem himself superior to others differently gifted. He should delight in their works, justly recognizing those works as of God's grace, and knowing that God distributes the measure of faith and this his grace not in one way, but in many ways." Paul's peculiar choice of words here, referring to all gifts as the grace of God and the measure of faith, is meant to teach that no man may regard his individual gift as a peculiar instance in that respect, as do they who are not of the common faith. It is the one same God, Spirit and Lord, the apostle tells us (1 Cor

12, 5-11), who effects in this work and that, whether small or great, in you or in me, in the one same faith, love and hope.

15. The importance, the nobleness and helpfulness of this doctrine is beyond our power of expression. The wretched condition of all Christendom, divided as it is into innumerable sects, is, alas, plain testimony that no body nor member, no faith nor love, seems longer to exist anywhere. Unity of mind in relation to the various gifts of God cannot exist in connection with human doctrines. Hence it is impossible for the orders and the doctrines of our ecclesiastical lords to stand with unity of mind; one or the other must fall.

16. "Measure of faith" may be understood as implying that God imparts to some more of faith itself; and to others, less. But I presume Paul's thought in employing the expression is that faith brings gifts, which are its chief blessing. These are said to be according to the measure of our faith, and not to the measure of our will or our merit. We have not merited our gifts. Where faith exists, God honors it with certain gifts, apportioned, or committed, according to his will. As we have it in First Corinthians 12, 11, "dividing to each one severally even as he will"; and in Ephesians 4, 16, "to each member according to his measure." The same reason may be assigned for Paul's words, "Having gifts differing according to the grace that was given to us," not "differing according to our merits." Grace as well as faith brings these noble jewels—our gifts—to each one according to his measure. It excludes in every respect our works and our merits, and directs us to make our works minister only to our neighbors.

"Whether prophecy, let us prophesy according to the proportion of our faith."

17. The apostle enumerates several gifts, or works of Christian members, mentioning prophecy first. Prophecy is of two kinds: One is the foretelling of future events, a gift or power possessed by all the prophets under the Old Testament dispensation, and by the apostles; the other is the explanation of the Scriptures. "Greater is he that prophesieth than he that speaketh with tongues." 1 Cor 14,

5. Now, the Gospel being the last prophetic message to be delivered previous to the time of the judgment, and to predict the events of that period, I presume Paul has reference here simply to that form of prophecy he mentions in the fourteenth of First Corinthians—explanation of the Scriptures. This form is common, ever prevails, and is profitable to Christians; the other form is rare. That reference is to this form, Paul implies in his words, "Let us prophesy according to the proportion of faith." Doubtless he means the Christian faith then arising. No other faith, no other doctrine, is to be introduced. Now, when he says prophecy must be according to the proportion of faith, it is plain enough he does not refer to the foretelling of future events.

18. The apostle's meaning, then, is: "They who have the gift of Scripture explanation must be careful to explain in conformity with the faith, and not to teach contrary to its principles." "Other foundation can no man lay than that which is laid, which is Jesus Christ." 1 Cor 3, 11. Let every man be careful not to build upon this foundation with wood, hay, stubble—things unsuited to such a foundation; let him build with gold, silver and precious stones.

Every doctrine, every explanation of the Scriptures, then, which leads us to rely upon our own works, and produces false Christians and self-righteous individuals, in the name of faith, is emphatically condemned. Any doctrine that teaches we are to exterminate our sins, to become happy and righteous and to obtain peace of conscience before God, in any other way than through faith alone—without works—is not in harmony with the Christian faith. For instance, all monastic life, and the doctrine of racketing spirits from purgatory, are in conflict with faith.

19. Paul, you will observe, does not attach so much importance to the prediction of future events; for instance, the prophecies of Lichtenberger, Joachim and others in these latter times. Such predictions, though they may gratify the curiosity of men concerning the fate of kings, princes and others of prominence in the world, are unnecessary prophecies under the New Testament dispensation. They neither

teach the Christian faith nor contribute to its strength.
Hence this form of prophecy may be regarded as among the
least of God's gifts. More, it sometimes proceeds from the
devil. But the ability to explain the Scriptures is the noblest, the best, prophetic gift. The Old Testament prophets
derived their title to the name chiefly because they proph-
esied concerning Christ—according to Peter (Acts 4, 25 and
1 Pet 1, 10)—and because they led the people of their day
in the way of faith by explaining—giving the sense of—the
divine Word. These things had much more to do with their
title than the fact of their making occasional predictions concerning earthly kings and temporal affairs. In general, they
did not make such predictions. But the first-mentioned form
of prophecy they daily delivered, without omission. The
faith whereto their prophecies conformed is perpetual.

20. It is of much significance that Paul recognizes faith
as the controlling judge and rule in all matters of doctrine
and prophecy. To faith everything must bow. By faith
must all doctrine be judged and held. You see whom Paul
would constitute doctors of the holy Scriptures—men of
faith and no others. These should be the judges and decid-
ers of all doctrines. Their decision should prevail, even
though it conflict with that of the Pope, of the councils, of
the whole world. Faith is and must be lord and God over
all teachers. Note, then, the conduct of the Church orders
who failed to recognize faith's right to judge, and assumed
that prerogative themselves, accepting only power, numbers
and temporal rank. But you know Pope, councils and all
the world, with their doctrines, must yield authority to the
most insignificant Christian with faith, even though it be
but a seven-year-old child, and his decision of their doctrines
and laws is to be accepted. Christ commands us to take
heed that we despise not one of these little ones that believe
in him. See Mt 18: 6, 10. Again, he says (Jn 6, 45), "They
shall all be taught of God." Now, it is inconsistent to reject the judgment of him whom God himself teaches. Rather,
let all men hearken to him.

"Or ministry, let us give ourselves to our ministry."

21. The office of the ministry is the second gift of God the apostle enumerates. With the early Christians the duties of this office were to serve poor widows and orphans, distributing to them temporal goods. Such were the duties of Stephen and his associates (Acts 6, 5), and such should be the duties of the stewards and provosts in monasteries today. Again, this was the office of those who ministered unto the prophets and apostles, the preachers and teachers: for instance, the women who followed Christ and served him with their substance; and Onesimus, Titus, Timothy and others of Paul's disciples. They made all necessary temporal provision, that the apostles and the preachers might give themselves uninterruptedly to preaching, teaching and prayer, and might be unencumbered with temporal affairs.

22. But things have changed, as we see. Now we have spiritual lords, princes, kings, who neglect, not alone to preach and to pray, but also to distribute temporal goods to the poor and the widow and the orphan. Rather, they pervert the rightful substance of these to add to their own pomp. They neither prophesy nor serve; yet they appropriate the position and the name of minister, their purpose being to restrain and persecute true preachers and servants, and to destroy Christianity everywhere and spend its possessions to foster their own luxury.

"Or he that teacheth, to his teaching; or he that exhorteth, to his exhorting."

23. We treated of these two gifts in the epistle lesson for Christmas night. Tit 2. Teaching consists in instructing those unacquainted with faith and the Christian life; exhortation, in inciting, arousing, impelling, reproving and beseeching with all perseverance, those having knowledge of the faith. We are enjoined (2 Tim 4, 2) to be urgent, to "reprove, rebuke and exhort," that Christians may not grow weary, indolent and negligent, as too often they do, knowing already what is required of them. But prophecy must furnish the store of information for the teachers and exhorters. Scripture expositors must supply these latter. Prophesying, then, is the source of all doctrine and exhortation.

"He that giveth, let him do it with liberality."

24. The mention here made of giving has reference to the fund contributed into a common treasury, in charge of servants and officers, for distribution among teachers, prophets, widows, orphans and the poor generally, as before stated. This was according to an Old Testament command. Beside the annual tithes, designed for the Levites, special tithes were to be set aside every third year for the poor, the widows and the orphans. There is no New Testament law for specific giving, for this is the day of grace, wherein everyone is admonished to give freely. Paul says (Gal 6, 6), "Let him that is taught in the word communicate unto him that teacheth in all good things." Again (verse 10), "Let us work that which is good toward all men, and especially toward them that are of the household of faith."

25. But giving is to be done with liberality—freely and gratuitously, to the honor of God alone, with no intent to secure favor, honor or profit; none shall dictate in the matter; and preference shall not be shown in giving much to the amiable and nothing to the uncongenial, as has been the case in the past in relation to the prebends and fiefs. These were distributed according to friendship and favor; for the sake of money, honor and profit. The same is true of nearly all paid services in the matter of purgatory and hell. Freely, freely, we are to give, being careful only that it be well pleasing to God and bestowed according to necessity.

Paul, you will observe, frequently commends such liberality. It is rarely manifest, however. True gifts are made beyond measure, but they are unprofitable because not made with a free, liberal spirit; for instance, contributions to monasteries and other institutions. Not being given with liberality, God does not permit these gifts to be used for Christian purposes. Given in an unchristian manner, they must, in an unchristianlike way, be wasted; as Micah says (ch. 1, 7): "Of the hire of a harlot hath she gathered them, and unto the hire of a harlot shall they return." Reference is to spiritual whoredom—unbelief—which never acts with liberality.

"He that ruleth, with diligence."

26. "Ruling," or overseeing, is to be understood as relating to the common offices in the Christian Church. Paul is not speaking of temporal rulers, as princes and heads of families, but of rulers in the Church. He says (1 Tim 3, 5): "If a man knoweth not how to rule his own house, how shall he take care of the church of God?" He means those who have oversight of Church officers generally; who take care that teachers be diligent, that deacons and ministers make proper and careful distribution of the finances, and that sinners are reproved and disciplined; in short, who are responsible for the proper execution of all offices. Such are the duties of a bishop. From their office they receive the title of bishops—superintendents and "Antistrites," as Paul here terms them; that is, overseers and rulers.

27. It is the especial duty of these to be concerned about others, not about themselves; the latter care is forbidden rather than enjoined. Mt 6, 25. Diligence in the connection in which it is used in the text, is prompted by love and not by self-interest. It being the duty of a bishop to readily assume oversight, to minister and control, and all things being dependent upon him as the movements of team and wagon are dependent upon the driver, the bishop has no time for indolence, drowsiness and negligence. He must be attentive and diligent, even though all others be slothful and careless. Were he inattentive and unfaithful, the official duties of all the others would likewise be badly executed. The result would be similar to that when the driver lies asleep and allows the team to move at will. Under such circumstances, to hope for good results is useless, especially considering the dangerous roads wherein Christians must travel here, among devils who would, in every twinkling of the eye, overthrow and destroy them.

28. Why should Paul reverse the seemingly proper order? He does not mention ruling first—give it precedence. He rather assigns to prophecy the first place, making ministering, teaching, exhorting and contributing follow successively, while ruling he places last or sixth, among the com-

mon offices. Undoubtedly, the Spirit designed such order in view of future abominations that should follow the devil's establishment of tyranny and worldly dominion among Christians. This is the case at present. Dominion occupies chief place. Everything in Christendom must yield to the wantonness of tyranny. Prophecy, ministry, teaching, exhortation, benevolence—all must give way to tyranny. Nothing may interrupt its sway; it must not yield to prophecy, teaching or any other office.

29. We must remember, however, that nothing takes precedence of the Word of God. The preaching of it transcends all other offices. Dominion is but a servant to arouse preaching to activity, like to the servant who wakes his master from sleep, or in other ways reminds him of his office. This principle confirms Christ's words (Lk 22, 26): "He that is the greater among you, let him become as the younger; and he that is chief, as he that doth serve." Teachers and prophets, however, are to be obedient to rulers and continue subject to them; each Christian work and office must subserve the others. Thus is carried out Paul's doctrine in this epistle: that one should not esteem himself better than others; should not exalt himself over men, thinking of himself more highly than he ought to think; though one gift or office is more honorable than another, yet it must also subserve that other. While the office of ruler is the lowest, yet every other appointment is subject to it; on the other hand, in care and oversight the ruler serves all others. Again, the prophet, who holds the highest office, submits to the ruler, etc.

"He that showeth mercy, with cheerfulness."

30. The six preceding obligations devolve upon the common governing powers of the Christian Church—at present known as the ecclesiastical order. Paul now proceeds to enumerate duties pertaining to every member of the Church. The six first-mentioned obligations are not, however, to be individualized to the extent of making but a single obligation devolve upon one individual. He who prophesies may also teach, admonish, serve and rule. And the same is true

of each office. Let every man discover unto how many offices he is called, and conduct himself accordingly. He must not exalt himself over others, as if better than they, and create sects from the common gifts of God; he must continue in the common faith of his fellows, allowing mutual service and subjection in the gifts.

31. "Mercy" implies all good deeds or benefits conferred by neighbors upon one another, aside from the regular contributions of which we have spoken. The Hebrew word the apostle uses for "mercy" is "hesed." In Latin it is "beneficium"; in Greek, "eleemosyna"; and in common parlance, "alms." It is in this sense that Christ employs the term throughout the Gospel: "When thou doest alms" (Mt 6, 2)—that is, thy good deeds, or favors; "I desire mercy, and not sacrifice" (Mt 12, 27); "He that showed mercy on him" (Lk 10, 37). And there are other similar passages where the word "mercy" is equivalent to "benefit" or "favor"; for instance (Mt 5, 7), "Blessed are the merciful."

32. Paul would say: "Let him who is himself so favored that he may confer benefits upon others, do it cheerfully and with pleasure." He declares (2 Cor 9, 7), "God loveth a cheerful giver." And he makes his meaning clear by another portion of the same verse, "not grudgingly, or of necessity." That is, the giver is not to twitter and tremble, not to be slow and tardy in his giving, nor to seek everywhere for reasons to withhold his gift. He is not to give in a way calculated to spoil the recipient's enjoyment of the favor. Nor is he to delay until the gift loses its sweetness because of the importunity required to secure it; rather he should be ready and willing. Solomon says (Prov 3, 28): "Say not unto thy neighbor, Go, and come again, and to-morrow I will give; when thou hast it by thee." "Bis dat qui cito dat." He gives doubly who gives quickly. Again, "Tarda gratia non est gratia," A tardy favor is no favor. The word "hilaris" in this connection does not imply joyful giving, but free, cheerful, willing and loving generosity, a generosity moved by slight entreaty.

THE WORKS OF CHRIST'S MEMBERS.

"Let love be without hypocrisy."

33. How aptly the apostle points out the danger of error in each obligation, as well as the right course! Prophecy is carried beyond its proper sphere when it does not accord with the faith. This is the danger-point in all prophecy. The common error in ministering lies in the indolence manifested therein, and the constant preference for some other occupation. Again, the prevailing error in teaching and exhorting is in giving attention to something besides those obligations; for instance, deceiving men with human nonsense. The mistake in giving is that it is seldom done with liberality. Rulers are prone to seek quiet and leisure, desiring to escape being burdened with care and anxiety. Favors are seldom bestowed cheerfully and with a willing heart. So, too, pure love is a rare thing on earth. Not that love in itself is impure, but too often it is mere pretense. John implies as much in his words (1 Jn 3, 18), "My little children, let us not love in word, neither with the tongue; but in deed and truth."

34. Now, they who harbor hatred while pretending to love, or are guilty of similar gross hypocrisies, fall far short of the spirit of this teaching. But Paul refers to those of liberated conscience, who conduct themselves like true Christians, well knowing how to teach concerning Christ; but who are careless of their works, not realizing that they neglect their neighbors and fail to assist the needy and to rebuke the wicked; who are generally negligent, bringing forth none of the fruits of faith; among whom the true Word of God is choked, like seed among thorns, as Christ says. Mt 13, 22. But we have elsewhere explained the nature of pure love.

"Abhor that which is evil."

35. While to abhor evil is one of the chief principles of love, it is rare. The principle is too often lost sight of through hypocrisy and false love. We ignore, wink at, even make light of and are undisturbed by the evil deeds of our neighbor. We are unwilling to incur his displeasure by manifesting indignation and offering rebuke for his wick-

edness, or by withdrawing from his society. Especially do we hesitate when we thus must endanger body or life; for instance, when the vices of those in high life demand our censure. By such weakness on our part we merely dissimulate love. Paul requires, not only a secret abhorrence of evil, but an open manifestation of it in word and deed. True love is not influenced by the closeness of the friend, by the advantage of his favors, or by the standing of his connections; nor is it influenced by the perverseness of an enemy. It abhors evil, and censures it or flees from it, whether in father or mother, brother or sister, or in any other. Corrupt nature loves itself and does not abhor its own evil; rather, it covers and adorns it. Anger is styled zeal; avarice is called prudence; and deception, wisdom.

"Cleave to that which is good."

36. The second feature of real, true love is that it cleaves to the good, even though found in the worst enemy, and though directly opposing love's desire. Love is no respecter of persons. It is not intimidated by the possible danger its expression might incur. But false love will dare, even for the sake of honor, profit or advantage, to forsake the good in its friend, particularly when danger threatens or persecution arises. Much less, then, will he whose love is false cleave to the good in an enemy and stand by and maintain it. And if it necessitated opposing his own interests, he would not support his enemy's deed, however good. Briefly, the proverb, "The world is false and full of infidelity," and that other saying, "Fair but empty words," clearly express the fact that the love of our corrupt human nature is false and hypocritical, and that where the Spirit of God dwells not, there is no real, pure love. These two principles—abhorring the evil and cleaving to the good—are clearly presented in Psalm 15, 4: "In whose eyes a reprobate is despised, but who honoreth them that fear Jehovah"—in other words, "Who cleaves to the good, even though it be in an enemy; and hates the evil, even though in a friend." Try men by these two principles in their lending, their dealing and giving, reproving and teaching, tolerating and suffering, and

their dissimulation and hypocrisy will be readily apparent.
"In love of the brethren be tenderly affectioned one to
another."

37. Christians exhibit perfect love when, in addition to
the love they manifest toward all men, they are themselves
united by a peculiar bond of Christian affection. The term
"tenderly affectioned" expresses the love parents have for
children, and brothers for each other. Paul would say:
"Christians are not simply to manifest a spirit of mutual
love, but they are to conduct themselves toward one another
in a tender, parental and brotherly way." Thus Paul boasts
of doing in the case of the people of Thessalonica. I Thes
1, 11. Isaiah declares (ch. 66, 13) that God will so comfort
the apostles: "As one whom his mother comforteth, so
will I comfort you." And Peter says (1 Pet 3, 8): "Loving
as brethren, tenderhearted, humbleminded." The nature of
the brotherly love we owe our neighbors is illustrated in
the love of an affectionate mother for her child. Such love
Christ has shown, and still shows, toward us. He sustains
us, frail, corrupt, sinful beings that we are. So imperfect
are we, we seem not Christians at all. But the love of
Christ makes us his, regardless of our imperfections.
"In honor preferring one another."

38. Christ's love and friendship for ourselves should lead
us to esteem one another precious. We should be dear to
one another for the sake of the Christ within us. We may
not reject any because of his imperfections. We must remember the Lord dwells in the weak vessel also, and honors
him with his presence. If Christ regards him worthy of
kindness and affection, and extends to him the same privilege in himself that we enjoy, we should bow before that
weak one, honoring him as the living temple of our Lord,
the seat of his presence. What matters to us the insignifi-
cance of the seat the Lord chooses? If it is not too humble
to be honored with his presence, why should we his servants
not honor it?
"In diligence not slothful."

39. "Diligence" here implies every form of righteous

work and business that occupies us. Paul requires us to be
diligent, skillful and active. We are not to proceed as do
they who undertake one thing today, and tomorrow another,
confining themselves to nothing and soon growing weary
and indolent. For instance, some readily and very zealously
engage in a good work, such as praying, reading, fasting,
giving, serving, disciplining the body. But after two or
three attempts they become indolent and fail to accomplish
the undertaking. Their ardor subsides with the gratification
of their curiosity. Such people become unstable and weak.
So Paul enjoins to be

"Fervent in spirit."

40. A weak and somewhat curious disposition may undertake with fervor, being ready to accomplish everything
at once; but in the very start it becomes faint and weak, and
voluntarily yields. It becomes silent when opposition, dis-
affection and persecution must be encountered. The fervor
that does not persevere in spiritual matters is carnal.
Spiritual fervor increases with undertaking and effort. It is
the nature of spirit not to know weariness. Spirit grows
faint and weary only by idleness. Laboring, it increases in
strength. Particularly does it gain in fervor through persecution and opposition. So it perseveres, and accomplishes
its projects, even though the gates of hell oppose.

"Serving the Lord." (Adapt yourselves to the time.)

41. Some renderings read, "Serve the Lord," for in the
Greek "Kairos" and "Kyrios" sound much alike. One means
"Time," the other "Lord." I am undecided which is prefer-
able. "Serve the time"—"adapt yourselves to the time"—
would be apt. And "Serve the Lord" would not be a bad
construction. Let each choose for himself. To serve the
Lord means to let all our acts be done as unto the Lord himself, in the effort to serve him, not seeking our own honor,
and not neglecting our duty for fear of men or because of
their favors; it means to follow the spirit of Nehemiah's
declaration when the temple was being built (Neh 2, 20)—
We are servants of the God of Heaven. Such was the reply
of the Jews to those who attempted to hinder them. Prac-

tically, the Jews said: "We do not serve ourselves. Our service is not designed for our own honor, but for the honor of the God of Heaven." I shall, however, adhere to the rendering, "Adapt yourselves to the time." It is equivalent to saying: Direct yourselves according to the time. That is, employ it well; be seasonable, in keeping with Solomon's words (Ec 3, 3-4): "A time to break down, and a time to build up; a time to weep, and a time to laugh," etc. There is a time for everything. The thought is, Exercise your privileges, confining yourself to no particular time; be able to do the duty that presents itself, as Psalm 1, 3 suggests: "He shall be like a tree . . . that bringeth forth its fruit in its season."

42. This valuable and excellent doctrine militates against the self-righteous, who confine themselves to set times, to the extent of making the time conform to them and adapt itself to their convenience. They observe particular hours for praying, for eating, for drinking. Should you, in dire need of aid, approach one of them, you might perish before he would disengage himself to assist you.

Note, the self-righteous man does not adapt himself to the time—does not rise to the occasion as he should. The opportunity to perform a work of love, he permits to pass. The time must be suited to him—which will never be. No opportunity to do good ever presents itself to this class, for they are so absorbed in themselves as to permit every such occasion to pass. Nor are they seasonable in things concerning themselves. They laugh when they should weep; they are gloomy when they should rejoice; they flatter when censure is due. All their efforts are untimely. It is their fortune to miss every opportunity in consequence of confining their endeavors to certain times. This is the way of the world.

"Rejoicing in hope."

43. Here is an occasion, truly, when we should be timely. The ungodly rejoice when satiate with wealth, honor and ease, but are filled with gloom at a change in the weather. Their joy is untimely as well as their grief. They rejoice

when they should grieve, and grieve when they should
rejoice. But Christians are capable of rejoicing, not in ease
and temporal advantage, but in God. They rejoice most
when their worldly condition is worst. The farther earthly
advantages are removed, the nearer is God with his eternal
blessings. Paul enumerates joy among the fruits of the
Spirit (Gal 5, 22); the flesh knows not such pleasure. In
Romans 14, 17, he speaks of "joy in the Holy Spirit."

"Patient in tribulation."

44. Throughout the Gospel we are taught that Christians
must endure crosses and evil days. Hence the Gospel arms
us with divine armor, and that alone. That is, it teaches us,
not how to avert temporal ills and to enjoy peace, but how
to endure and conquer these ills. We are not to oppose and
try to avert them, but patiently to endure them until they
wear themselves out upon us, and lose their power; as ocean
waves, dashing against the shore, recede and vanish of their
own accord. Not yielding, but perseverence, shall win here.
But of this topic we have treated during the Advent season.

"Continuing stedfastly in prayer."

45. Prayer has been sufficiently defined in the third
epistle for Advent. Paul does not allude to babbling out of
prayer-books, nor to bawling in the Church. You will never
offer true prayer from a book. To be sure, you may, by
reading a prayer, learn how and what to pray, and have
your devotion enkindled; but real prayer must proceed spon-
taneously from the heart, not in prescribed words; the language must be dictated by the fervor of the soul. Paul par-
ticuarly specifies that we are to be "stedfast in prayer." In
other words, we should not become remiss, even though we
do not immediately receive what we ask. The chief thing
in prayer is faith. Faith relies on God's promise to hear its
petition. It may not receive at once what it is confident of
receiving; but it waits, and though for a time there may
be indications of failure, yet the petition is granted. Christ
gives striking illustrations of such perseverence in the parable of the wicked judge (Lk 18), and in that of the friend's
importunity (Lk 11). He everywhere teaches the necessity

of faith in prayer. "Whatsoever ye shall ask in prayer, believing, ye shall receive," Mt 21, 22. And again, "Or what
man is there of you, who, if his son shall ask him for a loaf,
will give him a stone?" Mt 7, 9.

"Communicating to the necessities of the saints."

46. The meaning of this injunction is shamefully perverted. In our necessities we daily seek the assistance of
saints. Hence the numerous institutions, altars and services to these, everywhere in the world. Paul's teaching,
however, is that we are to "communicate to the necessity of
the saints." Since we ignore the sanctified ones of this life
who need our assistance, we are well rewarded by having
to go to the dead to solicit aid in our necessities. Paul
means the saints on earth—the Christians. He calls them
saints out of respect to the Word of God and his grace,
which, in faith, renders them holy without works.

47. It would be a great shame, a blasphemy, for a Christian to deny that he is holy. It would be equivalent to deny-
ing the holiness of the blood of Christ, of the Word, the
Spirit, the grace of God, and of God himself. And all these
God has applied to or conferred upon the Christian to render
him holy. Paul does not hesitate to call himself a saint
(Eph 3, 8): "Unto me who am less than the least of all
saints, was this grace given." And (1 Tim 5, 10) he would
relieve widows who washed the feet of the saints. It is
also said in Psalm 86, 2, "Preserve my soul; for I am godly
[holy]." Peter, too (1 Pet 1, 16), quoting from Moses,
speaks God's message, "Ye shall be holy; for I am holy."
The word "holy" in the Scriptures has reference only to
the living.

But we have had books other than the Scriptures to read.
Consequently we have been led by our seducers into the
humiliating wickedness of calling holy only the dead, and
regarding it the highest presumption to apply the term to
ourselves. At the same time we are all desirous of being
called "Christians," a sublimer title than "holy"; for Christ
is perfect holiness, and Christians are named after Christ—
after perfect holiness. The shameful abomination known as

"the exaltation of saints" is responsible for the deplorable
error here. The Pope's influence has created the belief that
only they are holy who are dead, or whose works have exalted them to the honor of the title. But how often is the
devil exalted as a saint, and how often we regard them
saints who are of hell!

48. Paul's design in mentioning "the necessities of the
saints" is to teach and move us to do as much for Christians
as we are inclined to do for the saints of heaven; to regard
such ministration as precious service, for so it is. He commends to us the real saints—those in want; who are of
saintly character, though they may be forsaken, hungry,
naked, imprisoned, half-dead, regarded by the world as ungodly evil-doers deserving of every form of misfortune;
who, unable to help themselves, need assistance. They differ much from those saints whose help we, staring heaven-
ward, implore. It is the poor Christians whom Christ will
array on the last day, saying, "Inasmuch as ye did it unto
one of these my brethren, even these least, ye did it unto
me." Mt 25, 40. Then they who so ostentatiously served
the blessed of heaven must stand shamed and afraid in the
presence of those whom in this life they scorned to respect
as they should. Nor will the saints whom they bound themselves to serve, and whom they worshiped, avail them anything.

"Given to hospitality."

49. Now, Paul specifies concerning the "necessities of the
saints" and names the treatment to be accorded them. Not
only in word are we to remember them, but in deed, extending hospitality as their necessities demand. "Hospitality"
stands for every form of physical aid when occasion calls
for it—feeding the hungry, giving drink to the thirsty, clothing the naked. In the early days of the Gospel, the apostles
and disciples did not sit in palaces, cloisters, institutions,
and torture the people with edicts and commands as do the
idolatrous bishops today. Pilgrim-like, they went about the
country, having no house nor home, no kitchen nor cellar,
no particular abiding-place. It was necessary that every-

where hospitality be extended the saints, and service rendered them, that the Gospel might be preached. This was as essential as giving assistance in their distresses and sufferings.

"Bless them that persecute you."

50. Incidental to the subject of the saints' necessities, the apostle reminds us we are to conduct ourselves in a Christian manner toward our persecutors, who, to great extent, are to blame for the distresses of the saints. It is well to observe here that we are not merely advised, but commanded, to love our enemies, to do them good and to speak well of them; such conduct is the fruit of the Spirit. We must not believe what we have heretofore been taught— that the admonition comes only to the perfect, and that they are merely counseled to bless their persecutors. Christ teaches (Mt 5, 44) that all Christians are commanded so to do. And to "bless" our persecutors means to desire for them only good in body and soul. For instance, if an enemy detracts from our honor, we should respond, "God honor you and keep you from disgrace." Or if one infringe upon our rights, we ought to say, "May God bless and prosper you." On this wise should we do.

"Bless, and curse not."

51. This is to be our attitude toward mankind generally, whether persecutors or otherwise. The meaning is: "Not only bless your persecutors, but live without curses for any, with blessings for all; wishing no one evil, but everyone only good." For we are children of blessing; as Peter says: "Hereunto were ye called, that ye should inherit a blessing." 1 Pet 3, 9. In our blessing, all the world is blessed—through Christ. "In thy seed shall all the nations of the earth be blessed." Gen 22, 18. It is inconsistent for a Christian to curse even his most bitter enemy and an evil-doer; for he is commanded to bear upon his lips the Gospel. The dove did not bring to Noah in the ark a poisonous branch or a thistle sprig; she brought an olive-leaf in her mouth. Gen 8, 11. The Gospel likewise is simply a gracious, blessed, glad and healing word. It brings only blessing and grace

to the whole world. No curse, but pure blessing, goes with the Gospel. The Christian's lips, then, must be lips of blessing, not of cursing. If they curse, they are not the lips of a Christian.

52. It is necessary, however, to distinguish between cursing and censuring or reproving. Reproof and punishment greatly differ from cursing and malediction. To curse means to invoke evil, while censuring carries the thought of displeasure at existing evil, and an effort to remove it. In fact, cursing and censuring are opposed. Cursing invokes evil and misfortune; censure aims to remove them. Christ himself censured, or reproved. He called the Jews a generation of vipers, children of the devil, hypocrites, blind dolts, liars, and so on. He did not curse them to perpetuate their evils; rather he desired the evils removed. Paul does similarly. He says of the sorcerer that he is a child of the devil and full of subtilty. Acts 13, 10. Again, the Spirit reproves the world of sin. Jn 16, 8.

53. But the strong argument is here urged that the saints of the Scriptures not only censured, but cursed. Jacob, the patriarch, cursed his sons Reuben, Simeon and Levi. Gen 49, 7. A great part of the Law of Moses is made up of curses, especially Deut 28, 15. Open cursing is commanded to be pronounced by the people, on Mount Ebal. Deut 27, 13. How much cursing we find in the Psalms, particularly Psalm 109. Again, how David cursed Joab, captain of his host! 2 Sam 3, 29. How bitterly Peter curses Simon (Acts 8, 20): "Thy silver perish with thee." Paul curses the seducers of the Galatians (Gal 5, 12), "I would they were even cut off." And he says (1 Cor 16, 22), "If any man loveth not the Lord, let him be anathema." Christ cursed the innocent fig-tree. Mt 21, 19. And Elisha cursed the children of Bethel. 2 Kings 2, 24. What shall we say to these things?

54. I answer: We must distinguish between love and faith. Love must not curse; it must always bless. But faith has power to curse. Faith makes us children of God, and is to us in God's place. Love makes us servants of men,

and occupies the place of a servant. Without the Spirit's direction, no one can rightly understand and imitate such examples of cursing. Cursing stands opposed to cursing—the curses of God to the curses of the devil. When the devil, through his followers, resists, destroys, obstructs, the Word of God—the channel of the blessing—the blessing is impeded, and in God's sight a curse rests upon the blessing. Then it is the office of faith to come out with a curse, desiring the removal of the obstruction that God's blessing may be unhindered.

55. Were one, with imprecation, to invoke God to root out and destroy popery—the order of priests, monks and nuns, together with the cloisters and other institutions, the whole world might well say, Amen. For these the devil's devices curse, condemn and impede everywhere God's Word and his blessing. These things are evils so pernicious, so diabolical, they do not merit our love. The more we serve the ecclesiasts and the more we yield to them, the more obdurate they become. They rant and rage against the Word of God and the Spirit, against faith and love. Such conduct Christ calls blasphemy—sin—against the Holy Spirit—unpardonable sin. Mt. 12, 31. And John says (1 Jn. 5, 16), "There is a sin unto death; not concerning this do I say that he should make request." With the ecclesiasts all is lost. They will not accept any love or assistance which does not leave them in their wickedness, does not strengthen and help—even honor and exalt—them in it. Any effort you may make otherwise will but cause them to rage against the Holy Spirit, to blaspheme and curse your teaching, declaring: "It proceeds not from love and fidelity to God, but from the hate, the malice, of the devil. It is not the Word of God, but falsehood. It is the devil's heresy and error."

56. In fact, cursing which contributes only to the service of God is a work of the Holy Spirit. It is enjoined in the first commandment, and is independent of and superior to love. Until God commands us to do a certain good work or obligation so to do. His will transcends all the good works to manifest our love toward our neighbor, we are under no

we can do, all the love we can show our neighbor. Even if
I could save the entire world in a single day and it were not
God's will I should, I would have no right to do it. Therefore, I should not bless, should not perform a good work,
should not manifest my love to any, unless it be consistent
with the will and command of God. The measure of our
love to our neighbors is the Word of God. Likewise, by
the first commandment all other commandments are to be
measured. We might, in direct violation of the commandments of the second table, were it consistent with God's will
and promotive of his honor, obey the first commandment in
killing, robbing, taking captive women and children and
disobeying father and mother, as did the children of Israel
in the case of their heathen enemies. Likewise the Holy
Spirit is able to, and does at times, perform works seemingly
opposed to all the commandments of God. While apparently there is violation in some respects, it is in reality only
of the commandments of the second table, concerning our
neighbor. The Spirit's works are in conformity with the
first three commandments of the first table, relating to God.
Therefore, if you first become a Peter, a Paul, a Jacob, a
David, an Elisha, you too may curse in God's name, and
with exalted merit in his sight.

"Rejoice with them that rejoice; weep with them that
weep."

57. There may be a direct connection between these two
commands and the injunction about "communicating to the
necessities of the saints" upon which Paul has been expatiat-
ing, teaching how we are to treat our persecutors, who are
largely to blame for the "necessities" of Christians. Yet I
am inclined to think he speaks here in an unrelated way, of
our duty to make ourselves agreeable to all men, to adapt
ourselves to their circumstances, whether good or ill, whether
or no they are in want. As common servants, we should minister to mankind in their every condition, that we may persuade them to accept the Gospel. Paul speaks further on this
point.

58. Now, if a fellow-man have reason to rejoice, it is not

for us to put on a stern countenance, as do the hypocrites, who assume to be somewhat peculiar. Their unnatural seriousness is meant to be indicative of their unrivaled wisdom and holiness, and of the fact that men who rejoice instead of wearing, as they do, a stern look, are fools and sinners. But no, we are to participate in the joy of our fellow-man when that joy is not inconsistent with the will of God. For instance, we should rejoice with the father who joys in the piety and sweetness of his wife, in her health and fruitfulness, and in the obedience and intelligence of his children; and when he is as well off as we are so far as soul, body and character, family and property, are concerned. These are gifts of God. According to Paul (Acts 14, 17), they are given that God may fill our hearts "with food and gladness." Though many such gifts and pleasures are improperly used, they are nevertheless the gifts of God and not to be rejected with a gloomy face as if we dare not, or should not, enjoy them. On the other hand, we ought to weep with our fellow-man when he is in sad circumstances, as we would weep over our own unhappy condition. We read (2 Sam 1, 17; 3, 33) that David lamented for Saul, Jonathan and Abner, and (Phil 2, 27) that Paul was filled with sorrow over the illness of Epaphroditus and grieved as if the affliction were his own.

"Be of the same mind one toward another."

59. The apostle has previously (verse 10) spoken concerning unity of mind in relation to God-ordained spiritual gifts, counseling that everyone should be content as to the offices and gifts of his fellows. Now Paul speaks of the temporal affairs of men, teaching likewise mutual appreciation of one another's calling and character, offices and works, and that none is to esteem himself better than another because of these. The shoemaker's apprentice has the same Christ with the prince or the king; the woman, the same Christ the man has. While there are various occupations and external distinctions among men, there is but one faith and one Spirit.

60. But this doctrine of Paul has long been dishonored.

Princes, lords, nobles, the rich and the powerful, reflect themselves in themselves, thinking they are the only men on earth. Even among their own ranks, one aspires to be more exalted, more noble and upright, than another. Their notions and opinions are almost as diverse as the clouds of heaven. They are not of the same mind concerning external distinctions. One does not esteem another's condition and occupation as significant and as honorable as his own. The individual sentiment apparently is: "My station is the best; all others are revolting."

The clumsy, booted peasant enters the strife. The baker aspires to be better than the barber; the shoemaker, than the bath-keeper. Should one happen to be illegitimately born, he is not eligible to a trade, though he even be holy. Certificates of legitimate birth must be produced, and such is the complex state of society, there are as many beliefs as masters and servants. How can there be unity of mind concerning spiritual offices and blessings with people so at variance upon trivial, contemptible worldly matters? True, there must be the various earthly stations, characters and employments; but it is heathenish, unchristian and worldly for one to entertain the absurd idea that God regards a certain individual a better Christian than another upon the contemptible grounds of his temporal station, and not to preceive that in God's sight these conditions make no inner difference.

61. Indeed, it is not only unchristian, but effeminate and childish, to hold such a view. A woman will win distinction for herself by handling the spindle or the needle more deftly than another, or by adjusting her bonnet more becomingly than her neighbor can; in fact, she may secure prominence by things even more insignificant. To say the least, no woman thinks herself less a woman than any other. The same is true of children; each is best satisfied with its own bread and butter, and thinks its own toy the prettiest; if it

And so it is with the world: one has more power, another does not, it will cry until it gets its prettiest.

is a better Christian, another is more illustrious; one has

more learning, another is more respectable; one is of this lineage, another that. These distinctions are the source of hatred, murder and every form of evil, so tenaciously does each individual adhere to his own notions. Yet, despite their separate and dissimilar opinions, men call themselves Christians.

"Set not your mind on high things."

62. Here Paul makes clear the preceding injunction. He would restrain men from their unholy conceits. As before stated, every man is best pleased with his own ideas. Hence foolishness pervades the land. One, seeing another honored above himself, is restlessly ambitious to emulate that other. But he acts contrary to both teachings of Paul: Comparing himself to his inferiors or to his equals, he thinks he is far above them, and his own station most honorable. Comparing himself with his superiors, he sees his pretended rank fail; hence he strives to rival them, devoting all his energies to attain the enviable position. Clinging to external distinctions, his changing notions and unstable heart impel him to such ambition and render him dissatisfied with the Christ whom all men possess alike.

But what does Paul teach? Not so. He says, "Set not your mind on what the world values." His meaning is: "Distinctions truly must there be in this life—one thing high, another low. Everything cannot be gold, nor can all things be straw. Nevertheless, among men there should be unity of mind in this relation." God treats men alike. He gives his Word and his Spirit to the lowly as well as to the high. Paul does not use the little word "mind" undesignedly. "High things" have their place and they are not pernicious. But to "mind" them, to be absorbed in them with the whole heart, to be puffed up with conceit because of our relation to them, enjoying them to the disadvantage of the less favored—this is heathenish.

"But condescend to things that are lowly."

63. In other words: Despise not lowly stations and characters. Say not, they must either be exalted or removed. God uses them; indeed, the world cannot dispense

with them. Where would the wealthy and powerful be if there were no poor and humble? As the feet support the body, so the low support the high. The higher class, then, should conduct themselves toward the lowly as the body holds itself with relation to the feet; not "minding," or regarding, their lofty station, but conforming to and recognizing with favor the station of the lowly. Legal equality is here made a figure of spiritual things—concerning the aspirations of the heart. Christ conducted himself with humility. He did not deny his own exaltation, but neither was he haughty toward us by reason of it. He did not despise us, but stooped to our wretched condition and raised us by means of his own exalted position.

Third Sunday After Epiphany

Text: Romans 12, 16-21.

16 "Be not wise in your own conceits. 17 Render to no man evil for evil. Take thought for things honorable in the sight of all men. 18 If it be possible, as much as in you lieth, be at peace with all men. 19 Avenge not yourselves, beloved, but give place unto the wrath of God: for it is written, Vengeance belongeth unto me; I will recompense, saith the Lord. 20 But if thine enemy hunger, feed him; if he thirst, give him to drink: for in so doing thou shalt heap coals of fire upon his head. 21 Be not overcome of evil, but overcome evil with good.

CHRISTIAN REVENGE.*

"Be not wise in your own conceits."

64. The lesson as read in the Church ends here. We shall, therefore, notice but briefly the remaining portion. "Conceits," as here used, signifies the obstinate attitude with regard to temporal things which is maintained by that individual who is unwilling to be instructed, who himself knows best in all things, who yields to no one and calls good whatever harmonizes with his ideas. The Christian should be more willing to make concession in temporal affairs. Let him not be contentious, but rather yielding, since the Word of God and faith are not involved, it being only a question of personal honor, of friends and of worldly things.

"Render to no man evil for evil."

*This and the last sermon are one in some editions. Hence the paragraphs are numbered as one sermon.

51

65. In the counsel above (verse 14) to "curse not," the writer of the epistle has in mind those unable to avenge themselves, or to return evil for evil. These have no alternative but to curse, to invoke evil upon their oppressors. In this instance, however, the reference is to those who have equal power to render one another evil for evil, malice for malice, whether by acts committed or omitted—and usually they are omitted. But the Christian should render good for evil, and omit not. God suffers his sun to shine upon the evil and upon the good. Mt 5, 45.

"Take thought for things honorable in the sight of all men."

66. This injunction is similar to that he gives the Thessalonians (1 Thes 5, 22), "Abstain from all appearance of evil"; and the Philippians (ch. 4, 8): "Whatsoever things are true, whatsoever things are honorable, whatsoever things are just, whatsoever things are pure, whatsoever things are lovely, whatsoever things are of good report; if there be any virtue, and if there be any praise, think on these things." The reference is purely to our outward conduct. Paul would not have the Christian think himself at liberty to do his own pleasure, regardless of others' approbation. Only in the things of faith is such the Christian's privilege. His outward conduct should be irreproachable, acceptable to all men; in keeping with the teaching of first Corinthians, 10, 32-33, to please all men, giving offense neither to Jews nor to Gentiles; and obedient to Peter's advice (1 Pet 2, 12), "Having your behavior seemly among the Gentiles."

"If it be possible, as much as in you lieth, be at peace with all men."

67. Outward peace among men is here intended—peace with Christians and heathen, with the godly and the wicked, the high and the low. We must give no occasion for strife; rather, we are to endure every ill patiently, never permitting peace to be disturbed on our account. We must not return evil for evil, blow for blow; for he who so does, gives rise to contention. Paul adds, "As much as in you lieth." We are to avoid injuring any, lest we be the ones to occasion

contention. We must extend friendliness to all men, even though they be not friendly to us. It is impossible to maintain peace at all times. The saying is, "I can continue in peace only so long as my neighbor is willing." But it lies in our power to leave others at peace, friends and foes, and to endure the contentions of all. "Oh yes," you say, "but where would we be then?" Listen:

> "Avenge not yourselves, beloved, but give place unto the wrath of God: for it is written, Vengeance belongeth unto me; I will recompense, saith the Lord."

68. Note, in forbidding us to return blow for blow and to resort to vengeance, the apostle implies that our enjoyment of peace depends on our quiet endurance of others' disturbance. He not only gives us assurance that we shall be avenged, but he intimidates us from usurping the office of God, to whom alone belong vengeance and retribution. Indeed, he rather deplores the fate of the Christian's enemies, who expose themselves to God's wrath; he would move us to pity them in view of the fact that we must give place to wrath and permit them to fall into the hands of God.

The vengeance and wrath of God are dispensed in various ways: through the instrumentality of political government; at the hands of the devil; by illness, hunger and pestilence; by fire and water; by war, enmity, disgrace; and by every possible kind of misfortune on earth. Every creature may serve as the rod and the weapon of God when he designs chastisement. As said in Wisdom of Solomon, 5, 17: "He shall . . . make the creature his weapon for the revenge of his enemies."

69. So Paul says, "Give place unto wrath." I have inserted the words "of God" to make clearer the meaning of the text; the wrath of God is intended, and not the wrath of man. The thought is not of giving place to the anger of our enemies. True, there may be occasion even for that, but Paul has not reference here to man's anger. Evidently, he means misfortunes and plagues, which are regarded as expressions of God's wrath. Possibly the apostle omitted the phrase to avoid giving the idea that only the final wrath of

God is meant—his anger at the last day, when he will inflict punishment without instrumentality. Paul would include here all wrath, whether temporal or eternal, to which God gives expression in his chastisements. This is an Old Testament way of speaking. Phinehas says (Jos 22, 18), "Tomorrow he will be wroth with . . . Israel." And Moses in several places speaks of God's anger being kindled. See Numbers 11: 1, 10, 33. I mention these things by way of teaching that when the political government wields the sword of punishment against its enemies, it should be regarded as an expression of God's wrath; and that the statement in Deuteronomy 32, 35, "Vengeance is mine," does not refer solely to punishment inflicted of God direct, without instrumentality.

> "But if thine enemy hunger, feed him; if he thirst, give him to drink; for in so doing thou shalt heap coals of fire upon his head."

70. This teaching endorses what I have already stated—that the Christian's enemies are to be pitied in that they are subjected to the wrath of God. Consequently it is not Christian-like to injure them; rather, we should extend favors. Paul here introduces a quotation from Solomon. Prov 25, 21-22. Heaping coals of fire on the head, to my thought, implies conferring favors upon the enemy. Being enkindled by our kindness, he ultimately becomes displeased with himself and more kindly disposed to us. Coals here are benefits, or favors. Coals in the censer likewise stand for the favors, or blessings, of God; they are a type of our prayers, which should rise with fervor. Some say that coals represent the Law and judgments of God (see Psalm 18, 8, "Coals were kindled by it"), reasoning that in consequence of the Christian's favors, his enemy is constrained to censure himself and to feel the weight of God's Law and his judgments. I do not think a Christian should desire punishment to fall upon his enemy, though such explanation of the sentence is not inapt. In fact, it rather accords with the injunction, "Give place unto wrath"; that is, do good and then wrath—the coals—will readily fall upon the enemy.

"Be not overcome of evil, but overcome evil with good."

71. With this concluding counsel, it strikes me, Paul himself explains the phrase "coals of fire" in harmony with the first idea—that the malice of an enemy is to be overcome with good. Overcoming by force is equivalent to lending yourself to evil and wronging the enemy who wrongs you. By such a course your enemy overcomes you and you are made evil like himself. But if you overcome him with good, he will be made righteous like you. A spiritual overcoming is here meant; the disposition, the heart, the soul—yes, the devil who instigates the evil—are overcome.

Fourth Sunday After Epiphany

Text: Romans 13, 8-10.

8 Owe no man anything, save to love one another: for he that loveth his neighbor hath fulfilled the law. 9 For this, Thou shalt not commit adultery, Thou shalt not kill, Thou shalt not steal, Thou shalt not covet, and if there be any other commandment, it is summed up in this word, namely, Thou shalt love thy neighbor as thyself. 10 Love worketh no ill to his neighbor; love therefore is the fulfilment of the law.

CHRISTIAN LOVE AND THE COMMAND TO LOVE.

1. This, like the two preceding epistle lessons, is admonitory, and directs our attention to the fruits of faith. Here, however, Paul sums up briefly all the fruits of faith, in love. In the verses going before he enjoined subjection to temporal government—the rendering of tribute, custom, fear and honor wherever due—since all governmental power is ordained of God. Then follows our lesson: "Owe no man anything," etc.

2. I shall ignore the various explanations usually invented for this command, "Owe no man anything, but to love one another." To me, clearly and simply it means: Not as men, but as Christians, are we under obligations. Our indebtedness should be the free obligation of love. It should not be compulsory and law-prescribed. Paul holds up two forms of obligation: one is inspired by law, the other by love.

Legal obligations make us debtors to men; an instance is when one individual has a claim upon another for debt. The

56

duties and tribute, the obedience and honor, we owe to political government are of this legal character. Though personally these things are not essential to the Christian—they do not justify him nor make him more righteous—yet, because he must live here on earth, he is under obligation, so far as outward conduct is concerned, to put himself on a level with other men in these things, and generally to help maintain temporal order and peace. Christ paid tribute money as a debt (Mt 17, 27), notwithstanding he had told Peter he was under no obligation to do so and would have committed no sin before God in omitting the act.

3. Another obligation is love, when a Christian voluntarily makes himself a servant of all men. Paul says (1 Cor 9, 19), "For though I was free from all men, I brought myself under bondage to all." This is not a requirement of human laws; no one who fails in this duty is censured or punished for neglect of legal obligations. The world is not aware of the commandment to love; of the obligation to submit to and serve a fellow-man. This fact is very apparent. Let one have wealth, and so long as he refrains from disgracing his neighbor's wife, from appropriating his neighbor's goods, sullying his honor or injuring his person, he is, in the eyes of the law, righteous. No law punishes him for avarice and penuriousness; for refusing to lend, to give, to aid, and to help his wronged neighbor secure justice. Laws made for restraint of the outward man are directed only toward evil works, which they prohibit and punish. Good works are left to voluntary performance. Civil law does not extort them by threats and punishment, but commends and rewards them, as does the Law of Moses.

4. Paul would teach Christians to so conduct themselves toward men and civil authority as to give no occasion for complaint or censure because of unfulfilled indebtedness to temporal law. He would not have them fail to satisfy the claims of legal obligation, but rather to go beyond its requirements, making themselves debtors voluntarily and serving those who have no claims on them. Relative to this topic, Paul says (Rom 1, 14), "I am debtor both to Greeks

and to Barbarians." Love's obligation enables a man to do
more than is actually required of him. Hence the Christian
always willingly renders to the state and to the individual
all service exacted by temporal regulations, permitting no
claims upon himself in this respect.

5.   Paul's injunction, then, might be expressed: Owe all
men, that you may owe none; owe everything, that you may
owe nothing. This sounds paradoxical. But one indebtedness is that of love, an obligation to God. The other is indebtedness to temporal law, an obligation in the eyes of the
world. He who makes himself a servant, who takes upon
himself love's obligation to all men, goes so far that no one
dares complain of omission; indeed, he goes farther than any
could desire. Thus he is made free. He lives under obligation to no one from the very fact that he puts himself under
obligation to all. This manner of presenting the thought
would be sustained by the Spirit in connection with other
duties; for instance: Do no good work, that you may do
only good works. Never be pious and holy, if you would
be always pious and holy. As Paul says (ch. 12, 16), "Be
not wise in your own conceits"; or (1 Cor 3, 18), "If any
man thinketh that he is wise among you in this world, let
him become a fool, that he may become wise." It is in this
sense we say: Owe all men that you may owe no man; or,
"Owe no man anything, but to love one another."

6.   Such counsel is given with the thought of the two obligations. He who would perform works truly good in the
sight of God, must guard against works seemingly brilliant
in the eyes of the world, works whereby men presume to
become righteous. He who desires to be righteous and
holy must guard against the holiness attained by works
without faith. Again, the seeker for wisdom must reject
the wisdom of men, of nature, wisdom independent of the
Spirit. Similarly, he who would be under obligation to none
must obligate himself to all in every respect. So doing, he
retains no claim of his own. Consequently, he soon rises
superior to all law, for law binds only those who have claims
of their own. Rightly is it said, "Qui cedit omnibus bonis,

omnibus satisfecit," "He who surrenders all his property, satisfies all men." How can one be under obligation when he does not, and cannot, possess anything? It is love's way to give all. The best way, then, to be under obligation to none is, through love to obligate one's self in every respect to all men. In this sense it may be said: If you would live, die; if you would not be imprisoned, incarcerate yourself; if you do not desire to go to hell, descend there; if you object to being a sinner, be a sinner; if you would escape the cross, take it upon yourself; if you would conquer the devil, let him vanquish you; would you overcome a wicked individual, permit him to overcome you. The meaning of it all is, we should readily submit to God, to the devil and to men, and willingly permit their pleasure; we are to insist on nothing, but to accept all things as they transpire. This is why Paul speaks as he does, "Owe no man anything," etc., instead of letting it go at the preceding injunction in verse 5, "Render therefore to all their dues, etc.

LOVE FULFILS THE LAW.

"For he that loveth his neighbor hath fulfilled the law."

7. Having frequently spoken of the character and fruits of love, it is unnecessary to introduce the subject here. The topic is sufficiently treated in the epistle lesson for the Sunday preceding Lent. We will look at the command to love, in the Law of God. Innumerable, endless, are the books and doctrines produced for the direction of man's conduct. And there is still no limit to the making of books and laws. Note the ecclesiastical and civil regulations, the spiritual orders and stations. These laws and doctrines might be tolerated, might be received with more favor, if they were founded upon and administered according to the one great law—the one rule or measure—of love; as the Scriptures do, which present many different laws, but all born of love, and comprehended in and subject to it. And these laws must yield, must become invalid, when they conflict with love.

Of Love's higher authority we find many illustrations in the Scriptures. Christ makes particular mention of the mat-

ter in Matthew 12, 3-4, where David and his companions ate
the holy showbread. Though a certain law prohibited all
but the priests from partaking of this holy food, Love was
empress here, and free. Love was over the Law, subjecting it to herself. The Law had to yield for the time being,
had to become invalid, when David suffered hunger. The
Law had to submit to the sentence: "David hungers and
must be relieved, for Love commands, Do good to your
needy neighbor. Yield, therefore, thou Law. Prevent not
the accomplishment of this good. Rather accomplish it thyself. Serve him in his need. Interpose not thy prohibitions." In connection with this same incident, Christ
teaches that we are to do good to our neighbor on the Sabbath; to minister as necessity demands, whatever the Sabbath restrictions of the Law. For when a brother's need
calls, Love is authority and the Law of the Sabbath is void.

8. Were laws conceived and administered in love, the
number of laws would matter little. Though one might not
hear or learn all of them, he would learn from the one or
two he had knowledge of, the principle of love taught in all.
And though he were to know all laws, he might not discover
the principle of love any more readily than he would in one.
Paul teaches this method of understanding and mastering
law when he says: "Owe no man anything, but to love one
another"; "He that loveth another hath fulfilled the law";
"If there be any other commandment, it is briefly comprehended in this saying, namely, Thou shalt love thy neighbor
as thyself"; "Love worketh no ill to his neighbor"; "Love is
the fulfilling of the law." Every word in this epistle lesson
proves Love mistress of all law.

9. Further, no greater calamity, wrong and wretchedness
is possible on earth than the teaching and enforcing of laws
without love. In such case, laws are but a ruinous curse,
making true the proverbs, "summum jus, summa injustitia,"
"The most strenuous right is the most strenuous wrong";
and again, Solomon's words (Ec 7, 17), "Noli nimium esse
justus," "Be not righteous overmuch." Here is where we
leave unperceived the beam in our own eye and proceed to

remove the mote from our neighbor's eye. Laws without love make the conscience timid and fill it with unreasonable terror and despair, to the great injury of body and soul. Thus, much trouble and labor are incurred all to no purpose.

10. An illustration in point is the before-mentioned incident of David in his hunger. 1 Sam 21, 6. Had the priest been disposed to refuse David the holy bread, had he blindly insisted on honoring the prohibitions of the Law and failed to perceive the authority of Love, had he denied this food to him who hungered, what would have been the result? So far as the priest's assistance went, David would have had to perish with hunger, and the priest would have been guilty of murder for the sake of the Law. Here, indeed, "summum jus, summa injustitia"—the most strenuous right would have been the most strenuous wrong. Moreover, on examining the heart of the priest who should be so foolish, you would find there the extreme abomination of making sin where there is no sin, and a matter of conscience where there is no occasion for it. For he holds it a sin to eat the bread, when really it is an act of love and righteousness. Then, too, he regards his act of murder—permitting David to die of hunger—not a sin, but a good work and service to God.

11. But who can fully portray this blind, perverted, abominable folly? It is the perpetration of an evil the devil himself cannot outdo. For it makes sin where there is no sin, and a matter of conscience without occasion. It robs of grace, salvation, virtue, and God with all his blessings, and that without reason, falsely and deceitfully. It emphatically denies and condemns God. Again, it makes murder and injustice a good work, a divine service. It puts the devil with his falsehoods in the place of God. It institutes the worst form of idolatry and ruins body and soul, destroying the former by hunger and the latter by a terrified conscience. It makes of God the devil, and of the devil God. It makes hell of heaven and heaven of hell; righteousness of sin, and sin of righteousness. This I call perversion—where strictest justice is the most strenuous wrong.

To this depravity Ezekiel has reference (ch. 13, 18-19):

"Thus saith the Lord Jehovah: Woe to the women that sew pillows upon all elbows, and make kerchiefs for the head of persons of every stature to hunt souls! Will ye hunt the souls of my people, and save souls alive for yourselves? And ye have profaned me among my people for handfuls of barley and for pieces of bread, to slay the souls that should not die, and to save the souls alive that should not live, by your lying to my people that hearken unto lies." What is meant but that the blind teachers of the Law terrify the conscience, and put sin and death in the place of grace and life, and grace and life where is only sin and death; and all for a handful of barley and a bit of bread? In other words, such teachers devote themselves to laws concerning strictly external matters, things that perish with the using, such as a drink of water and a morsel of bread, wholly neglecting love and harassing the conscience with fear of sin unto eternal death; as Ezekiel goes on to say (verses 22-23): "Because with lies ye have grieved the heart of the righteous, whom I have not made sad, and strengthened the hands of the wicked, that he should not return from his wicked way, and be saved alive; therefore ye shall no more see false visions, nor divine divinations: and I will deliver my people out of your hand; and ye shall know that I am Jehoviah."

12. Mark you, it is making the hearts of the righteous sad to load them with sins when their works are good; it is strengthening the hands of the wicked to make their works good when they are naught but sin. Relative to this subject, we read (Ps 14, 5): "There were they in great fear; for God is in the generation of the righteous." That is, the sting of conscience fills with fear where there is neither reason for fear nor for a disturbed conscience. That is feared as sin which is really noble service to God. The thought of the last passage is: When they should call upon God and serve him, they fear such conduct is sin and not divine service; again, when they have need to fear a service not divine, they are secure and unafraid. Isaiah's words (ch. 29, 13) are to the same effect: "Their fear of me is a

commandment of men which hath been taught them." Always the perverted people spoken of corrupt everything. They confidently call on God where is only the devil; they refrain in fear from calling on God where God is.

13. Such, mark you, is the wretched condition of them who are blindly occupied with laws and works and fail to comprehend the design of law and its mistress Love. Note, also, in the case of our miserable ecclesiasts and their followers, how rigidly they adhere to their own inventions! Though all the world meet ruin, their devices must be sustained; they must be perpetuated regardless of bodily illness and death, or of suffering and ruin for the soul. They even regard such destruction and ruin as divine service, and know no fear nor remorse of conscience. Indeed, so strongly entrenched are they in their wickedness, they will never return from it. Moreover, should one of their wretched number be permitted to alleviate the distress of his body and soul—to eat meat, to marry—he is afraid, he feels remorse of conscience; he is uncertain about sin and law, about death and hell; he calls not on God, nor serves him; all this, even though the body should die ten deaths and the soul go to the devil a hundred times.

14. Observe, then, the state of the world; how little flesh and blood can accomplish even in their best efforts; how dangerous to undertake to rule by law alone—indeed, how impossible it is, without great danger, to govern and instruct souls with mere laws, ignoring love and the Spirit, in whose hands is the full power of all law. It is written (Deut 33, 2), "At his right hand was a fiery law for them." This is the law of love in the Spirit. It shall regulate all laws at the left hand; that is, the external laws of the world. It is said (Ex 28, 30) that the priest must bear upon his breast, in the breastplate, "the Urim and the Thummim"; that is, Light and Perfection, indicative of the priest's office to illuminate the Law—to give its true sense—and faultlessly to keep and to teach it.

15. In the conception, the establishment and the observance of all laws, the object should be, not the furtherance

of the laws in themselves, not the advancement of works, but the exercise of love. That is the true purpose of law, according to Paul here, "He that loveth his neighbor hath fulfilled the law." Therefore, when the law contributes to the injury rather than the benefit of our neighbor, it should be ignored. The same law may at one time benefit our neighbor and at another time injure him. Consequently, it should be regulated according to its advantage to him. Law should be made to serve in the same way that food and raiment and other necessaries of life serve. We consider not the food and raiment themselves, but their benefit to our needy neighbor. And we cease to dispense them as soon as we perceive they no longer add to his comfort.

16. Suppose you were to come across an individual foolish enough to act with no other thought than that food and clothing are truly good things, and so proceed to stuff a needy one with unlimited food and drink unto choking, and to clothe him unto suffocation, and then not to desist. Suppose to the command, "Stop, you have suffocated, have already over-fed and over-clothed him, and all is lost effort now," the foolish one should reply: "You heretic, would you forbid good works? Food, drink and raiment are good things, therefore we must not cease to dispense them; we cannot do too much." And suppose he continued to force food and clothing on the man. Tell me, what would you think of such a one? He is a fool more than foolish; he is more mad than madness itself. But such is about the character of our ecclesiasts today, and of those who are so blind in the exercise of law as to act as if works were the only requisite, and to suffocate body and soul, being ignorant that the one purpose of law is to call forth the exercise of love. They make works superior to love, and a maid to her matron. Such perversion prevails to an extent distressing to think of, not to mention hearing and seeing it, or more, practicing and permitting it ourselves.

17. The commandment of love is not a long one; it is short. It is one injunction, not many. It is even not a commandment, and at the same time is all commandments.

Brief, and a unit in itself, its meaning is easily comprehended. But in its exercise, it is far-reaching, for it includes and regulates all commandments. So far as works are enjoined, it is no commandment at all; it names no peculiar work. Yet it represents all commandments, because properly the fulfilment of all commandments is the fulfilment of this. The commandment of love suspends every commandment, yet it perpetuates all. Its whole purpose is that we may recognize no commandment, no work, except as love dictates.

18.   As life on earth apart from works is an impossibility, necessarily there must be various commandments involving works. Yet Love is supreme over these requirements, dictating the omission or the performance of works according to its own best interests, and permitting no works opposed to itself.

To illustrate: A driver, holding the reins, guides team and wagon at will. If he were content merely to hold the reins, regardless of whether or no the team followed the road, the entire equipage—team, wagon, reins and driver— would soon be wrecked; the driver would be lying drowned in a ditch or a pool, or have his neck broken going over stumps and rocks. But if he dextrously regulates the movement of the outfit according to the road, observing where it is safe and where unsafe, he will proceed securely because wisely. Were he, in his egotism, to drive straight ahead, endeavoring to make the road conform to the movement of the wagon, at his pleasure, he would soon see how beautifully his plan would work.

19.   So it is when men are governed by laws and works, the laws not being regulated according to the people. The case is that of the driver who would regulate the road by the movements of the wagon. True, the road is often well suited to the straight course of the wagon. But just as truly the road is, in certain places, crooked and uneven, and then the wagon must conform to the course and condition of the road. Men must adapt themselves to laws and regulations wherever possible and where the laws are beneficial. But

where laws prove detrimental to men's interests, the former must yield. The ruler must wisely make allowance for love, suspending works and laws. Hence, philosophers say prudence—or circumspection or discretion as the ecclesiasts put it—is the guide and regulator of all virtues.

20. We read in a book of the ancient fathers that on a certain occasion of their assembling, the question was raised, which is really the noblest work? Various replies were given. One said prayer, another fasting; but St. Anthony was of the opinion that of all works and virtues, discretion is the best and surest way to heaven. These, however, were but childish, unspiritual ideas relating to their own chosen works. A Christian views the matter in quite a different light, and more judiciously. He concludes that neither discretion nor rashness avails before God. Only faith and love serve with him. But love is true discretion; love is the driver and the true discretion in righteous works. It always looks to the good of the neighbor, to the amelioration of his condition; just as the discretion of the world looks to the general welfare of the governed in the adjustment of political laws. Let this suffice on this point.

21. But the question arises: How can love fulfil the Law when love is but one of the fruits of faith and we have frequently said that only faith in Christ removes our sins, justifies us and satisfies all the demands of the Law? How can we make the two claims harmonize? Christ says, too (Mt 7, 12): "All things, therefore, whatsoever ye would that men should do unto you, even so do ye also unto them: for this is the law and the prophets." Thus he shows that love for one's neighbor fulfils both the Law and the prophets. Again, he says (Mt 22, 37-40): "Thou shalt love the Lord thy God . . . thy neighbor as thyself. On these two the whole law hangeth, and the prophets." Where, then, does Paul stand, who says (Rom 3, 31): "Do we then make the law of none effect through faith? God forbid: nay, we establish the law." Again (Rom 3, 28): "We reckon therefore that a man is justified by faith apart from the works of the law." And again (Rom 1, 17), "The righteous shall live by faith."

22. I reply: As we have frequently said, we must properly distinguish between faith and love. Faith deals with the heart, and love with the works. Faith removes our sins, renders us acceptable, justifies us. And being accepted and justified as to our person, love is given us in the Holy Spirit and we delight in doing good. Now, it is the nature of the Law to attack our person and demand good works; and it will not cease to demand until it gains its point. We cannot do good works without the Spirit and love. The Law constrains us to know ourselves with our imperfections, and to recognize the necessity of our becoming altogether different individuals that we may satisfy the Law. The Law does not exact so much of the heart as of works; in fact, it demands nothing but works and ignores the heart. It leaves the individual to discover, from the works required, that he must become an altogether different person. But faith, when it comes, creates a nature capable of accomplishing the works the Law demands. Thus is the Law fulfilled.

So Paul's sayings on the subject are beautiful and appropriate. The Law demands of us works; it must be fulfilled by works. Hence it cannot in every sense be said that faith fulfils the Law. However, it prepares the way and enables us to fulfil it, for the Law demands, not us, but our works. The Law constrains us—teaches us that we must be changed before we can accomplish its works; it makes us conscious of our inability as we are. On the other hand, love and works do not change us, do not justify us. We must be changed in person and justified before we can love and do good works. Our love and our works are evidence of justification and of a change, since they are impossible until the individual is free from sin and made righteous.

23. This explanation is given to enable us to perceive the true nature of the Law, of faith and of love; to ascribe to each its own mission; and rightly to understand the Scripture declarations in their harmonious relations that while faith justifies, it does not fulfil the Law, and that while love does not justify, it does fulfil the Law. The Law requires love and works, but does not mention the heart. The heart

is sensible of the Law, but love is not. Just as the Law, in requiring works before faith exists, is a sign to the individual leading him to recognize his utter lack of faith and righteousness, and to conclude he is conquered, so love in its fulfilment of the Law after faith intervenes is a sign and a proof to the individual of his faith and righteousness. Law and love, then, witness to him concerning his unrighteousness or his righteousness. After faith comes, love is evidence of righteousness. Before faith, man is sensible of the Law's oppression because he knows he does not possess what the Law requires. And the Law does not require a changed heart, but works. Love and works do not effect the fulfilment of the Law; they are themselves its fulfilment.

24. Now, though faith does not fulfil the Law, it contains that which effects its fulfilment; it secures the Spirit and love whereby the end is accomplished. On the other hand, if love does not justify us, it makes manifest the faith whereby we are justified. Briefly, as Paul says here, "Love is the fulfilment of the law." His thought is: Fulfilment of the Law is one thing, and effecting or furnishing its fulfilment another. Love fulfils the Law in the sense that love itself is its fulfilment; but faith fulfils it in the sense that it offers that by which it is fulfilled. For faith loves and works, as said in Galatians 5, 6, "Faith worketh through love." The water fills the pitcher; so does the cupbearer. The water fills of itself; the cupbearer fills with the water— "effective et formaliter implere," as the sophists would say.

25. Faith is ever the actor, and love the act. The law requires the act and thus forces the actor to be changed. The Law is then fulfilled by the act, which, however, the actor must perform. Thus Paul rejects the fancies of the sophists, who in the matter of love would make a distinction between the external work and the inner affection, saying: "Love is an inner affection that loves our neighbor when in our heart we wish him well." Its expression in works, however, they call the fruit of love. But we will not discuss this idea. Note, Paul terms love not only an affection, but an affectionate good act. Faith and the heart are

the actor and fulfiller of the Law. Paul says, "He that lov-eth his neighbor hath fulfilled the law." And love is the act, the fulfilling; for he says, "Love is the fulfilment of the law."

26. Another question arises: How can love for our neighbor be the fulfilment of the Law when we are required to love God supremely, even above our neighbor? I reply: Christ answers the question when he tells us (Mt 22, 39) the second commandment is like unto the first. He makes love to God and love to our neighbor the same love. The reason for this is, first: God, having no need for our works and benefactions for himself, bids us to do for our neighbor what we would do for God. He asks for himself only our faith and our recognition of him as God. The object of proclaiming his honor and rendering him praise and thanks here on earth is that our neighbor may be converted and brought into fellowship with God. Such service is called the love of God, and is performed out of love to God; but it is exercised for the benefit of our neighbor only.

27. The second reason why God makes love to our neighbor an obligation equal to love to himself is: God has made worldly wisdom foolish, desiring henceforth to be loved amid crosses and afflictions. Paul says (1 Cor 1, 21), "Seeing that in the wisdom of God the world through its wisdom knew not God, it was God's good pleasure through the foolishness of the preaching to save them that believe." Therefore, upon the cross he submitted himself unto death and misery, and imposed the same submission upon all his disciples. They who refused to love him before when he bestowed upon them food and drink, blessing and honor, must now love him in hunger and sorrow, in adversity and disgrace. All works of love, then, must be directed to our wretched, needy neighbors. In these lowly ones we are to find and love God, in them we are to serve and honor him, and only so can we do it. The commandment to love God is wholly merged in that to love our neighbors.

28. These facts restrain those elusive, soaring spirits that seek after God only in great and glorious undertakings.

It stops the mouths of those who strive after greatness like his, who would force themselves into heaven, presuming to serve and love him with their brilliant works. But they miss him by passing over him in their earthly neighbor, in whom God would be loved and honored. Therefore, they will hear, on the last day, the sentence (Mt 25, 42), "I was hungry, and ye did not give me to eat," etc. For Christ laid aside his divinity and took upon himself the form of a servant for the very purpose of bringing down and centering upon our neighbor the love we extend to himself. Yet we leave the Lord to lie here in his humiliation while we gaze open-mouthed into heaven and make great pretensions to love and service to God.

ALL COMMANDMENTS SUMMED UP IN LOVE.

"For this, Thou shalt not commit adultery, Thou shalt not kill, Thou shalt not steal, Thou shalt not covet; and if there be any other commandment, it is briefly summed up in this word, namely, Thou shalt love thy neighbor as thyself."

29. Love being the chief element of all law, it comprehends, as has been made sufficiently clear, all commandments. Its one concern is to be useful to man and not harmful; therefore, it readily discovers the way. Recognizing the fact that man, from his ardent self-love, seeks to promote his own interests and avoid injuring them, love endeavors to adopt the same course toward others. We will consider the commandment just cited, noticing how ingeniously and wisely it is arranged. It brings out four thoughts. First, it states who is under obligation to love: thou—the nearest, noblest, best individual we can command. No one can fulfil the Law of God for another; each must do it for himself. As Paul says (Gal 6, 5), "Each man shall bear his own burden." And (2 Cor 5, 10): "For we must all be made manifest before the judgment-seat of Christ; that each one may receive the things done in the body, according to what he hath done, whether it be good or bad." So it is said, "Thou, thou thyself, must love;" not, "Let someone else love for you." Though one can and should

pray that God may be gracious to another and help him, yet no one will be saved unless he himself fulfils God's command. It is not enough merely to pray that another may escape punishment, as the venders of indulgences teach; much rather, we should pray that he become righteous and observe God's precepts.

30. Second, the commandment names the most noble virtue—love. It does not say, "Thou shalt feed thy neighbor, give him drink, clothe him," all of which things are inestimably good works; it says, "Thou shalt love him." Love is the chief virtue, the fountain of all virtues. Love gives food and drink; it clothes, comforts, persuades, relieves and rescues. What shall we say of it, for behold he who loves gives himself, body and soul, property and honor, all his powers inner and external, for his needy neighbor's benefit, whether it be friend or enemy; he withholds nothing wherewith he may serve another. There is no virtue like love; there can be no special work assigned it as in the case of limited virtues, such as chastity, mercy, patience, meekness, and the like. Love does all things. It will suffer in life and in death, in every condition, and that even for its enemies. Well may Paul here say that all other commandments are briefly comprehended in the injunction, "Thou shalt love thy neighbor as thyself."

31. Third, the commandment names, as the sphere of our love, the noblest field, the dearest friend—our neighbor. It does not say, "Thou shalt love the rich, the mighty, the learned, the saint." No, the unrestrained love designated in this most perfect commandment does not apportion itself among the few. With it is no respect of persons. It is the nature of false, carnal, worldly love to respect the individual, and to love only so long as it hopes to derive profit. When such hope ceases, that love also ceases. The commandment of our text, however, requires of us free, spontaneous love to all men, whoever they may be, and whether friend or foe, a love that seeks not profit, and administers only what is beneficial. Such love is most active and powerful in serving the poor, the needy, the sick, the wicked, the simple-minded

and the hostile; among these it is always and under all circumstances necessary to suffer and endure, to serve and do good.

32. Note here, this commandment makes us all equal before God, without regard to distinctions incident to our stations in life, to our persons, offices and occupations. Since the commandment is to all—to every human being—a sovereign, if he be a human being, must confess the poorest beggar, the most wretched leper, his neighbor and his equal in the sight of God. He is under obligation, according to this commandment, not to extend a measure of help, but to serve that neighbor with all he has and all he controls. If he loves him as God here commands him to do, he must give the beggar preference over his crown and all his realm; and if the beggar's necessity requires, must give his life. He is under obligation to love his neighbor, and must admit that such a one is his neighbor.

33. Is not this a superior, a noble, commandment, which completely levels the most unequal individuals? Is it not wonderfully comforting to the beggar to have servants and lovers of such honor? wonderful that his poverty commands the services of a king in his opulence? that to his sores and wounds are subject the crown of wealth and the sweet savor of royal splendor? But how strange it would seem to us to behold kings and queens, princes and princesses, serving beggars and lepers, as we read St. Elizabeth did! Even this, however, would be a slight thing in comparison with what Christ has done. No one can ever equal him in the obedience wherewith he has exalted this commandment. He is a king whose honor transcends that of all other kings; indeed, he is the Son of God. And yet he puts himself on a level with the worst sinners, and serves them even to dying for them. Were ten kings of earth to serve to the utmost one beggar, it would be a remarkable thing; but of what significance would it be in comparison with the service Christ has rendered? The kings would be put to utter shame and would have to acknowledge their service unworthy of notice.

34. Learn, then, the condition of the world—how far it is, not only from Christ's immeasurable example, but from the commandment in this verse. Where are to be found any who comprehend the meaning of the little phrase "thy neighbor," notwithstanding there is, beside this commandment, the natural law of service written in the hearts of all men? Not an individual is there who does not realize, and who is not forced to confess, the justice and truth of the natural law outlined in the command (Mt 7, 12), "All things therefore whatsoever ye would that men should do unto you, even so do ye also unto them." The light of this law shines in the inborn reason of all men. Did they but regard it, what need have they of books, teachers or laws? They carry with them in the depths of their hearts a living book, fitted to teach them fully what to do and what to omit, what to accept and what to reject, and what decision to make.

Now, the command to love our neighbors as ourselves is equivalent to that other, "Whatsoever ye would that men should do unto you," etc. Every individual desires to be loved and not hated; and he also feels and sees his obligation to exercise the same disposition toward others. The carrying out of this obligation is loving another as himself. But evil lust and sinful love obscure the light of natural law, and blind man, until he fails to perceive the guide-book in his heart and to follow the clear command of reason. Hence he must be restrained and repelled by external laws and material books, with the sword and by force. He must be reminded of his natural light and have his own heart revealed to him. Yet admonition does not avail; he does not see the light. Evil lust and sinful love blind him. With the sword and with political laws he must still be outwardly restrained from perpetrating actual crimes.

35. The fourth thing the commandment presents is the standard by which we are to measure our love—an excellent model. Those are particularly worthy instructions and commandments which present examples. This commandment holds up a truly living example—"thyself." It is a better model than any example the saints have set. The saints are

dead and their deeds are past, but this example ever lives.
Everyone must admit a consciousness of his own love for
himself; of his ardent concern for his temporal life; of his
careful nourishment of his body with food, raiment and all
good things; of his fleeing from death and avoiding evil.
This is self-love; something we are conscious of in ourselves.
What, then, is the teaching of the commandment? To do
to another as you do to yourself; to value his body and his
life equally with your own body and life. Now, how could
God have pointed you to an example dearer, more pleasing
and more to the purpose than this example—the deep instinct of your nature? Indeed, your depth of character is
measured by the writing of this command in your heart.

36. How will you fare with God if you do not love your
neighbor? Feeling this commandment written within your
heart, your conscience will condemn you. Your whole conduct will be an example witnessing against you, testifying
to your failure to do unto others as the natural instinct of
your being, more forcibly than all the examples of the saints,
has taught you to do. But how will it go with the ecclesiasts in particular—the churchmen with their singing and
praying, their cowls and bald pates, and all their jugglery?
I make no comment on the fact that they have never observed the commandment. I ask, however, when has their
monastic fanaticism permitted them time and opportunity to
perceive for once this law in their hearts, to become sensible
of the example set them in their own human instinct, or
even to read the precept in books or hear it preached? Poor,
miserable people! Do you presume to think that God will
make void this, love's commandment, so deeply and clearly
impressed upon the heart, so beautifully and unmistakably
illustrated in your own natures, and in the many written and
spoken words as well—think you God will do this on account
of your cowls and bald pates, and regard what you have
been devising and performing?

37. Alas, how shamelessly the world has ignored this
beautiful and impressive commandment wherein are so skilfully presented the individual, the task, the model and the

sphere of labor! And, on the other hand, how shamefully it occupies itself with the very reverse of what is taught in this commandment! Its whole practice and tendency seem to be to place our responsibility upon others; monks and priests must be righteous for us and pray in our stead, that we may personally be excused. For the noblest virtue, love, we substitute self-devised works; in the place of our neighbors we put wood and stone, raiment and food, even dead souls—the saints of heaven. These we serve; with them we are occupied; they are the sphere wherein we exercise ourselves. Instead of the noblest example—"as thyself"—we look to the legends and the works of saints. We presume to imitate such outward examples, omitting the duty which our own nature and life present and which the command of God outlines, notwithstanding such duty offers more than we could ever fulfil. Even if we could accomplish all it offers, we would still not equal Christ.

LOVE WORKS ONLY GOOD TO ITS NEIGHBOR.

"Love worketh no ill to his neighbor: love, therefore, is the fulfilment of the law."

38. The Ten Commandments forbid doing evil to our neighbor—"Thou shalt not kill, Thou shalt not commit adultery," etc. The apostle, employing similar phraseology, says that love observes all these commands, injuring none. Not only that; it effects good for all. It is practically doing evil to permit our neighbor to remain in peril when we can relieve him, even though we may not have been instrumental in placing him where he is. If he is hungry and we do not feed him when it is in our power to do so, we practically permit him to die of hunger. We should take this view concerning any perilous condition, any adverse circumstance, with our neighbors. How love is the fulfilment of the Law, we have now heard.

Fifth Sunday After Epiphany

Text: Colossians 3, 12-17.

12 Put on therefore, as God's elect, holy and beloved, a heart of compassion, kindness, lowliness, meekness, longsuffering; 13 forbearing one another, and forgiving each other, if any man have a complaint against any; even as the Lord forgave you, so also do ye: 14 and above all these things put on love, which is the bond of perfectness. 15 And let the peace of Christ rule in your hearts, to the which also ye were called in one body; and be ye thankful. 16 Let the Word of Christ dwell in you richly; in all wisdom teaching and admonishing one another with psalms and hymns and spiritual songs, singing with grace in your hearts unto God. 17 And whatsoever ye do, in word or in deed, do all in the name of the Lord Jesus, giving thanks to God the Father through him.

THE GLORIOUS ADORNMENT OF CHRISTIANS.

1. This text is also a letter of admonition, teaching what manner of fruit properly results from faith. Paul deals kindly with the Colossians. He does not command, urge nor threaten, as teachers of the Law must do in the case of those under the Law. He persuades them with loving words in view of the blessing and grace of God received, and in the light of Christ's own example. Christians should act with readiness and cheerfulness, being moved neither by fear of punishment nor by desire for reward, as frequently before stated. This admonition has been so oft repeated in the preceding epistle lesson that we know, I trust, what constitutes a Christian. Therefore we will but briefly touch on the subject.

76

"Put on, therefore."

2. In the epistle for New Year's day we have sufficiently explained the meaning of "putting on"; how by faith we put on Christ, and he us; how in love we put on our neighbor, and our neighbor us. The Christian apparel is of two kinds —faith and love. Christ wore two manner of garments— one whole and typical of faith, the other divided and typical of love.

Paul here has reference to the latter garment, love. He would teach us Christians the manner of ornaments and apparel we are to wear in the world; not silk or precious gold. To women these are forbidden of Peter (1 Pet 3, 3), and of Paul (1 Tim 2, 9). Love for our neighbor is a garment well befitting us—that love which leads us to concern ourselves about the neighbor and his misfortunes. Such love is called the ornament of a Christian character—an ornament in the eyes of men.

3. Observe the tender and sacred style of the apostle's admonition, a style he is wont to use toward us. He does not drive us with laws, but persuades by reminding us of the ineffable grace of God; for he terms us the "elect of God," and "holy" and "beloved." He would call forth the fruits of faith, desiring them to be yielded in a willing, cheerful and happy spirt. The individual who sincerely believes and trusts that before God he is beloved, holy and elect, will consider how to sustain his honors and titles, how to conduct himself worthily of them; more, he will love God with a fervor enabling him to do or omit, or to suffer, all things cheerfully, and will never know how to do enough. But he who doubts such attitude of God toward himself will not recognize the force of these words. He will not feel the power of the statement that we are holy, beloved, elect, in the sight of God.

4. Let us disregard, therefore, the saints who elect and love themselves; who adorn themselves with the works of the Law; who observe fasts and discipline; who regard raiment and position, for they are unwilling to be sinners before God. Our ornaments are unlike these, and not as-

sociated with such mockeries. They are honesty, sincerity, good works, service to our neighbor. We are unfettered by laws regarding food, raiment, times, etc. We are holy in the sight of God, before whom none can be holy until he sees himself a sinner and rejects his own righteousness. But the class mentioned are holy in their own estimation; therefore, they ever remain wicked—sinners in the sight of God. We are beloved of God because we despise ourselves, we judge and condemn ourselves and reject our self-love. The others, because they love and esteem themselves, are despicable and unacceptable in the sight of God. Again, we are chosen of God for the reason that we despise ourselves as filth. Such God chooses, and has chosen from eternity. Because the would-be saints elect themselves, God will reject them, as indeed he has from eternity. Now, this is what Paul means by these words,

"A heart of compassion."

5. They stand for a part of the ornament, the beautiful, charming Christian jewel, that becomes us better in the sight of God than pearls, precious stones, silk and gold become us in the eyes of the world. "A heart of compassion" is evidence of the true Christian. Paul would say: "Not simply in external deed, or in appearance, are ye to be merciful, but in the inmost heart." He refers to that sincere and whole-souled mercy characteristic of the father and mother who witness the distress of a child for whom they would readily expose their lives or sacrifice all they possess. The Christian's mind and heart should be constantly devoted to merciful deeds, with an ardor so intense as to make him unaware he is doing good and compassionate acts.

6. With this single phrase Paul condemns the works and arbitrary rules of hypocritical saints, whose severity will not permit them to associate with sinners. Their rigorous laws must be all-controlling. They do nothing but compel and drive. They exhibit no mercy, but perpetual reproach, censure, condemnation, blame and bluster. They can endure no imperfection. But among Christians many are sinners, many infirm. In fact, Christians associate only with these;

not with saints. Christians reject none, but bear with all. Indeed, they are as sincerely interested for sinners as they would be for themselves were they the infirm. They pray for the sinners, teach, admonish, persuade, do all in their power to reclaim. Such is the true character of a Christian. So God, in Christ, has dealt with us and ever deals. So Christ dealt with the adulteress (Jn 8, 11) when he released her from her tormentors, and with his gracious words influenced her to repentance and suffered her to depart. We read of St. Antony having said that Paphrutius knew how souls are to be saved, because he rescued a certain individual from brethren who persecuted and oppressed him for his transgression. See "Lives of the Fathers."

Were God to deal with us according to the rigor of his laws, we should all be lost. But he mercifully suspends the Law. Isaiah says (ch. 9. 4): "For the yoke of his burden, and the staff of his shoulder, the rod of his oppressor, thou hast broken." God now only persuades.

7. Note how involved in the Law and in hypocrisy they still are who esteem themselves prominent saints and at the same time are intolerant of the infirmities of Christians. If they fail to find perfect holiness—a miracle of purity—in those who possess Christ and know the Gospel, then nothing is as it should be; the heavens are on the point of falling and the earth about to be destroyed. They can only judge, censure and deride, saying: "Oh, yes, he is truly evangelical; indeed, he is a visionary!" Thus they indicate their utter blindness. With the beam constantly in their own eyes, they show how little they know of Christ.

Know, then, when you meet one so ready to censure and condemn, one requiring absolute perfection in Christians— know that such a one is merely an enforcer of the Law, a base hypocrite, a merciless jailer, with no true knowledge of Christ. As, with Christians, there is no law but all is love, so neither can there be judgment, condemnation and censure. And he who calls another a visionary is certainly a visionary ten-fold himself. In the thing for which he judges and condemns another, he condemns himself. Since he ignores mercy and all but the Law, he finds no mercy in the sight of God; in fact, he has never experienced, never tasted, God's mercy. To his taste, both God and neighbor are bitter as gall and wormwood.

8. But tender mercy is to be shown only to Christians and only among Christians. With the rejecters and persecutors of the Gospel we must deal differently. It is not right that my charity be liberal enough to tolerate unsound doctrine. In the case of false faith and doctrine there is neither love nor patience. Against these it is my duty earnestly to contend and not to yield a hair's breadth. Otherwise—when faith is not imperiled—I must be unfailingly kind and merciful to all notwithstanding the infirmities of their lives. I may not censure, oppress nor drive; I must persuade, entreat and tolerate. A defective life does not destroy Christianity; it exercises it. But defective doctrine—false belief—destroys all good. So, then, toleration and mercy are not permissible in the case of unsound doctrine; only anger, opposition and death are in order, yet always in accordance with the Word of God.

9. On the other hand, they who are mercifully tolerated must not imagine that because they escape censure and force, their beliefs and practices are right. They must not construe such mercy as encouragement to become indolent and negligent, and to continue in their error. Mercy is not extended them with any such design. The object is to give them opportunity to recover zeal and strength. But if they be disposed to remain as they are, very well; let them alone. They will not long continue thus; the devil will lead them farther astray, until finally they will completely apostatize, even becoming enemies to the Gospel. Such will be their end if they permit mercy to be lavished upon them in vain. We may not be indolent and asleep in the matter of our false doctrines, relying upon the fact that we are not despised nor constrained of men. There is particular need to be active and diligent, for the devil neither sleeps nor rests. We need beware that he does not lead us where we will never enjoy God's mercy.

"Kindness, lowliness, meekness, longsuffering."

10.   These words represent the other elements of Christian character. Kindness you will find defined in the second epistle lesson for the early Christmas service. It characterizes the conduct of the individual who is gentle and sympathetic to all; who repels none with forbidding countenance, harsh words or rude deportment. We Germans would call such a one affable and friendly disposed. Kindness is a virtue not confined to certain works; it modifies the whole life. The kindly person is obliging to everyone, not displeased with any, and is attractive to all men. In contrast are those peculiar characters who have pleasure in nothing but their own conceits; who insist on others accommodating themselves to them and their ways, while they yield to none. Such individuals are termed "uncivil."

11.   But the liberality of kindness is not to be extended to false doctrine. Only relative to conduct and works is it to be exercised. As oft before stated, love with all its works and fruits has no place in the matter of unsound doctrine. I must love my neighbor and show him kindness whatever the imperfections of his life. But if he refuses to believe or to teach sound doctrine, I cannot, I dare not, love him or show him kindness. According to Paul (Gal 1, 8-9), I must hold him excommunicated and accursed, even though he be an angel from heaven.

Thus remarkably do faith and love differ and are distinct. Love will be, must be, kind even to the bitterest enemy so long as he assails not faith and doctrine. But it will not, it cannot, tolerate the individual who does, be it father, mother or dearest friend. Deut 13, 6-8. Love, then, must be exercised, not in relation to the doctrine and faith of our neighbor, but relative to his life and works. Faith, on the contrary, has to do, not with his works and life, but with his doctrine and belief.

12.   I think we must know by this time the meaning of "lowliness" of mind—esteeming one's self least and others greater. As Christ illustrates it, occupying the lowest seat at the wedding, and this cheerfully. We are to serve even

when our service is not desired, and to minister unto our enemies. So Christ humbled himself before Judas the betrayer, and before all of us. He came, not to be served, but to serve. That humbleness of mind is a rare virtue is not to be wondered at, for every Christian grace is a rarity. Particularly are graces lacking with those who, professing to know most of Christ, find something to censure in all Christians. Christianity Paul calls a mystery of God; and it is likely to continue so.

13. "Meekness" is opposed to anger. The meek man is not easily excited to exhibit anger, to curse, smite, hate, or wish evil to any, even an enemy. To refrain thus is an art. Hypocrites—in fact, all the world—can be meek toward friends and those who treat them well. But true meekness and humility will remain only among the elect and beloved saints of God, as Paul here implies. Even among these are many deficient in all, or at least a large part, of the Christian graces. Hypocrites may thus find something to censure, something whereat to be offended, in the beloved, elect saints of God. And the true saints have occasion to exercise mercy, humility, meekness and forbearance. They whom Paul here terms elect and beloved saints of God, though slightly deficient in humility, meekness and forbearance, are not therefore unholy, not rejected and despised.

14. Paul makes a distinction between longsuffering and forbearance, as in Romans 2, 4: "Despisest thou the riches of his goodness and forbearance and longsuffering?" In "longsuffering" we have the thought here and there expressed by God in the Psalms and elsewhere by the Hebrew "arich apaim"—"slow to wrath." God patiently bears with evil. Indeed, he repeatedly delays vengeance, apparently more ready to forgive than to punish, even under extreme provocation and having just reason to chastise. Longsuffering extends farther than patience. Patience bears evil and injustice; but longsuffering delays punishment. It does not design to punish; it would not take hasty revenge. Unlike the revengeful, it wishes no one evil. Many we see, indeed, who suffer much and are patient but at the same time trust

in a final avenging. The longsuffering Christian, however, is opposed to revenge, desiring the sinner to amend his ways.

"Forbearing one another, and forgiving each other, if any man have a complaint against any; even as the Lord forgave you, so also do ye."

15. In this verse all law is abolished among Christians. One is not permitted to demand, through process of law, the recovery of his property. He must forgive and yield. Christ's example enjoins this principle; he has forgiven us. And what is the extent of his forgiveness? He pardons past sins, but that is not all; as John says (1 Jn 2, 1-2), "If any man sin, we have an Advocate with the Father, Jesus Christ the righteousness and he is the propitiation for our sins."

16. Note, it is the true Christian saints whom Paul describes, but he looks upon them as infirm to the extent of offending and complaining against one another. This is a state of affairs by no means becoming Christians and saints. So I say Christ's kingdom is a mystery obscure beyond the power of our preaching and teaching sufficiently to explain. Unbelievers cannot be induced to work, but believers cannot be withheld from working. Some would not believe and some would not love.

It is true of Christ's kingdom that his Christians are not perfectly holy. They have begun to be holy and are in a state of progression. There are still to be found among them anger, evil desire, unholy love, worldly care and other deplorable infirmities, remains of the old Adam. Paul speaks of these things as burdens which one must bear for a neighbor (Gal 6, 2), and in Romans 15, 1, he admonishes us to "bear the infirmities of the weak." Likewise Christ loved his apostles much and suffered much from them, and he still daily bears with his own.

17. Some, enumerating the fruits of the Spirit mentioned in Galatians 5, 22-23, say a Christian should be gentle, meek, longsuffering, chaste; and they look upon this passage as a law commanding such fruits. Hence they refuse to recognize as Christians any who fail to possess the fruits in perfection. Now, such individuals cannot believe there is a

Christ, certain as the fact is. They judge malignantly, complaining that Christians do not exist. They take offense at Christ for his superior wisdom. For Christ has given us scriptural authority for knowing Christians by their fruits. He says (Mt 7, 16), "By their fruits ye shall know them." Here they are emphatic.

18. Can you locate the failure of such an individual? He fails in the fact that he understands absolutely nothing of Christ's kingdom. For he misinterprets the passages referring to Christians. He understands the statement that Christians should be kind and meek, to mean they must never become angry, must bear anything and show impatience toward none; if they do not so, they cannot be Christians, for they have not the fruits. Dear man, what but his own blindness can lead him to such a conclusion? He fancies Christianity to be a holy order of perfection, altogether without infirmity, a perfection as in heaven among the angels. But tell me, where do the Scriptures speak thus of Christians?

But whoso recognizes Christianity as a progressive order yet in its beginning, will not be offended at the occasional manifestation of ungentleness, unkindness and impatience on the part of a Christian; for he remembers that Christians are commanded to bear one another's burdens and infirmities. He knows that the enumeration of the fruits of the Spirit is not a record of laws the observance of which is imperative or Christ will be denied. He is aware the passage is to be interpreted as meaning that Christians are to strive to be kind; that is the mark at which they aim. However, even though they have made a beginning and some progress in this virtue, they often are unkind and bear fruits directly the opposite of the fruits of the Spirit. True, the text quoted says we should be kind, but it does not say we are kind. We are tending toward it, we are in a state of progression; but during the progress much of the old and as yet untransformed nature is intermingled.

19. Know, then, that in a mysterious way Christ is in his saints, and beware of judging or condemning anyone when you have not positive assurance that he believes and teaches

contrary to the Gospel. But whoso does oppose the Gospel, you may safely judge to be without Christ, and under the sway of the devil. Pray for such a one and admonish him, in the hope of his conversion. But in the case of one who endorses and honors the Gospel, observe Paul's comment (Rom 14, 4): "Who art thou that judgest the servant of another?. to his own lord he standeth or falleth. Yea, he shall be made to stand; for the Lord hath power to make him stand." And again (1 Cor 10, 12): "Wherefore let him that thinketh he standeth take heed lest he fall." Christ would be at the same time hidden and revealed, found and not found. He permits the intermingling of some infirmities with the fruits of the Spirit, that he may conceal himself, and that malicious judges may be offended.

"And above all these things put on love, which is the bond of perfectness."

20. From longsuffering and meekness the apostle distinguishes love and other jewels of spiritual beauty whereof we have already heard, though all are comprehended in love. As faith is the chief element of Christian character, so love is chief of the fruits of the Spirit, the jewel of surpassing beauty. Therefore Paul says, "Above all these things put on love." Love transcends mercy, kindness, meekness and humility. Paul calls it "the bond of perfectness" because it unites human hearts; not a partial unity, based on similarity or close relationship, but a complete unity among all men and in all relations. It makes us of one mind, one heart, one desire. It permits no one to originate a peculiar order of doctrine or faith. All who love are of the same belief. Consequently there is the same purpose of heart with the poor and the rich, with rulers and subjects, the ill and the well, the high and the low, the honored and the disgraced. The loving heart permits all to share in its good; more, it participates in the adversities of all men, regarding them as its own. Where love is, perfect unity and communion obtain in every event, good or bad. It is a most perfect bond.

21. Where love is lacking, hearts are united and aims single in but few relations; in most things there is disagree-

ment. For instance: Robbers have a common bond, but it
is no more than a common purpose in committing robbery
and murder. Worldly friends are of the same mind so far
as concerns their own interests. Monks are united in relation to their order and their honor. Herod and Pilate
agreed, but simply in regard to Christ. For the most part it
is exceptional that one monk, priest or layman agrees with
another. Their bond of union is weak; they are as chaff
bound with straw.

"And let the peace of Christ rule in your hearts, to
which also ye were called."

22. There is much to threaten the sundering of love's
bond. The devil never sleeps, but continually stirs up discord and unrest. Paul does not deny that the bond is assailed. But he exhorts us to resist, remembering that love
must be exercised by opposition. He admonishes us to let
the peace of Christ have dominion in our hearts. The
thought of the verse is: Though the peace of the world
and the flesh abides not, though you must witness the forces
of discord and disruption, nevertheless let your hearts have
peace in Christ.

We spoke of the peace of God in the epistle selection for
the Fourth Sunday in Advent—Philippians 4, 7. This is the
peace whereunto the Gospel calls; not the peace of the
world, the flesh or the devil, but the peace that passeth all
understanding, of which Paul tells us. We are to hold the
peace of God, not only when all is well, but when sin, death,
the flesh, the world and all calamities rage.

"And be ye thankful."

23. "Thankfulness" here may be taken in either of two
senses: First, thankfulness toward God, Paul's thought being: Let the remembrance of all God has done for you move
you to gratitude for his grace and mercy, a gratitude to
which shall succeed love and peace. Secondly, we may understand thankfulness toward men—gratitude for all the
benefits received from our fellows. The apostle elsewhere
(2 Tim 3, 2) speaks of there being, in the last days, among
other vices, that of "unthankfulness" of men toward each

other. Let everyone make choice for himself of the two applications. It is my opinion, since Paul later takes up the subject of gratitude to God, and since he is here handling that of love to our neighbor—it is my opinion he has reference here to gratitude to our fellowmen. This, I think, is his meaning.

Man is glad to have love shown him; he is quite willing to receive good from others and to be dealt with according to the Gospel. At the same time, he is not disposed to manifest love to his fellows: favors shown him are lost upon his ingratitude. Though love is not defeated by ungratefulness—for it bears all things (1 Cor 13, 7)—yet unthankfulness produces weariness and aversion; and it is a base, unjust and shameful thing for one who continually lends assistance not to be served in return.

24. Paul says on this topic (Gal 6, 6), "Let him that is taught in the Word communicate unto him that teacheth in all good things." And he declares (1 Tim 5, 17) that they who labor in the Word and doctrine are worthy of double honor. In the ninth chapter of First Corinthians he speaks at length on how teachers are entitled to support, saying the mouth of the threshing ox should not be muzzled; that would be gross ingratitude. Of such unthankfulness he here hints. It is true today, and ever has been, that preachers of the Word of God must in general seek their own bread, and receive ingratitude as their reward for the wonderful blessings they confer. Were it their part to celebrate masses and indulgences, gratitude would be forthcoming; great would be the gifts and service rendered them as expression of thankfulness. But just as ungratefully were the Levites treated under the old Law, in contrast with the favor shown the priests of idols and groves.

"Let the word of Christ dwell in you richly; in all wisdom teaching and admonishing one another with psalms and hymns and spiritual songs, singing with grace in your hearts unto God."

25. This verse appropriately follows the injunction to be thankful. Paul would say: Be careful to honor teachers

and preachers, being grateful that they handle the Word
and may richly impart it to you. I do not imagine Paul
refers to the giving of the Word of God from heaven, for
it is not within man's power to so give it; God alone can
commit it to us. So he has done and continues to do. On
every occasion when he permits the Gospel to be preached,
he showers the message upon us abundantly, withholding
no essential knowledge. But, after it is given, we ought to
be thankful and to faithfully read and hear it, sing and speak
it, and meditate upon it day and night. And it should be
our part to secure teachers enough to minister it to us liberally and continuously. This is what is meant by letting
the Word of God dwell among us richly.

26. Satiated, indolent spirits soon grow tired and dismiss
their pastors to go wherever they wish. The latter are forced
to seek a living by other work, and thus God's Word is
neglected and becomes rare and thinly sown in the land.
Nehemiah (ch. 13, 10) complains that the Levites, because of lack of support, were forced to leave their worship
and temple and flee to the fields or start false worship and
fables to mislead the people. They then received enough to
exist—they became wealthy.

It has come about in the Christian Church that as often
as the support of godly pastors and teachers has grown to
be a burden, as Augustine laments has been the case, these
have been either forced to neglect the Word to labor for
their own support, or forced to invent that wretched, accursed worship now prevalent throughout the world and
whereby the preachers have attained lordly position. With
the revival of the Gospel the financial difficulty mentioned
is recurring, and it will continue to recur. One hundred
dollars cannot now be raised for the support of a good
schoolmaster or preacher where formerly a thousand dollars—yes, incomputible sums—were contributed toward
churches, institutions, masses, vigils and the like. Once
more God punishes ingratitude by permitting his preachers
to withdraw wholly from the ministry and to engage in their
own support, or by sending upon the people even greater

delusions than ever, which defraud them of wealth and destroy body and soul. For they refuse to let the Word of God dwell among them richly. Paul adds the modifying phrase,

"In all wisdom."

27. Were we to have the Word of God so richly as to ring in every street corner, to be sung everywhere by all children—as they designed who into the pulpits and the lessons introduced canonical prayers and singing and reading—what would all this profit without an understanding mind—without wisdom? For the Word of God was given to make us wise. It was intended that we should understand it; that it should be preached and sung intelligibly. And they who minister it, who sing and speak it, ought to be wise, understanding everything pertaining to the salvation of the soul and the honor of God. That is what it means to have the Word of God dwell among us in all wisdom. Here Paul briefly overthrows the vociferous practices of the churches and monasteries where so much preaching and reading obtain while at the same time the Gospel is not understood. He seems to have foreseen the coming time when the Word of God should freely prevail, but with no resulting wisdom; the time when men should daily increase in ignorance and fanaticism until they should become mere dolts, so completely void of wisdom as to call vociferation and boasting divine worship, and to regard that preaching the salvation of souls.

28. What it is to teach and to admonish has been frequently explained. Here Paul makes the duty of instruction common to all Christians—"teaching and admonishing one another." That is, aside from the regular office of preaching, each is to teach himself and others, thus making everyday use of the Word of God, publicly and privately, generally and specially.

29. As I see it, the apostle's distinction of the three words —psalms, hymns and spiritual songs—is this: "psalms" properly indicates those productions of David and others constituting the Book of Psalms; "hymns" refers to the

songs of the prophets occasionally mentioned in the Scriptures—songs of Moses, Deborah, Solomon, Isaiah, Daniel,
Habakkuk, with the Magnificat, the Benediction, and the
like, called "Canticles"; "spiritual songs" are those not written in the Scriptures but of daily origin with men. Paul
calls these latter "spiritual" to a greater degree than psalms
and hymns, though he recognizes those as themselves spiritual. He forbids worldly, sensual and unbecoming songs, desiring us to sing of spiritual things. It is then that our
songs are calculated to benefit and instruct, as he says.

30. But what is the significance of Paul's phrase "with
grace"? I offer the explanation that he refers to the grace
of God and means that the singing of spiritual songs is to
be voluntary, uncompelled, spontaneous, rendered with
cheerfulness and prompted by love; not extorted by authority and law, as is the singing in our churches today. No one
sings, preaches or prays from a recognition of mercy and
grace received. The motive is a hope for gain, or a fear of
punishment, injury and shame; or again, the holiest individuals bind themselves to obedience, or are driven to it, for
the sake of winning heaven, and not at all to further the
knowledge of the Word of God—the understanding of it
richly and in all wisdom, as Paul desires it to be understood.
I imagine Paul has in mind the charm of music and the
beauty of poetry incident to song. He says in Ephesians 4,
29: "Let no corrupt speech proceed out of your mouth, but
such as is good for edifying as the need may be, that it may
give grace to them that hear." Likewise should songs be
calculated to bring grace and favor to them who hear. Foul,
unchaste and superfluous words have no place therein, nor
have any inappropriate elements, elements void of significance and without virtue and life. Hymns are to be rich in
meaning, to be pleasing and sweet, and thus productive of
enjoyment for all hearers. The singing of such songs is
very properly called in Hebrew singing "with grace," as
Paul has it. Of this character of songs are the psalms and
hymns of the Scriptures; they are good thoughts presented
in pleasing words. Some songs, though expressed in charm-

ing words, are worldly and carnal; while others presenting good thoughts are at the same time expressed in words inappropriate, unattractive and devoid of grace.

"Singing with grace in your hearts unto God."

31. Paul does not enjoin silence of the lips. He would have words of the mouth proceed from the heart sincerely and fervently; not hypocritically, as Isaiah mentions (ch. 29, 13), saying: "This people draw nigh unto me, and with their mouth and with their lips do honor me, but have removed their heart far from me." Paul would have the Word of God to dwell among Christians generally, and richly to be spoken, sung and meditated upon everywhere; and that understandingly and productive of spiritual fruit, the Word being universally prized. He would that men thus sing unto the Lord heartfelt praise and thanks. He says let the Word "dwell" among you. Not merely lodge as a guest for a night or two, but abide with you forever. He is constantly apprehensive of human doctrines.

"And whatsoever ye do, in word or in deed, do all in the name of the Lord Jesus, giving thanks to God the Father through him."

32. The works of Christians are not circumscribed by name, time nor place. Whatever Christians do is good; whenever done it is timely; wherever wrought it is appropriately. So Paul names no work. He makes no distinction, but concludes all works good, whether it be eating or drinking, speaking or keeping silence, waking or sleeping, going or staying, being idle or otherwise. All acts are eminently worthy because done in the name of the Lord Jesus. Such is Paul's teaching here. And our works are wrought in the name of the Lord Jesus when we by faith hold fast the fact that Christ is in us and we in him in the sense that we no longer labor but he lives and works in us. Paul says (Gal 2, 20), "It is no longer I that live, but Christ liveth in me." But when we do a work as of ourselves, then it is wrought in our own name and there is nothing good about it.

33. The expression "in the name of God," or "Go in the

name of Jesus," is frequently uttered falsely and in sheer hypocrisy. The saying is, "All misfortunes rise in the name of God." For teachers of false doctrines habitually offer their commodities in the name of God. They even come in the name of Christ, as he himself foretells. Mt 24, 24. To sincerely and earnestly speak and work in Jesus' name, necessarily the heart must accord with the utterances of the mouth. As the lips declare in the name of God, so must the heart confidently, with firm faith, hold that God directs and performs the work. Peter teaches the same (1 Pet 4, 11): "If any man ministereth [perform anything], ministering as of the strength which God supplieth." Then will the venture prosper. No Christian should undertake to do any deed in his own ability and directed by his own judgment. Rather let him be assured that God works with and through him. Paul says (1 Cor 9, 26): "I therefore so run, as not uncertainly; so fight I, as not beating the air."

34. Such an attitude will result in praise and thanks to God as the one to whom are due all honor and praise for every good thing. So Paul teaches and also Peter. Immediately after declaring that we are to work according to the ability which God gives, Peter adds "that in all things God may be glorified through Jesus Christ." But he who undertakes anything in his own ability, however he may glorify God with his lips, lies and deceives, like the hypocrite in the Gospel. Thankfulness, therefore, is the only duty we can perform unto God; and this is not to be rendered of ourselves, but through our Mediator, Jesus. Without him none can come to the Father, none can be accepted. Of this fact we have often spoken.

Third Sunday Before Lent

Text: 1 Cor 9, 24-27; 10, 1-5.

24 "Know ye not that they that run in a race run all, but one receiveth the prize? Even so run; that ye may attain. 25 And every man that striveth in the games exerciseth self-control in all things. Now they do it to receive a corruptible crown; but we an incorruptible. 26 I therefore so run, as not uncertainly; so fight I, as not beating the air: 27 but I buffet my body, and bring it into bondage: lest by any means, after that I have preached to others, I myself should be rejected. 1 For I would not, brethren, have you ignorant, that our fathers were all under the cloud, and all passed through the sea; 2 and were all baptized unto Moses in the cloud and in the sea; 3 and did all eat the same spiritual food; 4 and did all drink the same spiritual drink: for they drank of a spiritual rock that followed them: and the rock was Christ. 5 Howbeit with most of them God was not well pleased: for they were overthrown in the wilderness.

THE CHRISTIAN RACE FOR THE PRIZE.

1. This lesson is a part of the long four-chapter instruction Paul gives the Corinthians. Therein he teaches them how to deal with those weak in the faith, and warns rash, presumptuous Christians to take heed lest they fall, however they may stand at the present. He presents a forcible simile in the running of the race, or the strife for the prize. Many run without obtaining the object of their pursuit. But we should not vainly run. To faithfully follow Christ does not mean simply to run. That will not suffice. We must

93

run to the purpose. To believe, to be running in Christ's course, is not sufficient; we must lay hold on eternal life. Christ says (Mt 24, 13), "But he that endureth to the end, the same shall be saved." And Paul (1 Cor 10, 12), "Wherefore let him that thinketh he standeth take heed lest he fall."

2. Now, running is hindered in two ways; for one, by indolence. When faith is not strenuously exercised, when we are indolent in good works, our progress is hindered, so that the prize is not attained. But to such hindrance I do not think Paul here refers. He is not alluding to those who indolently run, but to them who run in vain because missing their object; individuals, for instance, who pursue their aim at full speed, but, deluded by a phantom, miss their aim and rush to ruin or run up against fearful obstacles. Hence Paul enjoins men to run successfully while in the race, that they may seize the prize and not lose it by default. In consequence the race is hindered when a false goal is set up or the true one removed. The apostle says (Col 2, 18), "Let no man rob you of your prize." It is true, however, that an indolent, negligent life will eventually bring about loss of the prize. While men sleep, the enemy very soon sows tares among the wheat.

3. The goal is removed when the Word of God is falsified and creations of the human mind are preached under the name of God's Word. And these things readily come about when we are not careful to keep the unity of the Spirit, when each follows his own ideas and yields to no other, because he prefers his own conceit.

Such must be the course of events where love is lacking. The strong and the learned desire to be looked upon as peculiarly commendable, while the weak in the faith are despised. Thus the devil has abundant opportunity to sow tares. Paul calls love the unity of the Spirit, and admonishes (Eph 4, 3) that we endeavor to keep the unity of the Spirit in the bond of peace. In Second Thessalonians 2, 10 he proclaims the coming of Antichrist "because they received not the love of the truth"; that is, true love.

"And every man that striveth in the games [that striv-eth for the mastery]."

4. Were he who competes in a race to attempt other things or to make a success of other matters at the same time, he would not gain much; rather he would soon be defeated, lose the race and everything. If he would truly strive, he must attend to no other thing. All else must be neglected and attention centered upon the contest alone. Even then the winner must have fortune's favor; for they who neglect all to run do not all gain the prize.

Likewise in the Christian contest it is necessary, and in an even higher degree, to renounce everything and to devote oneself only to the contest. He who would in addition seek his own glory and profit, who would find in the Word and Spirit of God occasion for his own praise and advantage after the manner of the dissenters and schismatics—what can such a one expect to win? He is wholly entangled in temporal glory and gain; bound hand and foot, a complete captive. The race he runs is the mere dream race of one lying upon his couch an indolent captive.

"I therefore so run, as not uncertainly; so fight I, as not beating the air."

5. Paul here points to himself as exemplar and hints at the cause of failure, viz., lapse from love and the use of the divine word in a wilful, ambitious and covetous spirit, whereas the faith which worketh by love is lacking. Under such conditions, false and indolent Christians run indeed a merry race; yet God's Word and ways in which they are so alert and speedy are merely a show, because they make them subserve their own interests and glory. They fail, however, to see that they race uncertainly and beat the air. They never make a serious attempt, nor do they ever hit the mark. While it is theirs to mortify ambition, to restrain their self-will and to enlist in the service of their neighbors, they do none of these things. On the contrary, they even do many things to strengthen their ambition and self-will, and then they swear by a thousand oaths that they are seeking not their own honor but the honor of God, their neighbor's welfare and not their own.

Peter says (2 Pet 1, 9-10) this class are blind and cannot
see afar and have forgotten they were purged from their old
sins, because they fail to make their calling sure by good
works.   Therefore, it comes about that, as Paul says, they
run uncertainly, beating the air.   Their hearts are unstable
and wavering before God, and they are changeable and fickle
in all their ways, James 1, 8.   Since they are aimless and
inconstant at heart, this will appear likewise as inconstancy
in regard to works and doctrines.   They undertake now this
and now that; they cannot be quiet nor refrain from factional
strife.   Thus they miss their aim or else remove the goal,
and cannot but deviate from the true and common path.

> "But I buffet [keep under] my body, and bring it into
> bondage [subjection]."

6.   The apostle's thought is the same as in his statement
above, "Every man that striveth in the games exerciseth
self-control in all things."   By "keeping under the body"
Paul means, not only subduing the carnal lusts, but every
temporal object as well, in so far as it appeals to bodily desire—love of honor, fame, wealth and the like.   He who gives
license to these things instead of subduing them will preach
to his own condemnation, however correct his preaching be.
Such do not permit the truth to be presented; this is true
particularly of temporal honor.   These words of the apostle,
then, are a fine thrust at ambitious and self-centered preachers and Christians.   Not only do they run in vain and fight
to no purpose; they become actual castaways with only the
semblance—the color—of Christianity.

EXAMPLES FROM SCRIPTURE.

> "For I would not, brethren, have you ignorant, that
> our fathers were all under the cloud."

7.   Paul cites a terrible example from Scripture to prove
that not all obtain the prize who run.   There were about
six hundred thousand of them, all of whom walked in the
way of God and enjoyed his word and his confidence so
completely as to be protected under the cloud and miracu-
lously to pass through the sea; yet among the vast number
who ran at that time only two, Joshua and Caleb, obtained

the prize. They alone of all that multitude reached the promised land.

Later on in the chapter (verses 11-12) Paul explains this fact, saying: "Now these things happened unto them by way of example; and they were written for our admonition . . . wherefore let him that thinketh he standeth take heed lest he fall." The design of these dealings of God with Israel is to terrify the pride, false wisdom and self-will; to deter men from despising their fellows and from seeking to make the Word of God minister to their own honor or profit in preference to the honor and profit of others. The intent is to have each individual put himself on an equality with others, each to bear with his fellow, the weak enduring the strong, and so on, as enjoined in the four chapters.

8. How many great and noble men may have been among the six hundred thousand, men to whom we would have been unworthy to hand a cup of water! They included the twelve princes of the twelve tribes, one of whom, Nahshon, Matthew (ch. 1, 4) numbers in the holy lineage of Christ. There were also the seventy elders who shared in the spirit of Moses, Eldad and Medad in particular (Num 11, 27), and all the other great men aside from the faction of Korah. All these, mark you, strove in the race. They did and suffered much. They witnessed many miracles of God. They aided in erecting a grand tabernacle and in instituting divine worship. They were full of good works. Yet they failed, and died in the wilderness. Who is so daring and haughty he will not be restrained and humbled by so remarkable an example of divine judgment? Well may it be said, "Let him that . . . standeth take heed lest he fall."

9. Well, the example of Israel is one readily understood. God grant we may heed it! Let us examine the apostle's text yet further—his mention of baptism and spiritual food, using Christian terms and placing the fathers upon the same plane with us Christians, as if they also had had Baptism and the Holy Supper.

He would have us know, first, the oft-repeated fact that God from the beginning led, redeemed and saved his saints

by two instrumentalities—by his own word and external
signs. Adam was saved by the word of promise (Gen 3, 15):
The seed of the woman shall bruise the serpent's head; that
is, Christ shall come to conquer sin, death and Satan for us.
To this promise God added the sign of sacrifice, sacrifice
kindled with fire from heaven, as in Abel's case (Gen 4, 4),
and in other cases mentioned in the Scriptures. The word
of promise was Adam's Gospel until the time of Noah and
of Abraham. In this promise all the saints down to Abraham believed, and were redeemed; as we are redeemed by
the word of the Gospel which we believe. The fire from
heaven served them as a sign, as baptism does us, which is
added to the word of God.

10. Such signs were repeated again and again at various
times, the last sign being given by Christ in his own person
—the Gospel with baptism, granted to all nations. For instance, God gave Noah the promise that he should survive
the flood, and granted him a sign in the ship, or ark, he built.
And by faith in the promise and sign Noah was justified and
saved, with his family. Afterward God gave him another
promise, and for a sign the rainbow. Again, he gave Abraham a promise, with the sign of circumcision. Circumcision
was Abraham's baptism, just as the ark and the flood were
that of Noah. So also our baptism is to us circumcision, ark
and flood, according to Peter's explanation. 1 Pet 3, 21.
Everywhere we meet the Word and the Sign of God, in
which we must believe in order to be saved through faith
from sin and death.

11. Thus the children of Israel had God's word that they
should inherit the promised land. In addition to that word
they were given many signs, in particular those Paul here
names—the sea, the cloud, the bread from heaven, the water
from the rock. These he calls their baptism; just as our
baptism might be called our sea and cloud. Faith and the
Spirit are the same everywhere, though the signs and the
words vary. Signs and words indeed change from time to
time, but faith in the one and same God continues. Through
various signs and revelations, God at different times bestows

the same faith and the same Sp.rit, effecting through these in all saints remission of sins, redemption from death, and salvation, whether they lived in the beginning or at the end of time, or while time progressed.

12. Such is Paul's meaning when he says the fathers did eat the same meat, and drink the same drink as we. He, however, qualifies with the word "spiritual." Externally and individually Israel had signs and revelations different from ours; but the Spirit and their faith in Christ was identical with our own. Spiritual eating and drinking is simply believing in God's Word and sign. Christ says (Jn 6, 56), "He that eateth my flesh and drinketh my blood abideth in me, and I in him." And in the preceding verse, "My flesh is meat indeed, and my blood is drink indeed." That is, He that believeth in me shall live.

> "For they drank of a spiritual rock that followed them."

13. In other words, they believed in the same Christ in whom we believe, though he was yet to come in the flesh; and the sign of their faith was the material rock, from which they physically drank water, just as we in partaking of the material bread and wine at the altar spiritually eat and drink the true Christ. With the outward act of eating and drinking we exercise inward faith. Had the Israelites not possessed the word of God and faith as they drank from the rock, the act of drinking would not have benefited their souls. Neither would it profit us to receive bread and wine at the altar if we were without faith. Indeed, had not the Word of God come first, the rock would not have yielded water and command faith. Likewise, if God's Word did not accompany bread and wine, they would not be spiritual food nor exercise faith.

14. So it is ever the same spiritual meat and drink which God embodies in his word and sign, whatever its material and external form may be. Were he to command me to lift up a mere straw, immediately the straw would hold for me spiritual food and drink. Not because of any virtue in the straw, but because it is a revelation and sign of the

divine truth and presence. Again, if God's Word and his
sign be lacking or unrecognized, the very presence of God
himself has no effect. Christ says of himself (Jn 6, 63),
"The flesh profiteth nothing." He makes that statement because his hearers pay no heed to the words in which he
speaks of his flesh, though it is these which make his body
the true meat, according to his declaration (v. 58), "This
is the bread which came down out of heaven." Therefore
we are not to regard unduly, as blind reason does, the works,
signs and miracles of God; rather we are to recognize his
message therein. This is the act of faith.

15. The apostle refers to a single type—the rock, saying:
"They drank of a spiritual rock that followed them: and the
rock was Christ." By this statement he makes all the figures and signs granted to the people of Israel by the Word
of God refer to Christ; for where the Word of God is, there
Christ is. All the words and promises of God are concerning Christ. Christ himself refers the serpent of Moses to
himself, giving it a typical significance, Jn 3, 14. We may
truly say the Israelites looked upon the same serpent we
behold, for they saw the spiritual serpent that followed
them, or Christ on the cross. Their beholding was believing in the Word of God, with the serpent for a sign; even as
their spiritual drinking was believing in the Word of God
with the rock for a sign. Without the Word of God, the
serpent could have profited them nothing; nor could brazen
serpents innumerable, had the Israelites gazed upon them
forever. Likewise the rock would have profited them nothing without the word of God; they might have crushed to
powder all the rocks of the world or drank from them to no
purpose.

16. According to the general principle here laid down by
Paul, by using the rock as illustration, we may say the Israelites partook of the same bread of heaven whereof we eat;
and they ate of the spiritual bread of heaven which followed
them—Christ. With them, eating was believing in the
Word of God, while they had for their sign the bread from
heaven whereof they physically partook. Had not this

Word accompanied the bread, it would have been simply material food, incapable of profiting the soul or calling forth faith. Christ says (Jn 6, 32), "It was not Moses that gave you the bread out of heaven; but my Father giveth you the true bread out of heaven." And (verse 58), "Not as the fathers ate [manna], and died." Even Moses says (Deut 8, 3), "And fed thee with manna . . . that he might make thee know that man doth not live by bread only, but by everything that proceedeth out of the mouth of Jehovah."

In other words, "In the material manna you must not merely see the work—the act of satisfying the appetite—but much rather the word of promise bringing you the bread of heaven; for by that word you live forever if you have faith."

17. We may say the same concerning the sea and the cloud. The children of Israel walked under the same cloud that shadows us; that means, they walked under the spiritual cloud that followed them—Christ. Otherwise expressed, walking under the cloud was simply believing in the word of God, the word they had in their hearts, which told them to follow the cloud. Without that word they would have been unable to believe or to follow; indeed, with the word lacking, the cloud would never have appeared. Therefore, the cloud was called the glory of the Lord whose appearance had been promised.

So we see how we must in all things have regard to the word of God. To it faith must attach itself. Without it, either there are no signs and works of God, or else, existing, and regarded with the physical eyes only, without reference to the Word, they cause one to open his mouth in wonderment for a while like everything else which is new, but they do not profit the soul nor do they appeal to faith.

18. Some take the words "which followed them" to mean that the spiritual rock accompanied the children of Israel, companioning with them—"comitante petra," not "petra consequente," Christ being spiritually present in the word and by faith. This view they endeavor to base upon the Greek text. I have rendered it: "the rock following." The point is not worth contention. Let each understand it as he may.

Both interpretations given are correct. I hold to what I have offered because all the circumstances of the incident, and earlier words of God, pointed to a future Christ, a Christ who should follow, in whom they should all believe. Thus Abraham saw behind him the ram in the thicket and took and sacrificed him; that is, he believed in the Christ who afterward should come and be sacrificed.

19. Again, some say the common noun in the clause "and the rock was Christ" means the material rock; and since Christ cannot be material rock they explain the inconsistency by saying the rock signifies Christ. They here make the word "was" equivalent to "signifies." The same reasoning they apply to certain words of Christ; for instance, they say where Christ, referring to the Holy Supper (Mt 26, 26), commands, "Take, eat; this is my body"—they say the meaning is, "This bread signifies, but is not truly, my body." They would thereby deny that the bread is the body of Christ. In the same manner do they deal with the text (Jn 15, 1) "I am the true vine," in making it "I am signified by the vine." Beware of such reasoners. Their own malice has led them to such perverting of Scripture. Paul here expressly distinguishes between material and spiritual rocks, saying: "They drank of a spiritual rock that followed them: and the rock was Christ." He does not say the material rock was Christ, but the spiritual rock. The material rock was not spiritual, and did not follow or go with them.

20. The explanations and distortions of such false reasoners are not needed here. The words are true as they read; they are to be understood in substance and not figuratively. So in John 15, 1, Christ's reference is not to a material but a spiritual vine. How would this read, "I am signified by a spiritual vine"? Christ is speaking of that which exists, and must so be understood—"I am"; here is a true spiritual vine. Similar is John 6, 55, "My flesh is meat indeed." The thought is not, "My flesh signifies, or is signified by, true meat"; spiritual meat is spoken of and the meaning is, "My flesh is substantially a food; not for the stomach, physically, but for the soul, spiritually." Neither

must you permit the words "This is my body" to be perverted to mean that the body is but signified by the bread,
as some pretend; you must accept the words precisely as
they mean—"This bread is essentially, by a real presence,
my body." The forcing of Scripture to meet one's own
opinions cannot be tolerated. A clear text proving that the
infinitive "to be" is equivalent to "signify" would be needed;
and, even though this might be proven in a few instances,
it would not suffice. It would still have to be indisputably
shown true in the place in question. This can never be
done. Now, the proposition being impossible, we must surrender to the Word of God and accept it as it stands.

21. Christ has been typified by various signs and objects
in the Old Testament, and the rock is one of them. Note
first, the material rock spoken of had place independently of
man's labor and far from man's domain, in the wilderness,
in desolate solitude. So Christ is a truly insignificant object in the world, disregarded, unnoticed; nor is he indebted
to human labor.

22. Further, water flowing from the rock is contrary to
nature; it is purely miraculous. The water typifies the
quickening spirit of God, who proceeds from the condemned,
crucified and dead Christ. Thus life is drawn from death,
and this by the power of God. Christ's death is our life, and
if we would live we must die with him.

23. Moses strikes the rock at the command of God and
points to it, thus prefiguring the ministerial office which by
word of mouth strikes from the spiritual rock the Spirit.
For God will give his Spirit to none without the instrumentality of the Word and the ministerial office instituted by
him for this purpose, adding the command that nothing be
preached but Christ. Had not Moses obeyed the command
of God to smite the rock with his rod, no water would ever
have flowed therefrom. His rod represents rod of the mouth
whereof Isaiah speaks (ch. 11, 4): "He shall smite the
earth with the rod of his mouth; and with the breath of his
lips shall he slay the wicked." "A sceptre of equity is the
sceptre of thy kingdom." Ps 45, 6.

Second Sunday Before Lent

Text: 2 Cor 11, 19-33; 12, 1-9.

19 For ye bear with the foolish gladly, being wise yourselves. 20 For ye bear with a man, if he bringeth you into bondage, if he devoureth you, if he taketh you captive, if he exalteth himself, if he smiteth you on the face. 21 I speak by way of disparagement, as though we had been weak. Yet whereinsoever any is bold (I speak in foolishness), I am bold also. 22 Are they Hebrews? so am I. Are they Israelites? so am I. Are they the seed of Abraham? so am I. 23 Are they ministers of Christ? (I speak as one beside himself) I more; in labors more abundantly, in prisons more abundantly, in stripes above measure, in deaths oft. 24 Of the Jews five times received I forty stripes save one. 25 Thrice was I beaten with rods, once was I stoned, thrice I suffered shipwreck, a night and a day have I been in the deep; 26 in journeyings often, in perils of rivers, in perils of robbers, in perils from my countrymen, in perils from the Gentiles, in perils in the city, in perils in the wilderness, in perils in the sea, in perils among false brethren; 27 in labor and travail, in watchings often, in hunger and thirst, in fastings often, in cold and nakedness. 28 Besides those things that are without, there is that which presseth upon me daily, anxiety for all the churches. 29 Who is weak, and I am not weak? who is caused to stumble, and I burn not? 30 If I must needs glory, I will glory of the things that concern my weakness. 31 The God and Father of the Lord Jesus, he who is blessed for evermore knoweth that I lie not. 32 In Damascus the governor under Aretas the king guarded the city of the Damascenes in order to

take me: 33 and through a window was I let down in a basket by the wall, and escaped his hands.

1 I must needs glory, though it is not expedient; but I will come to visions and revelations of the Lord. 2 I know a man in Christ, fourteen years ago (whether in the body, I know not; or whether out of the body, I know not; God knoweth), such a one caught up even to the third heaven. 3 And I know such a man (whether in the body, or apart from the body, I know not; God knoweth), 4 how that he was caught up into Paradise, and heard unspeakable words, which it is not lawful for a man to utter. 5 On behalf of such a one will I glory: but on mine own behalf I will not glory, save in my weakness. 6 For if I should desire to glory, I shall not be foolish; for I shall speak the truth: but I forbear, lest any man should account of me above that which he seeth me to be, or heareth from me. 7 And by reason of the exceeding greatness of the revelations, that I should not be exalted overmuch, there was given to me a thorn in the flesh, a messenger of Satan to buffet me, that I should not be exalted overmuch. 8 Concerning this thing I besought the Lord thrice, that it might depart from me. 9 And he hath said unto me, My grace is sufficient for thee: for my power is made perfect in weakness. Most gladly therefore will I rather glory in my weaknesses, that the power of Christ may rest upon me.

PAUL'S GLORY IN HIS LABOR AND SUFFERING.

1. They who praise themselves are fools according to the views and speech of the world. The saying is, "Self-praise is unsavory." It is forbidden by Solomon in Proverbs 27, 2: "Let another man praise thee, and not thine own mouth." And Christ says (Jn 8, 54), "If I glorify myself, my glory is nothing." Paul acknowledges that he had to become a fool, something for which he had no desire, by reason of the necessity laid upon him to praise himself. The false apostles, as false spirits habitually do, delivered great, fine, splendid speeches to the multitude, in their vainglorious attempt to raise themselves above Paul, thereby to make contemptible and insignificant that apostle and his doctrine.

2. Paul was little concerned that he personally should be lightly esteemed and the false apostles highly honored, but he could not bear to have the Gospel perish in that way and his Corinthian converts seduced. Therefore he exerts himself to the utmost, at the risk of becoming a fool by his boasting. But he, in his strong spiritual wisdom, glories in a masterly manner, and skilfully puts to shame the boasts of the false apostles.

First, he shows them he can glory in the very things wherein they glory, and in even more. At the same time he declares himself a fool for glorying. He might have said: "Foolish, indeed, are they, and boorish creatures, who glory in themselves. They should feel shame to the very depth of their heart. No true, sane man boasts of what he is. The wicked and the frivolous do that." But the apostle's attack is not quite so severe and harsh. He addresses them civilly and delicately in that he makes himself appear a fool, as if to say: "Look! how becoming self-praise is in myself, although I have grounds for my glorying. But how much more disgraceful for you to boast when perhaps none of your claims are true." So Paul wears the foolscap, that those coarse fools might have a mirror in which to behold their real selves. This is wisely making foolishness minister to the good of the neighbor and to the honor of the Gospel. To the just, even folly is wisdom, just as all things are pure and holy unto him.

3. Second, Paul deals the false apostles a stout blow when he shows them to be ignorant of the grounds in which a true Christian seeks his glory. For, as he teaches them, a Christian glories in the things whereof other men are ashamed—in the cross and in his sufferings. This is the true art of glorying. To this he refers when he says (Gal 6, 14), "Far be it from me to glory, save in the cross of our Lord Jesus Christ." But the false apostles are careful to avoid glorying thus; for they flee with alacrity from reproach and affliction, rather seeking a life of ease and honor. They ever would have prominence over their fellows, be superior to and unlike others—certain indication that they lack the

right spirit and are not of God. Christ testifies (Jn 5, 44), "How can ye believe, who receive glory one of another, and the glory that cometh from the only God ye seek not?"

4. The main point of this lesson is that in a preacher or a teacher no vice is more injurious and venomous than vainglory. It is true, however, that avarice also is an evil characteristic of false teachers, being found hand in hand with vainglory. For the sake of profit, for the purpose of gain, the false teachers aspire to prominence, to honor and position. With them, nothing but current coin will pass, and what does not pay dividend is unprofitable. Any other vice is more endurable in a preacher than these two, though none is compatible with goodness, blamelessness and perfection being required in the ministry according to Paul, Titus 1, 7. This is not surprising, for the two vices under consideration are essentially and directly opposed to the nature of the ministry. The ministry is ordained to have as its aim the glory of God and its promotion. Psalm 19, 1 affirms, "The heavens declare the glory of God." And ministers must, for God's glory, suffer reproach and shame. Jeremiah complains (ch. 20, 8), "The word of Jehovah is made a reproach unto me, and a derision, all the day." The world will not endure the Word. For him who in preaching seeks his own honor, it is impossible to remain in the right path and preach the pure Gospel. Consequently he avoids striving for God's honor; he must preach what pleases the people, what brings honor to himself and magnifies his skill and wisdom.

5. Avarice, too, is, according to its very nature, opposed to the interests of the ministry. Just as the ministry is to be devoted to God's honor at the expense of our own, so is it to be devoted to the interests of our neighbor and not to our own. Otherwise it is an injury rather than a benefit. With the false teacher seeking only his own good, it is impossible for him to preach the truth. He is compelled to speak what is pleasing to men in order to gratify his appetites. Therefore Paul (Rom 16, 18) says of such preachers that they serve their own bellies. And in many places the

Scriptures reprove avarice. Let him, then, who would be a preacher guard vigilantly against vainglory and avarice. But, should he feel himself in the clutch of these sins, let him avoid the ministry. For under such conditions he will accomplish no good; he will only dishonor God, seduce souls and be a thief and robber in the acquisition of property. With this explanation, the lesson is now easily understood, but we will consider a few points."

"For ye bear with the foolish gladly, being wise yourselves."

6. Paul commends the Corinthians for their patience and wisdom in six points: as wise men, they cheerfully endure the foolish; they bear with those who bring them into bondage and oppress them; with those who devour them; with those who take from them [or take them captive]; with those who exalt themselves; with those who smite them in the face. But his commendation is meant to pave the way for his folly—to prepare them to suffer him the more readily. He would say, "Since you suffer so much from them who injure you—and you are wise in that—I trust you will bear with me who have wrought you only good, when I act the fool for a little; particularly when my object in it is your good—to preserve the Gospel among you in opposition to the false apostles." Note how tenderly and patiently he deals with the Corinthians when he might have severely reproved them for tolerating the false apostles. He commends them as does a father a timid child, and yet, while commending them he censures both them and their false teachers. He handles them as tenderly as if he held a raw egg in his hand, in order not to distract or terrify them.

7. Paul delivers a masterly stroke when with the same words he praises the Corinthians and rebukes them and their false apostles. His commendation of their patience is in reality reproof, blows and wounds for the false teachers. He would say:

"I have preached the Gospel to you at my own expense and jeopardy. By my labor have ye attained to its blessing. Ye have done nothing for me in return, and I have been no tax upon you. Now, upon my departure, others come and exploit you, and seek honor and profit from my labor. They would be your masters and I am to be ignored. They boast as if the accomplishment were all theirs. Of these ye must be disciples and pupils. Their preaching ye must accept, while my Gospel must become odious. My case is that of the bee who labors to make honey and then the idle drones and the earthworms come and consume the sweet not of their making. In me is illustrated Christ's proverb (Jn 4, 37), 'one soweth, and another reapeth.' Continually one enters into the fruits of another's labor. One must toil and incur danger, while another reaps the benefit in security.

8. "Ye can suffer these false apostles, though they be fools and teach only foolishness. In this ye display wisdom and patience. But ye do not so suffer me, who taught you true wisdom. Nor do ye permit me much enjoyment of my labor. Further, ye can permit them to make servants of you, to be your lords and to order you to do their bidding. And ye obey. But I who have made myself your servant, I who have served you without profit to myself, that ye might be lords with Christ, must now be ignored and all my labors be lost. They rule you at their pleasure, and their pleasure is all they consult. You suffer yourselves to be devoured. That is, your property is consumed; for ye bestow it upon them abundantly, as Psalm 14, 4 has it, 'Who eat up my people.' Upon such as these ye can shower goods and gifts, and can permit them to devour you as they please. But I have never enjoyed aught of your property. All my service has been without recompense, that ye might become rich in Christ.

"Again, ye suffer the false teachers to take from you beyond your consent; to exalt themselves above you, to esteem themselves better than you and me, and to exercise their arrogance upon you. But ye deal not so with me, who have sacrificed my own substance, and have taken from others, that I might bring the Gospel to you; who have not exalted myself above any, but have yielded to all and served them. The false apostles permit you to serve them; in fact, trample you beneath their feet. They even smite you in the face; that is, they reproach you publicly, put you to shame, and abuse you with rude and insolent words. They act as if ye were beasts of burden and they your real masters. All this ye suffer. But my patience with you, my parental tenderness, past and present, is remembered no more. Paul is now represented as having wrought no good at Corinth."

PAUL'S DESCRIPTION OF FALSE TEACHERS.

9. Note the master hand wherewith Paul portrays the character of false teachers, showing how they betray their avarice and ambition. First, they permit true teachers to lay the foundation and perform the labor; then they come and desire to do the work over, to reap the honors and the benefits. They bring about that the name and the work of the true teachers receive no regard and credit; what they themselves have brought—that is the thing. They make the poor, simple-minded people to stare open-mouthed while they win them with flowery words and seduce them with fair speeches, as mentioned in Romans 16, 18. These are the idle drones that consume the honey they will not and cannot make. That this was the condition of affairs at Corinth is very clear from this epistle—indeed, from both epistles. Paul continually refers to others having followed him and built upon the foundation he has laid. Messengers of the devil, he terms them.

10. And such false teachers have the good fortune that all their folly is tolerated, even though the people realize how these act the fool, and rather rudely at that. They have success with it all, and people bear with them. But no patience is to be exercised toward true teachers! Their words and their works are watched with the intent of entrapping them, as complained of in Psalm 17, 9 and elsewhere. When only apparently a mote is found, it is exaggerated to a very great beam. No toleration is granted. There is only judgment, condemnation and scorn. Hence the office of preaching is a grievous one. He who has not for his sole motive the benefit of his neighbor and the glory of God, cannot continue therein. The true teacher must labor, and permit oth-

ers to have the honor and profit of his efforts, while he receives injury and derision for his reward. Here the saying holds true: "To love without guerdon, nor wearying of the burden." Only the Spirit of God can inspire such love. To flesh and blood it is impossible. Paul here scores the false prophets when he says, "Ye suffer fools gladly"; in other words, "I know the false preachers often act as fools, nor can they help it, because their teaching is false; yet ye excuse them."

11. In the second place such teachers are disposed to bring the people into downright bondage and to bind their conscience by forcing laws upon them and teaching work-righteousness. The effect is that fear impels them to do what has been pounded into them, as if they were bond-slaves, while their teachers command fear and attention. But the true teachers, they who give us freedom of conscience and create us lords, we soon forget, even despise. The dominion of false teachers is willingly tolerated and patiently endured; indeed, it is given high repute. All those conditions are punishments sent by God upon them who do not receive the Gospel with love and gratitude. Christ says (Jn 5, 43): "I am come in my Father's name, and ye receive me not: if another shall come in his own name, him ye shall receive." The Pope, with his spiritual office, became our lord, and we became his captives, through his doctrine of human works. And our present-day schismatics pursue the same object with their fanciful doctrine concerning their works.

12. In the third place, false teachers flay their disciples to the bone, and cut them out of house and home, but even this is taken and endured. Such, I opine, has been our experience under the Papacy. But true preachers are even denied their bread. Yet this all perfectly squares with justice! For, since men fail to give unto those from whom they receive the Word of God, and permit the latter to serve them at their own expense, it is but fair they should give the more unto preachers of lies, whose instruction redounds to their injury. What is withheld from Christ must be given in

tenfold proportion to the devil. They who refuse to give the servant of the truth a single thread, must be oppressed by liars.

13.   Fourth, false apostles forcibly take more than is given them. They seize whatever and whenever they can, thus enhancing their insatiable avarice. This, too, is excused in them. Thus, the great establishments of the Pope did not suffice for him; with various artifices, bulls, laws and indulgences, he has brought under his power land and people and all they possess, exhausting the world by usury. And so it should be, for this state of affairs was richly deserved by men for despising the Gospel and its preachers.

14.   Fifth, these deceitful teachers, not satisfied with having acquired our property, must exalt themselves above us and lord it over us. Not only do they possess all property, but they must for that very reason become our superiors; must have precedence and receive honor. We bow our knees before them, worship them and kiss their feet. And we suffer it all, yes, with fearful reverence regard it just and right. And it is just and right, for why did we not honor the Gospel by accepting and preserving it?

15.   Sixth, our false apostles justly reward us by smiting us in the face. That is, they consider us inferior to dogs; they abuse us, and treat us as foot-rags. I venture to say we became sensible of such treatment when, under the Papacy, we were readily put in the van, cursed, condemned and delivered to the devil. We endured it all, suffered most patiently, and yielded up property, honor, body and soul. Fault in a sincere teacher, however, could by no means be tolerated. Very well, then; God is just, and it is his judgment that we must honor the messengers of Satan a thousand times more than his own, and do and suffer everything.

"I speak by way of disparagement [speak as concerning reproach], as thought we had been weak."

16.   There are two ways of interpreting this sentence: First, as meaning: "I speak as one of the weak whose folly you must endure; for which I deserve reproach, since I ought to bear with you." From such meaning I to this

day have seen no cause to swerve. The other interpretation is: "I speak as one reproached—after the manner of the weak." Or, more fully expressed: "I can speak in two ways of myself and my class: First, with honor, because of our strength in the sight of God and the spiritually-minded, worthy of honor, noble; not weak but strong, able. But I will not at present employ this way, for we are now despised; we are not known as honorable. And all because of the false prophets. I will, then, present myself in the other light, as I am regarded—despised, held in reproach and disrespect, weak and incapable. But even this condition shall be an occasion of glory for me; my reproach and weakness is more honorable than their honor, power and strength. What would my glory be should my actual strength inspire my speech! "Weakness," according to Paul's own later interpretation, implies being regarded worthless, unfit, a failure. The apostle's meaning, then, is: "I, too, will be one of the boasting fools. You will excuse it in me for I speak from the standpoint of my critics, that of a man contemptible, foolish, incompetent. Before God, however, I feel that I am a quite different being."

17. And recollect, Paul says, "Because ye are wise, ye suffer fools gladly," implying that one fool cannot tolerate another. The saying is, "Two fools in one house will not do." Reason and wisdom are required, to bear with another's infirmities and to excuse them.

"Yet whereinsoever any is bold."

18. That is, in whatever the false apostles can boast, I can likewise glory. Here we are shown what is the ground of the false apostles' boasting: their outward respectability —being of Abraham's seed, children of Israel, Christ's preachers. Therein they think to far excel the Corinthians, claiming their doctrine and works to be of greater weight because they have Moses and the prophets for their teachers. But they failed to perceive that their boast is of mere externals, that render no one righteous or better before God. The majority of the Hebrews, of the Israelites, of the seed of Abraham, and of the preachers of Christ are lost. Names

are of no consequence; they only make a fine show and serve to seduce the simple-minded. Paul boasts of his origin and yet derides his boasting, calling it fool's work. His object is to destroy the boasting of the false prophets, that the people might not be deceived.

19. Note how, even in Paul's time, great men erred concerning the true sense of the Gospel, and many noble preachers would have estimated Christian life by a merely external appearance and name. The true spiritual preachers must have been few. Should it be strange, then, that in our time sincere preachers are not numerous, and that the majority of ministers riot in what they themselves seem and do? It cannot and shall not be otherwise. The thievish drones, which are prone to riot, let them riot! We will resist to the utmost of our power, commending the matter to God, who doubtless will grant us sufficient honor and profit, both temporally and eternally, though we must labor gratuitously, accepting injury and derision as our reward. Our adversaries will not long continue their persecutions, for, as Paul says just preceding our lesson, they will eventually receive their deserts.

20. Again, Paul boasts of certain temporal afflictions wherein he excels the false apostles, who suffer nothing, for the sake of either the word or of souls, but only boast of name and person. Among the afflictions he mentions, he names having been a night and a day in the deep. Some refer this allusion to the voyage of which Luke writes (Acts 27, 20-21), when for fourteen days Paul and his companions ate nothing and saw never a star, being day and night continually covered by the surges and waves of the sea. Others think Paul was, like Jonah, personally sunk into the deep sea, though but for a day and a night. Such is the clear meaning of the text. Yet others interpret it as having reference to a prison or dungeon, because the Greek text makes no mention of the sea—simply "the deep."

"Who is weak, and I am not weak?"

21. Of external afflictions affecting not his own person, but distressing others, Paul mentions two: he is weak if

another is weak, and burns if another is offended. Thereby
he plainly portrays the ardor of his heart—how full of love
he is; the defects and sorrows of others pain him as his own.
By "weakness," I imagine, he means, not bodily infirmity,
but weakness of faith. He refers to those who, young in the
faith, have a tender and frail conscience, thereby betokening
immaturity and feebleness of faith. He says (Rom 14, 2),
"He that is weak eateth herbs"; and in First Corinthians 8,
12, that we sin against Christ if we wound a weak conscience. These weak ones Paul does not reject. He receives
them and conducts himself as if he, too, were weak. He asserts (1 Cor 9, 22), "To the weak I became weak, that I
might gain the weak."

22. This interpretation of the sentence is borne out in his
allusion to "that which presseth upon me daily, anxiety for
all the churches." Paul would say: "I exert myself, I have
a continual care, I urge and admonish constantly, that offenses and false doctrine may not invade and destroy my
planting; may not violate and ruin the weak consciences.
As seen in his epistle to the Corinthians, directed against the
false apostles, and in that to the Thessalonians, such is his
vigilant anxiety to guard them from the tempter that he
sends them a special messenger, and he exultingly declares
it is life to him to learn of their steadfastness.

23. Likewise, by the assertion that he burns, we are to
understand that he is exceedingly grieved and pained if one
is offended; that is, if through misleading doctrines or examples one in any wise falls from the faith. Of the offense
to faith, he says much in Romans 14. Not desiring to be
offended with the offended, as he became weak with the
weak, he says: "I burn and sorrow for them."

"I know a man in Christ, fourteen years ago."

24. Of the translation of Paul into the third heaven
many have written, perplexing themselves over what con-
stituted the first, second and third heavens, and the paradise. Paul himself, who had the experience, does not tell,
and declares no man can tell, for none may utter the words
he heard. Therefore, we must humbly acknowledge we do

not know the nature of these things. And it matters **not**.
Paul does not boast of his experience for the purpose **of** imparting knowledge to us or of enabling us to duplicate it.
The purpose of his boasting is simply to stop the mouths of
the fanatics and to show how paltry was their glory in comparison with his own. Certain it is, however, that Paul **was**
ravished from this life into a life ineffable; otherwise **his**
expression would be meaningless.

PAUL'S THORN IN THE FLESH AND HUMILITY.

"There was given to me a thorn in the flesh, a messenger of Satan."

25. And must this mighty apostle, O merciful God, be
subject to trials lest he exalt himself because of his great
revelations? Then how should others, how should such infirm beings as we, be free from self-exaltation? Many teachers have explained Paul's thorn to be the temptations of the
flesh. The Latin text is responsible for this interpretation;
it reads, "stimulus carnis," a spear, or thorn for the flesh.
Yet that rendering does not do justice to the words. Paul
is not in the habit of terming temptations of the flesh
"thorns." The thorn stands rather for something painful
and afflicting. In "a thorn of the flesh" the thought is not
of an instrumentality whereby the flesh stings, but of something that stings the flesh. The Greek text impels us to the
thought of a thorn for the flesh, or a thorn upon or in the
flesh. The idea is much like that in the German proverb,
"The clog is bound to the dog's neck." We may imagine
Paul expressing himself: "As a clog to a dog's neck, as a
ring in a bear's nose, a bit in a horse's mouth or a gag in
the mouth of a swine, in order to restrain them from running, biting and general mischief,—so is my thorn a clog to
my body lest I exalt myself."

26. But Paul himself explains the nature of the clog, or
thorn. He calls it "a messenger of Satan," a devil, to "buffet" him, or to flay and jog him. Hence a spiritual trial cannot be meant. The explanation appeals to me that the persecutions and sufferings the apostle recounts above constitute the devil's flaying. Thus his meaning would be: "I

have received great revelations, for which reason the clog
is bound to the dog; that is, the many dangers and misfortunes with which the angel of the devil buffets and humil-
iates my body will make me forget to exalt myself. They
are the thorn in my flesh, or upon my body; for God will
not permit it to come upon my soul."

27. Yet the text seems to imply some peculiar work of
the devil upon Paul's body, for it says the thorn, or clog, is
the messenger Satan employs to beat his body; and also
that the apostle diligently but unavailingly thrice besought
the Lord to remove it. I do not imagine him praying for
the cessation of persecutions in a spirit of unwillingness to
suffer them. But since he does not specify the affliction, we
must let it remain a secret one, a distress known only to
himself. It is enough for us to know that while God had
given him great revelations, revelations beyond human ken,
he also bound the clog to him—gave him a thorn for his
body—to prevent his exaltation of himself; and that the
knowledge of the buffetings and flaying caused by this clog,
or devil, are likewise beyond human ken.

"My power is made perfect in weakness."

28. It is a strange sort of strength which is weak and by
its weakness grows stronger. Who ever heard of weak
strength? or more absurd still, that strength is increased by
weakness? Paul would here make a distinction between human strength and divine. Human strength increases with
enhancement and decreases with enfeeblement. But God's
power—his Word in us—rises in proportion to the pressure
it receives. It is characteristic of God the Creator that he
creates all things from naught, and again reduces to naught
all created things. Human power cannot do this. The power
of God is the true palm-wood which buoys itself in proportion as it is burdened and weighted.

29. Note here, "weakness" is not to be understood in a
spiritual sense, as on a previous occasion, but externally; as
not illness alone, but every sort of evil, misfortune, suffering and persecution calculated to buffet and humble the
body. The power of Christ, in connection with which spirit-

ual weakness cannot exist, is invoked against this weakness likewise. He says, "Most gladly will I glory in my weaknesses, that the power of Christ may rest upon me." And his weaknesses he immediately explains as infirmities, injuries, necessities, persecutions and distresses. The thought, then, is: Christ is not mighty within us, his word and his faith are not strong in us, unless our bodies suffer affliction. The false apostles, however, take excellent care to escape suffering.

Sunday Before Lent

1 If I speak with the tongues of men and of angels, but have not love, I am become sounding brass, or a clanging cymbal. 2 And if I have the gift of prophecy, and know all mysteries and all knowledge; and if I have all faith, so as to remove mountains, but have not love, I am nothing. 3 And if I bestow all my goods to feed the poor, and if I give my body to be burned, but have not love, it profiteth me nothing. 4 Love suffereth long, and is kind; love envieth not; love vaunteth not itself, is not puffed up, 5 doth not behave itself unseemly, seeketh not its own, is not provoked, taketh not account of evil; 6 rejoiceth not in unrighteousness, but rejoiceth with the truth; 7 beareth all things, believeth all things, hopeth all things, endureth all things. 8 Love never faileth: but whether there be prophecies, they shall be done away; whether there be tongues, they shall cease; whether there be knowledge, it shall be done away. 9 For we know in part, and we prophesy in part; 10 but when that which is perfect is come, that which is in part shall be done away. 11 When I was a child, I spake as a child, I felt as a child, I thought as a child: now that I am become a man, I have put away childish things. 12 For now we see in a mirror, darkly; but then face to face: now I know in part; but then shall I know fully even as also I was fully known. 13 But now abideth faith, hope, love, these three; and the greatest of these is love.

PAUL'S PRAISE OF CHRISTIAN LOVE.

1. Paul's purpose in this chapter is to silence and humble

haughty Christians, particularly teachers and preachers.
The Gospel gives much knowledge of God and of Christ,
and conveys many wonderful gifts, as Paul recounts in
Romans 12 and in First Corinthians 12. He tells us some
have the gift of speaking, some of teaching, some of Scripture exposition; others of ruling; and so on. With Christians are great riches of spiritual knowledge, great treasures
in the way of spiritual gifts. Manifest to all is the meaning
of God, Christ, conscience, the present and the future life,
and similar things. But there are to be found few indeed
who make the right use of such gifts and knowledge; who
humble themselves to serve others, according to the dictates of love. Each seeks his own honor and advantage, desiring to gain preferment and precedence over others.

2. We see today how the Gospel has given to men knowledge beyond anything known in the world before, and has
bestowed upon them new capabilities. Various gifts have
been showered upon and distributed among them which
have redounded to their honor. But they go on unheeding.
No one takes thought how he may in Christian love serve
his fellow-men to their profit. Each seeks for himself glory
and honor, advantage and wealth. Could one bring about
for himself the distinction of being the sole individual
learned and powerful in the Gospel, all others to be insignificant and useless, he would willingly do it; he would be
glad could he alone be regarded as Mister Smart. At the
same time he affects deep humility, great self-abasement,
and preaches of love and faith. But he would take it hard
had he, in practice, to touch with his little finger what he
preaches. This explains why the world is so filled with
fanatics and schismatics, and why every man would master
and outrank all others. Such as these are haughtier than
those that taught them. Paul here attacks these vainglorious spirits, and judges them to be wholly insignificant,
though their knowledge may be great and their gifts even
greater, unless they should humble themselves and use
their gifts in the service of others.

To these coarse and mean people he addresses himself

with a multitude of words and a lengthy discourse, a subject he elsewhere disposes of in a few words; for instance, where he says (Phil 2, 3-4), "In lowliness of mind each counting other better than himself; not looking each of you to his own things, but each of you also to the things of others." By way of illustration, he would pass sentence upon himself should he be thus blameworthy; this more forcibly to warn others who fall far short of his standing. He says,

"If I speak with the tongues of men and of angels."

4. That is, though I had ability to teach and to preach with power beyond that of any man or angel, with words of perfect charm, with truth and excellence informing my message—though I could do this, "but have not love [charity]," and only seek my own honor and profit and not my neighbor's, "I am become sounding brass, or a clanging cymbal." In other words, "I might, perhaps, thereby teach others something, might fill their ears with sound, but before God I would be nothing." As a clock or a bell has not power to hear its own sound, and does not derive benefit from its stroke, so the preacher who lacks love cannot himself understand anything he says, nor does he thereby improve his standing before God. He has much knowledge, indeed, but because he fails to place it in the service of love, it is the quality of his knowledge that is at fault. 1 Cor 8, 1-12. Far better he were dumb or devoid of eloquence, if he but teach in love and meekness, than to speak as an angel while seeking but his own interests.

"And if I have the gift of prophecy."

5. According to chapter 14, to prophesy is to be able, by the Holy Spirit's inspiration, correctly to understand and explain the prophets and the Scriptures. This is a most excellent gift. To "know mysteries" is to be able to apprehend the spiritual meaning of the Scriptures, or its allegorical references, as Paul does where (Gal 4, 24-31) he makes Sarah and Hagar representative of the two covenants, and Isaac and Ishmael of the two peoples—the Jews and the Christians. Christ does the same (Jn 3, 14) when he makes the brazen serpent of Moses typical of himself on the cross;

again, when Isaac, David, Solomon and other characters of
sacred history appear as figures of Christ. Paul calls it
"mystery"—this hidden, secret meaning beneath the primary
sense of the narrative. But "knowledge" is the understanding of practical matters, such as Christian liberty, or the
realization that the conscience is not bound. Paul would
say, then: "Though one may understand the Scriptures,
both in their obvious and their hidden sense; though he may
know all about Christian liberty and a proper conversation;
yet if he have not love, if he do not with that knowledge
serve his neighbor, it is all of no avail whatever; in God's
sight he is nothing."

6. Note how forcibly yet kindly Paul restrains the disgraceful vice of vainglory. He disregards even those exalted
gifts, those gifts of exceeding refinement, charm and excellence, which naturally produce pride and haughtiness though
they command the admiration and esteem of men. Who
would not suppose the Holy Spirit to dwell visibly where
such wisdom, such discernment of the Scriptures, is present?
Paul's two epistles to the Corinthians are almost wholly directed against this particular vice, for it creates much mischief where it has sway. In Titus 1, 7, he names first among
the virtues of a bishop that he be "non superbus," not
haughty. In other words that he do not exalt himself because of his office, his honor and his understanding, and despise others in comparison. But strangely Paul says,

"If I have all faith, so as to remove mountains, but
have not love, I am nothing."

LOVE THE SPIRIT'S FRUIT RECEIVED BY FAITH.

7. We hold, and unquestionably it is true, that it is faith
which justifies and cleanses. Rom 1, 17; 10, 10; Acts 15, 9.
But if it justifies and ·purifies, love must be present. The
Spirit cannot but impart love together with faith. In fact,
where true faith is, the Holy Spirit dwells; and where the
Holy Spirit is, there must be love and every excellence.
How is it, then, Paul speaks as if faith without love were
possible? We reply, this one text cannot be understood
as subverting and militating against all those texts which

ascribe justification to faith alone. Even the sophists have not attributed justification to love, nor is this possible, for love is an effect, or fruit, of the Spirit, who is received through faith.

8. Three answers may be given to the question. First, Paul has not reference here to the Christian faith, which is inevitably accompanied by love, but to a general faith in God and his power. Such faith is a gift; as, for instance, the gift of tongues, the gift of knowledge, of prophecy, and the like. There is reason to believe Judas performed miracles in spite of the absence of Christian faith, according to John 6, 70: "One of you is a devil." This general faith, powerless to justify or to cleanse, permits the old man with his vices to remain, just as do the gifts of intellect, health, eloquence, riches.

9. A second answer is: Though Paul alludes to the true Christian faith, he has those in mind who have indeed attained to faith and performed miracles with it, but fall from grace through pride, thus losing their faith. Many begin but do not continue. They are like the seed in stony ground. They soon fall from faith. The temptations of vainglory are mightier than those of adversity. One who has the true faith and is at the same time able to perform miracles is likely to seek and to accept honor with such eagerness as to fall from both love and faith.

10. A third answer is: Paul in his effort to present the necessity of love, supposes an impossible condition. For instance, I might express myself in this way: "Though you were a god, if you lacked patience you would be nothing." That is, patience is so essential to divinity that divinity itself could not exist without it, a proposition necessarily true. So Paul's meaning is, not that faith could exist without love, but on the contrary, so much is love an essential of faith that even mountain-moving faith would be nothing without love, could we separate the two even in theory.

The third answer pleases me by far the best, though I do not reject the others, particularly the first. For Paul's very first premise is impossible—"if I speak with the tongues of angels." To speak with an angelic tongue is impossible for a human being, and he clearly emphasizes this impossibility by making a distinction between the tongues of men and those of angels. There is no angelic tongue; while angels may speak to us in a human tongue men can never speak in those of angels.

11. As we are to understand the first clause—"If I speak with the tongues of angels"—as meaning, Were it as possible as it is impossible for me to speak with the tongues of angels; so are we to understand the second clause—"If I have all faith, so as to remove mountains"—to mean, Were it as possible as it is impossible to have such faith. Equally impossible is the proposition of understanding all mysteries, and we must take it to mean, Were it possible for one to understand all mysteries, which, however, it is not. John, in the last chapter of his Gospel, asserts that the world could not contain all the books which might be written concerning the things of the kingdom. For no man can ever fathom the depths of these mysteries. Paul's manner of expressing himself is but a very common one, such as: "Even if I were a Christian, if I believed not in Christ I would be nothing"; or, "Were you even a prince, if you neither ruled men nor possessed property you would be nothing."

"And if I bestow all my goods to feed the poor."

12. In other words, "Were I to perform all the good works on earth and yet had not charity—having sought therein only my own honor and profit and not my neighbor's—I would nevertheless be lost." In the performance of external works so great as the surrender of property and life, Paul includes all works possible of performance, for he who would at all do these, would do any work. Just so, when he has reference to tongues he includes all good words and doctrines; and in prophecy, understanding and faith he comprises all wisdom and knowledge. Some may risk body and property for the sake of temporal glory. So Romans and pagans have done; but as love was lacking and they sought only their own interests, they practically gave nothing. It being generally impossible for men to give away all their

property, and their bodies to be burned, the meaning must be: "Were it possible for me to give all my goods to the poor, and my body to be burned."

13. The false reasoning of the sophists will not stand when they maliciously deduct from this text the theory that the Christian faith is not effectual to blot out sin and to justify. They say that before faith can justify it must be garnished with love; but justification and its distinctive qualities as well are beyond their ken. Justification of necessity precedes love. One does not love until he has become godly and righteous. Love does not make us godly, but when one has become godly love is the result. Faith, the Spirit and justification have love as effect and fruitage, and not as mere ornament and supplement. We maintain that faith alone justifies and saves. But that we may not deceive ourselves and put our trust in a false faith, God requires love from us as the evidence of our faith, so that we may be sure of our faith being real faith.

THE NATURE OF CHRISTIAN LOVE.

"Love suffereth long, and is kind."

14. Now Paul begins to mention the nature of love, enabling us to perceive where real love and faith are to be found. A haughty teacher does not possess the virtues the apostle enumerates. Lacking these, however many gifts the haughty have received through the Gospel, they are devoid of love.

First, love "suffereth long." That is, it is patient; not sudden and swift to anger, not hasty to exercise revenge, impatience or blind rage. Rather it bears in patience with the wicked and the infirm until they yield. Haughty teachers can only judge, condemn and despise others, while justifying and exalting themselves.

15. Second, love is "kind." In other words, it is pleasant to deal with; is not of forbidding aspect; ignores no one; is kind to all men, in words, acts and attitude.

16. Third, love "envieth not"—is not envious nor displeased at the greater prosperity of others; grudges no one property or honor. Haughty teachers, however, are envious

and unkind. They begrudge everyone else both honor and possessions. Though with their lips they may pretend otherwise, these characteristics are plainly visible in their deeds.

17. Fourth, love "vaunteth not itself." It is averse to knavery, to crafty guile and double-dealing. Haughty and deceptive spirits cannot refrain from such conduct, but love deals honestly and uprightly and face to face.

18. Fifth, love is not "puffed up," as are false teachers, who swell themselves up like adders.

19. Sixth, love "doth not behave itself unseemly" after the manner of the passionate, impatient and obstinate, those who presume to be always in the right, who are opposed to all men and yield to none, and who insist on submission from every individual, otherwise they set the world on fire, bluster and fume, shriek and complain, and thirst for revenge. That is what such inflating pride and haughtiness of which we have just spoken lead to.

20. Seventh, love "seeketh not her own." She seeks not financial advancement; not honor, profit, ease; not the preservation of body and life. Rather she risks all these in her is no such thing as the Church of Christ nor as true Christians. Many erring spirits, especially strong pretenders to

21. Eighth, love "is not [easily] provoked" by wrong and ingratitude; it is meek. False teachers can tolerate nothing; they seek only their own advantage and honor, to the injury of others.

22. Ninth, love "taketh not account of [thinketh no] evil." It is not suspicious; it puts the best construction on everything and takes all in good faith. The haughty, however, are immeasurably suspicious; always solicitous not to be underrated, they put the worst construction on everything, as Joab construed Abner's deeds. 2 Sam 3, 25. This is a shameful vice, and they who are guilty of it are hard to handle.

23. Tenth, love "rejoiceth not in unrighteousness [iniquity]." The words admit of two interpretations: First, as having reference to the delight of an individual in his

own evil doings. Solomon (Prov 2, 14) speaks of those who "rejoice to do evil." Such must be either extremely profligate and shameless, characters like harlots and knaves; or else they must be hypocrites, who do not appreciate the wickedness of their conduct; characters like heretics and schismatics, who rejoice when their knavery succeeds under the name of God and of the truth. I do not accept this interpretation, but the other. Paul's meaning is that false teachers are malicious enough to prefer to hear, above all things, that some other does wrong, commits error and is brought to shame; and their motive is simply that they themselves may appear upright and godly. Such was the attitude of the pharisee toward the publican, in the Gospel. But love's compassion reaches far beyond its own sins, and prays for others.

24. Eleventh, love "rejoiceth with [in] the truth." Here is evidence that the preceding phrase is to be taken as having reference to malicious rejoicing at another's sin and fall. Rejoicing in the truth is simply exulting in the right-doing and integrity of another. Similarly, love is grieved at another's wrong-doing. But to the haughty it is an affliction to learn of uprightness in someone else; for they imagine such integrity detracts from their own profit and honor.

25. Twelfth, love "beareth all things." It excuses every failing in all men, however weak, unjust or foolish one may be apparently, and no one can be guilty of a wrong too great for it to overlook. But none can do right in the eyes of the haughty, who ever find something to belittle and censure as beyond toleration, even though they must hunt up an old fence to find the injury.

26. Thirteenth, love "believeth all things." Paul does not here allude to faith in God, but to faith in men. His meaning is: Love is of decidedly trustful disposition. The possessor of it believes and trusts all men, considering them just and upright like himself. He anticipates no wily and crooked dealing, but permits himself to be deceived, deluded, flouted, imposed upon, at every man's pleasure, and asks, "Do you really believe men so wicked?" He measures

all other hearts by his own, and makes mistakes with utmost cheerfulness. But such error works him no injury. He knows God cannot forsake, and the deceiver of love but deceives himself. The haughty, on the contrary, trust no one, will believe none, nor brook deception.

27. Fourteenth, love "hopeth all things." Love despairs of no man, however wicked he may be. It hopes for the best. As implied here, love says, "We must, indeed, hope for better things." It is plain from this that Paul is not alluding to hope in God. Love is a virtue particularly representing devotion to a neighbor; his welfare is its goal in thought and deed. Like its faith, the hope entertained by love is frequently misplaced, but it never gives up. Love rejects no man; it despairs of no cause. But the proud speedily despair of men generally, rejecting them as of no account.

28. Fifteenth, love "endureth all things." It endures whatever harm befalls, whatever injury it suffers; it endures when its faith and hope in men have been misplaced; endures when it sustains damage to body, property or honor. It knows that no harm has been done since it has a rich God. False teachers, however, bear with nothing, least of all with perfidy and the violation of plighted faith.

29. Sixteenth, love never faileth; that means, it abides forever, also in the life to come. It never gives up, never permits itself to be hindered or defeated by the wickedness or ingratitude of men, as do worldly individuals and false saints, who, immediately on perceiving contempt or ingratitude, draw back, unwilling to do further good to any, and, rendering themselves quite inhuman, become perfect misanthropes like Timon in his reputation among the Greeks. Love does not so. It permits not itself to be made wicked by the wickedness of men, nor to be hindered in well-doing. It continues to do good everywhere, teaching and admonishing, aiding and serving, notwithstanding its services and benefits must be rewarded, not by good, but by evil. Love remains constant and immovable; it continues, it endures, in this earthly life and also in the life to come. The apostle adds, "Whether there be prophecies, they shall be done

away; whether there be tongues, they shall cease; whether there be knowledge, it shall be done away." Love he commends above all other endowments, as a gift that can never pass, even in the life to come. Those other gifts, the boast of the false apostles, are bestowed only for this present life, to serve in the administering of the ministerial office. Prophecy, tongues, knowledge, all must cease; for in yonder life each individual will himself perceive perfectly and there will be no need for one to teach another. Likewise, all differences, all inequalities, shall be no more. No knowledge and no diversity of gifts is necessary; God himself will be all in every soul. 1 Cor 15, 28.

30. Here Paul gives utterance to the distinction between the life of faith here below and that heavenly life of divine vision. He would teach that we have in this life and the other the same possession, for it is the same God and the same treasures which we have here by faith and there by sight. In the objects themselves there is no difference; the difference consists in our knowledge. We have the same God in both lives, but in different manner of possession. The mode of possessing God in this life is faith. Faith is an imperfect, obscure vision, which makes necessary the Word, which, in turn, receives vogue through the ministry, tongues and prophecy. Without the Word, faith cannot live. But the mode of possessing God in the future life is not faith but sight. This is perfect knowledge, rendering unnecessary the Word, and likewise preaching, tongues and prophecy. These, then, must pass. Paul continues,

"We know in part, and we prophesy in part."

31. "We know in part"; that is, in this life we know imperfectly, for it is of faith and not of sight. And we "prophesy in part"; that is, imperfectly, for the substance of our prophecy is the Word and preaching. Both knowledge and prophecy, however, reveal nothing short of what the angels see—the one God. "But when that which is perfect is come, that which is in part shall be done away."

He proves this by way of illustration and contrasts the child with the man. To children, who are yet weak, play is a necessity; it is a substitute for office and work. Similarly, we in the present life are far too frail to behold God. Until we are able, it is necessary that we should use the medium of Word and faith, which are adapted to our limitations.

> "For now we see in a mirror [through a glass] darkly;
> but then face to face."

32. Faith, Paul tells us, is like a mirror, like a riddle. The actual face is not in the glass; there is but the image of it. Likewise, faith gives us, not the radiant countenance of eternal Deity, but a mere image of him, an image derived through the Word. As a dark riddle points to something more than it expresses, so faith suggests something clearer than that which it perceives. But in the life to come, mirror and riddle, faith and its demonstration, shall all have ceased to be. God's face and our own shall be mutually and clearly revealed. Paul says, "Now I know in part; but then shall I know fully even as also I was fully known [know even also as I am known]." That is, God now knows me perfectly, clearly and plainly; no dark veil is upon myself. But as to him, a dark veil hides him from me. With the same perfect clearness wherewith he now knows me, I shall then know him—without a veil. The veil shall be taken away, not from him, but from me; for upon him is no veil.

THE GREATEST CHRISTIAN VIRTUE IS LOVE.

> "But now abideth faith, hope, love, these three; and
> the greatest of these is love."

33. The sophists have transgressed in a masterly manner as regards this verse. They have made faith vastly inferior to love because of Paul's assertion that love is greater than faith and greater than hope. As usual, their mad reason blindly seizes upon the literal expression. They hack a piece out of it and the remainder they ignore. Thus they fail to understand Paul's meaning; they do not perceive that the sense of Paul concerning the greatness of love is expressed both in the text and the context. For surely it cannot be disputed that the apostle is here referring to the permanent or temporary character respectively of love and

other gifts, and not to their rank or power. As to rank, not faith only, but the Word, surpasses love; for the Word is the power of God unto salvation to all that believe. Rom 1, 16. Yet the Word must pass. But though love is the fruit of the Word and its effect, it shall never be abolished. Faith possesses God himself. It possesses and can accomplish all things; yet it must cease. Love gives and blesses the neighbor, as a result of faith, and it shall never be done away.

34. Now, Paul's statement that love is greater than faith and hope is intended as an expression of the permanence, or eternal duration, of love. Faith, being limited as to time in comparison with love, ranks beneath it for the reason of this temporary duration. With the same right I might say that the kingdom of Christ is greater upon earth than was Christ. Thereby I do not mean that the Church in itself is better and of higher rank than Christ, but merely that it covers a greater part of the earth than he compassed; for he was here but three years and those he spent in a limited sphere, whereas his kingdom has been from the beginning and is coextensive with the earth. In this sense, love is longer and broader than either faith or hope. Faith deals with God merely in the heart and in this life, whereas the relations of love both to God and the whole world are eternal. Nevertheless, as Christ is immeasurably better and higher and more precious than the Christian Church, although we behold him moving in smaller limits and as a mere individual, so is faith better, higher and more precious than love, though its duration is limited and it has God alone for its object.

35. Paul's purpose in thus extolling love is to deal a blow to false teachers and to bring to naught their boasts about faith and other gifts when love is lacking. His thought is: "If ye possess not love, which abides forever, all else whereof ye boast being perishable, ye will perish with it. While the Word of God, and spiritual gifts, are eternal, yet the external office and proclamation of the Word, and likewise the employment of gifts in their variety, shall have an end, and thus your glory and pride shall

become as ashes." So, then, faith justifies through the Word and produces love. But while both Word and faith shall pass, righteousness and love, which they effect, abide forever; just as a building erected by the aid of scaffolding remains after the scaffolding has been removed.

36. Observe how small the word "love" and how easily uttered! Who would have thought to find so much precious virtue and power ascribed by Paul to this one excellence as counterpart of so much that is evil? This is, I imagine, magnifying love, painting love. It is a better discourse on virtue and vice than are the heathen writings. The model the apostle presents should justly shame the false teachers, who talk much of love but in whom not one of the virtues he mentions is found.

Every quality of love named by him means false teachers buffeted and assaulted. Whenever he magnifies love and characterizes her powers, he invariably makes at the same time a thrust at those who are deficient in any of them. Well may we, then, as he describes the several features, add the comment "But you do very differently."

37. It is passing strange that teachers devoid of love should possess such gifts as Paul has mentioned here, viz., speaking with tongues, prophesying, understanding mysteries; that they should have faith, should bestow their goods and suffer themselves to be burned. For we have seen what abominations ensue where love is lacking; such individuals are proud, envious, puffed up, impatient, unstable, false, venomous, suspicious, malicious, disdainful, bitter, disinclined to service, distrustful, selfish, ambitious and haughty. How can it consistently be claimed that people of this stamp can, through faith, remove mountains, give their bodies to be burned, prophesy, and so on? It is precisely as I have stated. Paul presents an impossible proposition, implying that since they are devoid of love, they do not really possess those gifts, but merely assume the name and appearance. And in order to divest them of those he admits for the sake of argument that they are what in reality they are not.

First Sunday In Lent

Text, Second Corinthians 6, 1-10.

1 And working together with him we entreat also that ye receive not the grace of God in vain 2 (for he saith, At an acceptable time I hearkened unto thee, and in a day of salvation did I succor thee: behold, now is the acceptable time; behold, now is the day of salvation): 3 giving no occasion of stumbling in anything, that our ministration be not blamed; 4 but in everything commending ourselves, as ministers of God, in much patience, in afflictions, in necessities, in distresses, 5 in stripes, in imprisonments, in tumults, in labors, in watchings, in fastings; 6 in pureness, in knowledge, in longsuffering, in kindness, in the Holy Spirit, in love unfeigned, 7 in the word of truth, in the power of God; by the armor of righteousness on the right hand on the left, 8 by glory and dishonor, by evil report and good report; as deceivers, and yet true; 9 as unknown, and yet well known; as dying, and behold, we live; as chastened, and not killed; 10 as sorrowful, yet always rejoicing; as poor, yet making many rich; as having nothing, and yet possessing all things.

AN ENTREATY TO LIVE AS CHRISTIANS.

1. This lesson is an admonition to the Corinthians calculated to stimulate them in the performance of the duties they already recognize. The words are easily enough said, but execution is difficult and practice rare. For Paul gives a strange description of the Christian life, and the color and characteristics with which he exhibits it render it decidedly unprepossessing. First he says:

133

"And working together with him we entreat also that ye receive not the grace of God in vain."

2. He calls the Corinthians co-workers, as in First Corinthians 3, 9, where he puts it: "We are God's fellow-workers; ye are God's husbandry, God's building." That is, we labor upon you with the external Word—teaching and admonishing; but God, working inwardly through the Spirit, gives the blessing and the success. He permits not our labor with the outward Word to be in vain. Therefore, God is the true Master, performing inwardly the supreme work, while we aid outwardly, serving him through the ministry.

The apostle's purpose in praising his co-laborers is to prevent them from despising the external Word as something inessential to them, or well enough known. For though God is able to effect everything without the instrumentality of the outward Word, working inwardly by his Spirit, this is by no means his purpose. He uses preachers as fellow-workers, or co-laborers, to accomplish his purpose through the Word when and where he pleases. Now, since preachers have the office, name and honor of fellow-workers with God, no one may be considered learned enough or holy enough to ignore or despise the most inferior preaching; especially since he knows not when the hour may come wherein God will, through preachers, perform his work in him.

3. Secondly, Paul shows the danger of neglecting the grace of God. He boldly declares here that the preaching of the Gospel is not an eternal, continuous and permanent mode of instruction, but rather a passing shower, which hastens on. What it strikes, it strikes; what it misses, it misses. It does not return, nor does it stand still. The sun and heat follow and dry it up. Experience shows that in no part of the world has the Gospel remained pure beyond the length of man's memory. Only so long as its pioneers lived did it stand and prosper. When they were gone, the light disappeared; factious spirits and false teachers followed immediately.

Thus Moses announces (Deut 31, 29) that the children of

Israel will corrupt themselves after his death; and the book of Judges testifies that so it really came to pass. Each time a judge died in whose days the Word of God obtained sway, the people fell away and became more wicked than before. King Joash did what was right so long as the high priest Jehoiada lived, but after the latter's death this had an end. And following the time of Christ and his apostles, the world was filled with seditious spirits and false teachers. Paul, in fact, declares (Acts 20, 29): "I know that after my departing grievous wolves shall enter in among you, not sparing the flock." So also we now have the pure Gospel. This is a time of grace and salvation and the acceptable day; but should the world continue, this condition, too, will soon pass.

4. To receive the grace of God in vain can be nothing else than to hear the pure word of God which presents and offers his grace, and yet to remain listless and irresponsive, undergoing no change at all. Thus, ungrateful for the Word and unworthy of it, we merit the loss of the Word. Such as these are described in the parable (Lk 14, 16-24) where the guests bidden to the supper refused to come and went about their own business, thus provoking the master's anger until he swore they should not taste his supper.

Similar is Paul's threat here, that we may take heed and accept the Gospel with fear and gratitude. Christ says (Jn 12, 35), "Walk while ye have the light, that darkness overtake you not." I should think we might have learned wisdom from experience—from the darkness we suffered under the Papacy. But that is all forgotten; we show neither gratitude nor amendment of life. Very well, we shall find out the consequences.

SALVATION WHEREVER THE GOSPEL IS SENT.

"Behold, now is the acceptable time; behold, now is the day of salvation."

5. These words portray the richness of the salvation wherever the Gospel goes: nothing but grace and help; no wrath or punishment. Indeed, these are words of unutterable meaning the apostle here employs.

First, he tells us that it is an "acceptable time," as the Hebrew expresses it. Our own way of putting it would be: "This is a gracious time, a time when God turns away his wrath and is moved only by love and benevolence toward us and is pleased to do us good." All our sins are forgotten; he takes no note of the sins of the past nor of those of the present. In short, we are in a realm of mercy, where are only forgiveness and reconciliation. The heavens are now open. This is the true golden year when man is denied nothing. So Paul says, "At an acceptable time I hearkened unto thee"; that is: "I am kindly disposed toward thee. Whatsoever thou shalt even desire and ask for, thou shalt surely receive. Be not neglectful, therefore, and ask while the acceptable time continues."

6. Second, Paul declares that it is a day of blessing, "a day of salvation." It is a day of help, wherein we are not only acceptable and assured of God's favor and good will toward us, but we experience even as we have been assured —that God really does help us. He verifies his assurance, for his beneficence gives testimony that our prayers are heard. We call it a happy day, a blessed day, a day of abundance; for these two truths are inseparably related— that God is favorable toward us, and that his kindness is the proof of his favor. God's favor toward us is revealed in the first clause, which speaks of an acceptable time; that he extends help to us is revealed in the second clause, telling of a blessed day of succor. Both these facts are to be apprehended by faith and in good conscience; for a superficial judgment would lead to the view that this period of blessing is rather an accursed period of wrath and disfavor. Words like these, of spiritual meaning, must be understood in the light of the Holy Spirit; thus shall we find that these two glorious, beautiful expressions refer to the Gospel dispensation and are intended to magnify all the treasures and the riches of the kingdom of Christ.

"Giving no occasion of stumbling [no offense] in anything."

7. Since this is a time of blessing, let us make right use

·of it, not spending it to no purpose, and let us take serious heed to give offense to none; thus avoiding reproach to our ministry. It is evident from the connection to what kind of offense the apostle has reference; he would not have the Gospel doctrine charged with teaching anything evil.

8. Two kinds of offense bring the Gospel into disgrace: In one case it is the heathen who are offended, and this because of the fact that some individuals would make the Gospel a means of freedom from temporal restraint, substituting temporal liberty for spiritual. They thus bring reproach upon the Gospel as teaching such doctrine, and make it an object of scandal to the heathen and worldly people, whereby they are misled and become enemies to the faith and to the Word of God without cause, being the harder to convert since they regard Christians as licentious knaves. And the responsibility for this must be placed at the door of those who have given offense in this respect.

In the other case, Christians are offended among themselves. The occasion is the indiscreet exercise of Christian liberty, which offends the weak in faith. Concerning this topic much is said in First Corinthians 8 and Romans 14. Paul here hints at what he speaks of in First Corinthians 10, 32-33: "Give no occasion of stumbling, either to Jews, or to Greeks, or to the church of God: even as I also please all men in all things, not seeking mine own profit, but the profit of the many that they may be saved." He takes up the same subject in Philippians 2, 4, teaching that every man should look on the things of others. Then no offense will be given.

"That our ministration [the ministry] be not blamed."

9. Who can prevent our office being vilified? for the Word of God must be persecuted equally with Christ himself. That the Word of God is reviled by unbelievers ignorant of faith in God is something we cannot prevent. For, according to Isaiah 8, 14 and Romans 9, 33, the Gospel is a "rock of offense." This is the offense of the faith; it will pursue its course and we are not responsible.

But for love's offense, offense caused by shortcomings in

our works and fruits of faith, the things we are commanded
to let shine before men, that, seeing these, they may be al-
lured to the faith—for offense in this respect we cannot dis-
claim responsibility. It is a sin we certainly must avoid,
that the heathen, the Jews, the weak and the rulers of the
world may never be able to say: "Behold the knavery and
licentiousness of these people! Surely their doctrine cannot be true." Otherwise our evil name and fame and the
obstacles we place before others will extend to the innocent
and holy Word God has given us to apprehend and to proclaim; it must bear our shame and in addition become un-
fruitful in the offended ones. Grievous is such a sin as this.

MARKS OF CHRISTIANS AS MINISTERS OF GOD.

"But in everything commending ourselves, as ministers of God, in much patience."

10. The apostle here portrays the Christian life in its
outward expression. Not that it is possible for anyone
thereby to become a Christian, or godly; but, being servants
of God, or Christians and godly people, we furnish in this
manner, according to Paul's statement here, the evidence
thereof as by fruits and signs.

Mark his phrase "ministers of God." What a remarkable service for God is this wherein we must endure so
much suffering, so much affliction, privation, anxiety,
stripes, imprisonment, tumult or sedition, labor, watching,
fasting, and so on! No mass here, no vigil, no hallucina-
tions of a fictitious service of God; it is the true service of
God, which subdues the body and mortifies the flesh. Not,
indeed, as if fasting, watching and toiling are to be despised
because they do not make just. Though we are not thereby justified, we must nevertheless practice those things, instead of giving rein to the flesh and indulging our idleness.

11. Paul also mentions sedition. Not that by our teaching or life we should be guilty of sedition against others;
rather, we should be quiet and obedient. See Romans 13.
Christ says (Mt 22, 21), "Render therefore unto Cæsar the
things that are Cæsar's." Paul's meaning is that when we
become victims of sedition on the part of others we should

submit; just as we are not to inflict upon others privations, distresses, stripes or imprisonment, but rather to accept them at their hands. So Paul heads the list with patience; which does not produce sedition, but endures it.

It is a consolation in these times when we are charged with raising seditions, to reflect that it is the very nature and color of the Christian life that it be criticised as seditious when the fact is it patiently bears sedition directed against itself. Thus was it with Elijah, who was accused by King Ahab of troubling Israel and exciting turbulence. 1 Kings 18, 17-18. Then, when we are charged with guilt in this respect, let us remember that not only did the apostles have to hear the same accusation, but even Christ himself, with all his innocence, was so accused. More than that, he was falsely reviled upon the cross with a superscription charging sedition; in fact, he was even put to death as a Jewish king guilty of opposition to Cæsar and of enticing and inciting the people.

12. The remaining marks of the Christian life—patience, affliction, necessities, distresses, stripes, imprisonments, labor, watching, fasting, purity, etc., are easily interpreted; it is readily seen how they are instrumental in our service to God. God will not have indolent, idle gluttons, nor sleepy and impatient servants. Most adroitly does Paul score in particular our fine idle youths who draw interest from their money, have an easy life, and imagine their tonsures, their long robes and their howling in the churches excuse them from labor. All men should labor and earn their bread, according to Paul. 2 Thes 3, 12. By labor, our text teaches, we serve God; more than that, our labor is testimony to the fact that we serve God.

"In knowledge."

13. What is meant here? With Paul, knowledge signifies discretion, understanding, reason. He speaks of the Jews (Rom 10, 2) as having "a zeal for God, but not according to knowledge"; that is, a zeal without reason, without understanding, without discretion. His message here, then, is: "We should conduct ourselves in Christian affairs with

becoming reason and moderation lest we give offense·to the
weak by a presumptuous use of Christian liberty. Rather
we should, with discretion and understanding, adapt ourselves to that which promotes the neighbor's welfare. Likewise, when we labor, fast, or when we regulate our sexual
relations, we are to exercise reason, lest the body should be
injured by too much fasting, watching and toil, and also by
needless abstention from sexual intercourse. Let everyone
take heed to remain within bounds by using reason and discretion. The apostle counsels the married (1 Cor 7, 5) not
to defraud each other too long, lest they be tempted. In
all such matters, he would impose no measures and rules,
no limits and laws, after the manner of the councils, the
popes and the monks. He leaves it wholly to each individual's discretion to decide and to test for himself all questions of time and quantity bearing upon the restraints of
his flesh.

"In longsuffering, in kindness."

14. The meaning of these phrases has been stated in
many other places, particularly in connection with Romans
2 and Galations 5.

"By the Holy Spirit."

15. What are we to understand here? The words may
have one of two meanings: First, the apostle may have reference to the Holy Spirit in person, who is God. Second,
he may have reference to the spirit of individuals, or their
spiritual condition. "Holy Spirit" may be intended to stand
for "spirituality," Paul's meaning being: "Beware of the
professedly spiritual, or of things glittering and purporting
to be spiritual; beware of them who make great boast of
the Spirit and nevertheless betray only a false, unclean, unholy spirit, productive of sects and discord. Abide ye in
that true, holy spirituality proceeding from God's Holy
Spirit, who imparts unity and harmony, determination and
courage." As Paul expresses it elsewhere (Eph 4, 3), "Giving diligence to keep the unity of the Spirit in the bond of
peace." They, then, who continue in one faith, one mind
and disposition, give testimony by the reality and saintli-

ness of their spiritual life and by the presence of the Holy
Spirit that they are servants of God. For true spirituality,
or a holy walk in the Spirit, means to be in heart and mind
at one with the Spirit, through faith.

"In love unfeigned, in the word of truth."

16.   As the apostle opposes the Holy Spirit to false sects
and false prophets, so he opposes unfeigned love to indolent Christians who in true faith and unity of mind possess
marks of true spirituality, but are nevertheless indolent,
cold, in fact false as regards love.

Again, he opposes the "Word of Truth" to abusers of the
Word of God, who misconstrue it and comment upon it according to their own fancy, and for their own honor and
profit. While much that purports to be spiritual has not
the Word as source and gives honor to the Spirit at the expense of the Word, the class under consideration profess to
magnify the Word; they would be master interpreters of
the Scriptures, confident that their explanations are correct
and superior. In condemnation of this class, Peter says (1
Pet 4, 11), "If any man speaketh, speaking as it were oracles
of God," and not his own word. In other words, let him be
assured he speaks the Word of God and not his own. God's
Word Paul here terms the "Word of truth"; that is, the true
Word of God and not our own misconstrued, falsified word
palmed off as God's Word. In our idiom we would say "the
real Word" where the Hebrew has "Word of truth," or
"true Word."

"In the power of God."

17.   Peter speaks also of this power, in the verse before
mentioned: "If any man ministereth, ministering as of the
strength which God supplieth." And Paul elsewhere declares (Col 1, 29): "Whereunto I labor also, striving according to his working, which worketh in me mightily";
and again (Rom 15, 18): "For I will not dare to speak of
any things save those which Christ wrought through me,
for the obedience of the Gentiles." Christians should have
the assurance that they are the kingdom of God, and that
in whatever they do, especially in undertakings of a spirit-

ual character, which have the salvation of souls as aim, they beware of everything not absolutely known as true, so that the work be not theirs but God's.

In God's kingdom God alone is to speak, reign and act. Christ says (Mt 5, 16): "Even so let your light shine before men, that they may see your good works and glorify your Father who is in heaven"—may glorify him as the worker, and not yourselves. Seductive spirits, however, come cavorting in their own power, throw the pictures out of the churches and establish rules of their own, without caring whether it is done in the power of God. The consequence is that their work is neither permanent nor fruitful.

THE ARMOR OF RIGHTEOUSNESS.
"By the armor of righteousness."

18. This armor Paul more fully describes in Ephesians and in Thessalonians. Sufficient explanation of it has been given in the lesson for Advent. There is the "shield of faith," the "helmet of salvation," the shoes of "the preparation of the Gospel of peace," and so on. Paul includes them all under the term "armor of righteousness," and, in his epistle to the Ephesians, under the phrase "armor of God," to teach Christians to eschew and to forsake carnal, worldly weapons for these. He would have them know themselves a spiritual people, spiritually warring against the spiritual enemies enumerated here and pointed out on the right hand and on the left.

19. On the left hand he places dishonor and evil report, in that we appear to men as deceivers, unknown, in conflict with death, chastened, sorrowful, poor and needy. Scorn is hurled in our faces and the reputation accorded us is that of deceivers. The Christian must not only be unknown, friendless and a stranger, but men will also be ashamed of him—even his best friends—in consequence of the reproach and evil report under which he lies in the eyes of the great, the wealthy, the wise and the powerful of the world.

He must be as one dying—continually expecting death by reason of the hatred and envy directed against him, and the various persecutions he suffers. He must be beaten and scourged; must at times feel the weight of the enmity and envy wherewith the world inflicts torment. He is like the sorrowful, for so ill does he fare in the world, he has reason to sorrow. He resembles the poor in that nothing is given him but injuries; he possesses nothing, for if he has not been deprived of all his possessions he daily expects that extremity.

Lest he despair of his hope in God and grow faint, he must be armed on the left hand against these enemies with a divine armor: with a firm faith, with the comfort of the divine Word, with hope, so that he may endure and exercise patience. Thereby he proves himself to be a true servant of God, inasmuch as false teachers and hypocrites, with all their pompous worship, are incapable of these things.

20. On the right he places honor and good report, inasmuch as we are after all true, well known, alive, defiant of death, full of joy, rich, possessing all things. The Christian will have always a few to honor and commend him; some there will be to give him a good report, to praise him as true and honest in doctrine. And there will be some who receive and acknowledge him, who are not ashamed of him. Life remains in spite of death oft faced, even in scourgings. He rejoices when things with him are at the worst, for his heart remains joyful in God, that joy finding expression in words, deeds and manner. Though poor in the goods of the world, he does not die of hunger, and he makes many spiritually rich through the Word. Even though he have no possessions at all, he suffers no lack but has in hand all things; for all creatures must serve the believer. As Christ promised (Mk 9, 23), "All things are possible to him that believeth." For himself, it is true, he possesses nothing, and gladly he endures his need; but for his neighbor's sake he can do all things, and all he has he is ready to place at the disposal of his neighbor whenever need requires. These blessings also give occasion for a powerful armor, for we must guard against pride and haughtiness.

21. Thus the Christian is quite untrammeled. His eyes are fixed upon God alone. Always choosing the safe middle

path he steers clear of danger on the right and on the left. He permits not the evil to overthrow him nor the good to exalt, but makes use of both to the honor of God and the benefit of his neighbor. This, Paul instructs us, should be the manner of our life now while the season of grace continues; nor must we fail to heed this! This is the true service of God, the service well pleasing to him; unto which may God help us. Amen.

Second Sunday In Lent

Text: First Thessalonians 4, 1-7.

1. Finally then, brethren, we beseech and exhort you in the Lord Jesus, that, as ye received of us how ye ought to walk and to please God, even as ye do walk,— that ye abound more and more. 2 For ye know what charge we gave you through the Lord Jesus. 3 For this is the will of God, even your sanctification, that ye abstain from fornication; 4 that each one of you know how to possess himself of his own vessel in sanctification and honor, 5 not in the passion of lust, even as the Gentiles who know not God; 6 that no man transgress, and wrong his brother in the matter: because the Lord is an avenger in all these things, as also we forewarned you and testified. 7 For God called us not for uncleanness, but in sanctification.

EXHORTATION TO HOLINESS.

1. This lesson is easy of interpretation. It is a general and earnest admonition on the part of Paul, enjoining us to an increasing degree of perfection in the doctrine we have received. This admonition, this exhortation, is one incumbent upon an evangelical teacher to give, for he is urging us to observe a doctrine commanded of God. He says, "For ye know what charge [commandments] we gave you through the Lord Jesus." Whatever Christians do, it should be willing service, not compulsory; but when a command is given, it should be in the form of exhortation or entreaty. Those who have received the Spirit are they from whom obedience is due; but those not inclined to a willing performance, we should leave to themselves.

145

2. But mark you this: Paul places much value upon the gift bestowed upon us, the gift of knowing how we are "to walk and to please God." In the world this gift is as great as it is rare. Though the offer is made to the whole world and publicly proclaimed, further exhortation is indispensable, and Paul is painstaking and diligent in administering it. The trouble is, we are in danger of becoming indolent and negligent, forgetful and ungrateful—vices menancing and great, and which, alas, are altogether too frequent.

Let us look back and note to what depths of darkness, of delusion and abomination, we had sunk when we knew not how we ought to walk, how to please God. Alas, we have forgotten all about it; we have become indolent and ungrateful, and are dealt with accordingly. Well does the apostle say in the lesson for the Sunday preceding this (2 Cor 6, 1): "And working together with him we entreat also that ye receive not the grace of God in vain, for he saith, At an acceptable time I hearkened unto thee, and in a day of salvation did I succor thee."

3. In our present lesson he treats chiefly of two vices: unchastity, which is a sin against oneself and destructive of the fruits of faith; and fraud in business, which is a sin against the neighbor and likewise destructive of faith and charity. Paul would have every man keep himself chaste and free from wrong against every man, pronouncing the wrath of God on offenses of this character.

4. It was a fact reflecting much credit and honor on the Thessalonians in contrast to the Corinthians and the Galatians, that they continued upright in doctrine and true in the knowledge of the faith, though perhaps deficient in the above-mentioned two self-evident features of Christian life. While it is true that if sins of immorality are not renounced God will punish, yet punishment in such cases is for the most part temporal, these sins being less pernicious than such gross offenses as error in faith and doctrine.

5. Paul, however, threatens such sins with the wrath of God, lest anyone become remiss and indolent, imagining the kingdom of Christ a kingdom to tolerate with impunity

such offenses. As Paul expresses it, "God called us not for uncleanness, but in sanctification [holiness]." The thought is: Unchastity does not come within the limits of Christian liberty and privilege, nor does God treat the offender with indulgence and impunity. No, indeed. In fact, he will more rigorously punish this sin among Christians than among heathen. Paul tells us (1 Cor 11, 30) that many were sickly and many had succumbed to the sleep of death in consequence of eating and drinking unworthily. And Psalm 89, 32 testifies, "Then will I visit their transgression with the rod."

6. True, they who sin through infirmity, who, conscious of their transgressions, suffer themselves to be reproved, repenting at once—for these the kingdom of Christ has ready pity and forbearance, commending them to acceptance and toleration (Rom 15; Gal 6, 1; 1 Cor 13, 7); but that such vices be regarded generally lawful and normal—this will not do! Paul declares, "This is the will of God, even your sanctification." And he speaks of "how ye ought to . . . please God." His thought is: Some consider these sins a matter of little moment, treat them as if the wind blew them away and God rather had pleasure in them as trivial affairs. But this is not true. While God really bears with the fallen sinner, he would have us perceive our errors and strive to mend our lives and to abound more and more in righteousness. His grace is not intended to cloak our shame, nor should the licentious abuse the kingdom of Christ as a shield for their knavery. Paul commands (Gal 5, 13), "Use not your freedom for an occasion to the flesh"; and Peter (1 Pet 2, 16), "As free, and not using your freedom for a cloak of wickedness, but as bondservants of God."

7. Paul, following the Hebrew way of speaking, has reference to chastity where he says "your sanctification." He terms the body "holy" when it is chaste, chastity being, in God's sight, equivalent to holiness. "Holiness," in the Old Testament, is a synonym for "purity." Again, "holiness" and "purity" are regarded as the same thing in First Cor-

inthians 7, 14: "Else were your children unclean; but now are they holy."

8. The nature of the holiness and purity whereof he speaks he makes plain himself in the words: "That ye abstain from fornication; that each one of you know how to possess himself of his own vessel in sanctification and honor." The apostle does not here prohibit matrimony, but licentiousness, and unchastity outside the marriage state. He who is careful to keep his vessel—his body—chaste, who does not commit adultery and is not guilty of whoredom—this man preserves his body in holiness and purity, and properly is called chaste and holy. The same thought is borne out in the succeeding verse:

"Not in the passion of lust [in the lust of concupiscence], even as the Gentiles."

9. The Gentiles, who know not God, give themselves up to all manner of uncleanness, or disgraceful vices, as Paul records in Romans 1, 29-31. Not that all gentiles are guilty in that respect. Paul is not saying what all heathen do; he merely states that with the gentiles such conduct is apparent, and quite to be expected from people "who know not God." Under such conditions, one allows the sin to pass unreproved, as does Paul himself. Notwithstanding he censures them who consent to sin of this character when knowing better, and who do not restrain the evil-doers. Rom 1, 32. But in the case of Christians, when any fall into such sin they are to be reproved and the sin resisted; the offense must not be allowed to pass as with the gentiles. In the case of the latter the lust of concupiscence holds sway; no restraints are exercised and the reins are given to lust, so that its nature and passion are given free expression, just as if this were a provision of nature, when the fact is it is a pest to be healed, a blemish to be removed. But there is none to heal and deliver, so the gentiles decay and go to ruin through evil lust. "Lust of concupiscence" would be, with us, "evil lust." The conclusion is simple:

"That no man transgress and wrong his brother in the matter."

10. In other words, that no one take for himself what belongs to another, or use the property of another for his own benefit, which may be done by a variety of tricks. To "defraud in any matter" is to seek gain at the expense of a neighbor. On this latter subject much has been written elsewhere, particularly in the little treatise on Merchants and Usury, showing the great extent to which extortion is practiced and how charity is rarely observed. It is on this topic that Paul here would fix our attention.

Third Sunay In Lent

Text: Ephesians 5, 1-9.

1. Be ye therefore imitators of God, as beloved children; 2 and walk in love, even as Christ also loved you, and gave himself up for us, an offering and a sacrifice to God for an odor of a sweet smell. 3 But fornication, and all uncleanness, or covetousness, let it not even be named among you, as becometh saints; 4 nor filthiness, nor foolish talking, or jesting, which are not befitting: but rather giving of thanks. 5 For this ye know of a surety, that no fornicator, nor unclean person, nor covetous man, who is an idolater, hath any inheritance in the kingdom of Christ and God. 6 Let no man deceive you with empty words: for because of these things cometh the wrath of God upon the sons of disobedience. 7 Be not ye therefore partakers with them; 8 for ye were once darkness, but are now light in the Lord: walk as children of light 9 (for the fruit of the light is in all goodness and righteousness and truth).

EXHORTATION TO BE IMITATORS OF GOD.

1. This is a letter of admonition, instructing Christians, according to the plan underlying Paul's epistles, not to become sluggish and careless, but by their deeds to evince their faith, and honor and proclaim the Word he has taught them; for the sake of the gentiles and unbelievers, that these may not take offense at the doctrine of Christ.

2. To begin with, having shown that we were made children of God through Christ, he admonishes us to be followers, or imitators, of the Father, as beloved children. He employs the most endearing of terms—"beloved children"—to

150

persuade us by the Father's love to love even as we are loved. But what manner of love has God manifested toward us? It was not simply that love manifest in the fact that he gives temporal support to us unworthy beings in common with all the wicked on earth; that he permits his sun to rise on the just and on the unjust and sends rain on the grateful and on the ungrateful, as Christ mentions (Mt 5, 45) in connection with his command to be perfect even as our Father in heaven is perfect. Not only thus did God love us, but in a special way: he has given his Son for us. In addition to showering upon us both temporal and eternal blessings he has given his own self; he has completely poured out himself for us, with all he is, with all he has, with all he does,— and we were nothing but sinners, unworthy creatures, enemies and servants of the devil. More than this would be beyond even his grace and power.

He who despises such glow of love, which fills all heaven and earth and is beyond all power to comprehend it; who does not permit this love to kindle and incite in him love for his neighbor whether enemy or friend—such a one is not likely ever to become godly or loving by such measures as laws or commandments, instruction, constraint or compulsion.

3. "Walk in love," counsels the apostle. He would have our external life all love. But not the world's love is to be our pattern, which seeks only its own advantage, and loves only so long as it is the gainer thereby; we must love even as Christ loved, who sought neither pleasure nor gain from us but gave himself for us, not to mention the other blessings he bestows daily—gave himself as a sacrifice and offering to reconcile God unto ourselves, so that he should be our God and we his children.

Thus likewise should we give, thus should we lend, or even surrender our goods, no matter whether friends claim them or enemies. Nor are we to stop there; we must be ready to give our lives for both friends and enemies, and must be occupied with no other thought than how we can serve others, and how both our life and property can be made to minister to them in this life, and this because we know that Christ is ours and has given us all things.

"To God for an odor of a sweet smell [for a sweet-smelling savor]."

4. This expression Paul takes from the Old Testament. There the temporal sacrifices are described as being "a sweet-smelling savor" unto God: that is, they were acceptable and well-pleasing to him; but not, as the Jews imagined, because of the value of the work or of the sacrifices in themselves. For such thoughts they were chastised by the prophets often enough. They were acceptable on the ground of the true sacrifice which they foreshadowed and encircled. Paul's thought is this: The sacrifices of the Old Testament have passed. Now all sacrifices are powerless but that of Christ himself; he is the sweet-smelling savor. This sacrifice is pleasing to God. He gladly accepts it and would have us be confident it is an acceptable offering in our stead. Moreover, there is no other sacrifice the Christian Church can offer for us. The once-offered Christ alone avails. Although, following his example, we present our bodies a sacrifice, as taught in Romans 12, 1, yet we do not do so in behalf of ourselves or others; that is the function of the one sacrifice alone—Christ. Therefore, all sacrifices offered in the mistaken notion that they avail for us, or even secure forgiveness of sin, are wicked and unsavory. But more of this elsewhere.

SINS NOT TO BE NAMED AMONG CHRISTIANS.

"But fornication, and all uncleanness, or covetousness, let it not even be named among you, as becometh saints."

5. In naming uncleanness in addition to fornication, the reference is to all sensual affections in distinction from wedded love. They are too unsavory for him to mention by name, though in Romans 1, 24 he finds it expedient to speak of them without disguise. However, also wedded love must be characterized by moderation among Christians. While there is a conjugal duty to be required by necessity, it is for the very purpose of avoiding unchastity and unclean-

ness. The ideal and perfect condition, it is true, would be cohabitation with a sole view to procreation; however, that is too high for attainment by all.

6. Paul declares that the sin he indicates should not be named of the Ephesians. Unquestionably, among Christians there will always be some infirm one to fall; but we must labor diligently, correcting, amending and restraining. We must not suffer the offense to go unchallenged, but curtail and remedy it, lest, as remarked in the preceding lesson, the heathen stumble, saying: "Christians tolerate such vices among themselves; their conduct is not different from our own." An occasional fall among Christians must be borne with so long as right prevails in general, and such things are neither tolerated nor taught, but reproved and amended. Paul gives the counsel (Gal 6, 1) that the brethren restore the fallen in a spirit of meekness; and he blames the Corinthians for not reproving them who sin. 1 Cor 5, 2. A sin, once punished, is as if the sin did not exist; it is no longer a matter of reproach.

7. Likewise with covetousness: we are to understand that it is not to be named of Christians. That is, should one be covetous, should one defraud another or contend with him about temporal advantage, as evidently was true of the Corinthians (1 Cor 6, 1), the offense must not be suffered to go unreproved and uncorrected. The Gospel must be carefully upheld and preserved among the multitude, "that our ministration be not blamed." 2 Cor 6, 3.

I make this point for the sake of those who, so soon as they observe that all Christians are not perfectly holy, but will occasionally stumble and fall, imagine there is no such thing as a Christian and the Gospel is impotent and fruitless. Just as if to be a Christian meant the mountain already climbed and complete, triumphant victory over sin! The fact is, it is rather a contest, a battle. Wherever there is a contest, or a battle, some of the combatants will flee, some will be wounded, some will fall and some even be slain. For warfare is not unaccompanied by disaster if it be real warfare.

8. The writer of the epistle goes on to assign the reason why it does not sound well to hear such things concerning Christians—because they are saints and it behooves saints to be chaste and moderate, and to practice and teach these virtues. Note, he calls Christians "saints," notwithstanding that in this life they are clothed with sinful flesh and blood. Doubtless the term is not applied in consequence of their good works, but because of the holy blood of Christ. For Paul says (1 Cor 6, 11): "But ye were washed, but ye were sanctified, but ye were justified in the name of the Lord Jesus Christ, and in the Spirit of our God." Being holy, we should manifest our holiness by our deeds. Though we are still weak, yet we ought duly to strive to become chaste and free from covetousness, to the glory and honor of God and the edifying of unbelievers.

"Nor filthiness, nor foolish talking, or jesting, which are not befitting."

9. "Filthiness"—scandalous talk—is unchaste language suggestive of fornication, uncleanness and carnal sins. It is common in taverns and generally found as accompaniment of gluttony, drunkenness and gambling. Especially were the Greeks frivolous and adepts in this respect, as their poets and other writers attest. What Paul refers to in particular is the lewd conversation uttered in public without fear and self-restraint. This will excite wicked thoughts and give rise to serious offenses, especially with the young. As he states elsewhere (1 Cor 15, 33), "Evil companionships [communications] corrupt good morals." Should there be any Christians forgetful enough to so transgress, the offense must be reproved; otherwise it will become general and give the congregation an ill repute, as if Christians taught and tolerated it the same as the heathen.

FOOLISH TALKING AND JESTING.

10. By "foolish talking" is indicated the fables and tales and other lore in which the Greeks particularly abound—a people who possess a special faculty for fiction of this sort. Similar are the tales commonly related by our women and maidens while spinning at the distaff, also those which

knaves are fond of relating. Here belong also worldly songs which either relate lewd matters or turn upon slippery, frivolous themes. Such are "The Priest of Kalenburg," "Dietrich of Berne" and innumerable others.

11. Particularly unchristian is every kind of such buffoonery in the church when men are gathered to hear and learn the Word of God. But the practice is common where many come together. Even where at first things of a serious nature are discussed, men soon pass to frivolous, wanton, foolish talk, resulting in a waste of time and the neglect of better things. For instance, on the festival of Easter, foolish, ridiculous stories have been introduced into the sermon to arouse the drowsy. And at the Christmas services, the absurd pantomime of rocking a babe, and silly declamations in rhyme, have found vogue. Similarly the festivals commemorating the three holy kings, the passion of Christ, Dorothy and other saints were characterized.

12. In this category should also be classed the legends of the saints and the confused mass of lies concerning miracles, pilgrimages, masses, worship of saints, indulgencies, and so on, which once dominated the pulpit. Yet these falsehoods are too gross to be called merely foolish. They are not just frivolous lies merely destructive of good morals, such as Paul refers to here, but they completely overthrow faith and the Word of God, making sainthood impossible. Such kind of jesting is altogether too serious. Those, however, who have seen into them treat them as lies of the same frivolous and abominable character as the fables or old women's tales mentioned by Paul 1 Tim 4, 7. But while the latter are mere human tales which nobody believes, which no one will place reliance on, serving as mere occasion of merriment, without becoming a source of general moral corruption, an obstacle to improvement and a cause of cold, indolent Christianity, the falsehoods of the pulpit are diabolical tales held as truth in all seriousness, but a comedy for the devil and his angels.

13. "Jesting" has reference to those conversational expedients which pander to gaiety in the form of scandal;

they are called among us banter and badinage. Laughter,
mirth and gaiety is their purpose, and we meet with them
generally in society and high life. Among the heathen,
jesting was counted a virtue, and therefore received the
title "eutrapelia" by Aristotle. But Paul calls it a vice among
Christians, who certainly may find conversational expedients of a different kind, such as will inspire a cheerful and
joyous spirit in Christ. True, Christians are not all so pure
but that some may err in this matter; but the Christian
Church does not command jesting, nor suffer any member
to abandon himself to the practice. It reproves and prohibits it, particularly in religious assemblies, and in teaching and preaching. For Christ says (Mt 12, 36) that at the
last day men must give account of every idle, unprofitable
word they have spoken. Christians should be a very firm,
though courteous, people. Courtesy should be coupled with
seriousness, and seriousness with courtesy, according to the
pattern of the life of Christ supplied in the Gospel.

"Which are not befitting."

14. Paul apparently would include in the catalog all unprofitable language of whatever name. I would call those
words unprofitable which serve not to further the faith nor
to supply the wants of the body and preserve it. We have
enough else to talk about during this short lifetime, if we
desire to speak, enough that is profitable and pleasant, if
we talk only of Christ, of love and of other essential things.
The apostle mentions the giving of thanks. It should be our
daily and constant employment to praise and thank God,
privately and publicly, for the great and inexpressible treasures he has given us in Christ. But it appears that what is
needful is relegated to the rear, while objects of indifference
are brought to the fore.

Now, mark you, if Paul will not tolerate banter and suggestive conversation among Christians, what would he say
of the shameful backbiting which is heard whenever people
meet, though but two individuals? Yes, what would be his
judgment of those who in public preaching clinch and claw,
attack and calumniate each other?

FRUITLESS CHRISTIANS ARE HEATHEN.

"For this ye know of a surety, that no fornicator, nor unclean person, nor covetous man, who is an idolater, hath any inheritance in the kingdom of Christ and God."

15. Hereby he declares in dry words that the man who does not exhibit the fruits of faith is a heathen under the name of a Christian. Here is absolute condemnation in a word. The whoremonger is a denier of the faith; the unclean person is a denier of the faith; the covetous individual is a denier of the faith: all are rebellious, perjured and faithless toward God. Paul tells Timothy (1 Tim 5, 8): "But if any provideth not for his own, and specially his own household, he hath denied the faith, and is worse than an unbeliever." How could he utter anything more severe, more terrifying?

He begins, "For this ye know." In other words: Doubt not; do not find vain comfort in the thought that this is a jest or an aspersion. A Christian name, and association with Christians, will count for nothing. It will profit you as little as it profits the Jews to be Abraham's seed and disciples of Moses. Christ's words (Mt 7, 21) concern every man: "Not every one that saith unto me, Lord, Lord, shall enter into the kingdom of heaven." There must be performance; faith must be manifested by works.

16. If the great fire of divine love which he uses as his first argument will not draw us, then may the terrible threat of hell fire prove a sufficient incentive. In other words, if men follow not God, walking in love and showing their faith by their deeds, let them know they are not God's children, not heirs in his kingdom, and therefore are unquestionably heirs of the evil one in hell. He who is unmoved by the threats of hell fire must truly be a stick or a stone; indeed, he must have a heart like an anvil, as Job says.

17. The writer of the epistle passes unusually severe sentence upon the covetous man, for he calls him an idolater, or a worshiper of a false God. Plainly, Paul entertained special enmity against the covetous, for in Colossians 3, 5 he defines this sin in a similar manner. His reasoning, I judge, is this: All other sinners turn to use what they have

and make it subservient to their lusts. Fornicators and the unclean make their bodies serve their pleasure. The haughty employ property, art, reputation and men to secure honor to themselves. The unhappy idolater alone is servant to his possessions; his sin is to save, guard and preserve property. He dare not make use of it either for himself or for others, but worships it as his god. Rather than touch his money, he would suffer both the kingdom of God and of the world to perish. He will not give a farthing to the support of a preacher or a schoolmaster for the sake of advancing God's kingdom. Because he places his confidence, his trust, in his money rather than in the living God, whose promises concerning ample support are abundant, his real God is his money, and to call him an idolater is entirely just. And, in addition, he must renounce heaven! A shameful vice, indeed! O contemptible Unbelief! what a dangerous vice art thou!

DECEPTION BY EMPTY WORDS.

"Let no man deceive you with empty words."

18. This applies to those who gloss their unchastity over, as if it were but a trivial sin. And some have been even such vulgar teachers as to consider no unchastity evil except adultery, and to accept it as a normal function, like eating and drinking. The Greek philosophers and poets were of this class. And Terence says, "It is neither a sin nor a shame for a youth to commit fornication." To obey such doctrine would be to know nothing of God and to live in the lust of concupiscence, like the gentiles who know not God, of whom we heard in the preceding lesson. All arguments of this character are vain words; they may fascinate the reason after a fashion; yet they are vain and futile, unable to profit their authors.

Covetousness likewise has much false show and glitter. When one defrauds another or seeks his own advantage to the injury of others, his act is not at all called sin, but cleverness, economy and sagacity, though meanwhile the poor must suffer want and even die of hunger. Such arguments are merely the specious and blind utterances of heathen, contrary to Christian love.

19.   But we have additional light upon this subject, showing that because of such practices the wrath of God comes upon the unbelieving.   In First Corinthians 10, 18 are cited numerous examples of punishment for the sin of fornication. See also Num 25.   Again, because of wantonness, covetousness and unchastity, the entire world was destroyed by the flood.   This is a severe utterance but true and indubitable.

"For because of these things cometh the wrath of God upon the sons of disobedience."

"Sons of disobedience"—in other words, they who have fallen from the faith.   Thus we see that he who does not show his faith by his deeds, is accounted practically an infidel.   In fact, he is worse than an infidel; he is an apostate Christian, or an apostate from the faith.   Therefore comes the wrath of God upon such, even here on earth.   This is why we Germans must suffer so much famine, pestilence, war and bloodshed to come upon us.

20.   Among these idle chatterers and misleading teachers the sluggards and drones should beware of being classified, who, with better light than the heathen, know full well that covetousness and unchastity are sin.   While they teach nothing to controvert this, they notwithstanding trust for salvation in a faith barren of works, on the ground that works cannot effect salvation.   They know full well that a faith barren of works is nothing, is a false faith; that fruit and good works must follow a genuine faith of necessity. Nevertheless they go on in carnal security, without fear of the wrath and judgment of God, who wants the old Adam to be crucified, and to find good fruit on good trees.

It is possible that St. Paul does not refer in this passage to those who, like the heathen, teach and maintain by specious arguments that unchastity is no sin; nevertheless there is reason to apprehend that the reward of the heathen will be meted out to them likewise; for they live like the heathen, being strangers to both chastity and kindness.   And our apprehension is so much more justified because they have a better knowledge of the wrong they commit. This is Paul's standpoint when he asks (Rom 2, 3): "And reckonest thou this, O man, who judgest them that practice such things, and doest the same, that thou shalt escape the judgment of God?" "After thy hardness and impenitent heart," he adds, thou "treasurest up for thyself wrath."

"Be not ye therefore partakers with them; for ye were once darkness, but are now light in the Lord."

21. Peter similarly counsels (1 Pet 4, 3) to let the time past of our lives suffice us to have wrought the will of the gentiles, and no longer be partakers with them, but live the rest of our time to the will of God. While we were gentiles we knew not that all those things were sin, because of the darkness of unbelief, which prevented our knowing God. But now we have become a light in the Lord. That is, we have been so amply enlightened through Christ that we not only know God and what he desires, and understand what sin and wrong are, but we are also able to light others, to teach them what we know. Paul commends the Philippians for being a light in the world, among an evil and untoward generation. Phil. 2, 15. And, similarly, when we were gentiles we not only were darkened, not only were ignorant and went astray, but we were darkness itself, leading others into the same condition by our words and deeds. We have reason, then, to be thankful unto him who has called us out of darkness into his marvelous light (1 Pet 2, 9), and to "walk as children of light."

"For the fruit of the light [Spirit] is in all goodness and righteousness and truth."

22. Since Paul is speaking of light, it would have been more to the point had he said "fruit of the light," in accordance with the Latin version, than "fruit of the Spirit," the Greek rendering. And who knows but it may, in the Greek, have been altered to harmonize with Galatians 5, 22, where Paul speaks of the "fruit of the Spirit"? It matters little. however; evidently "Spirit" and "light" are synonymous in this place.

"Goodness" is the fruit of light, or of the Spirit, as op-

posed to covetousness. The Christian is to be good; that is,
useful, gladly working his neighbor's good. "Righteousness," as fruit of the Spirit among men—for the Spirit also
is righteous before God—is opposed to covetousness. The
Christian must not take another's possessions by force,
trickery or fraud, but must give to each his due, his own,
even to the heathen authorities. See Rom 13, 1. "Truth"
is the fruit of the Spirit as opposed to hypocrisy and lies. A
Christian is not only to be truthful in word, but honest in
life. He should not bear the name without the works; he
cannot be a Christian and yet live a heathenish life, a life of
unchastity, covetousness and other vices.

Fourth Sunday In Lent

Text: Galatians 4, 21-31.

21. Tell me, ye that desire to be under the law, do ye not hear the law? 22. For it is written, that Abraham had two sons, one by the handmaid, and one by the free-women. 23 Howbeit the son by the handmaid is born after the flesh; but the son by the freewoman is born through promise. 24 Which things contain an allegory: for these women are two covenants; one from mount Sinai, bearing children unto bondage, which is Hagar, 25 Now this Hagar is mount Sinai in Arabia, and answereth to the Jerusalem that now is: for she is in bondage with her children. 26 But the Jerusalem that is above is free, which is our mother. 27 For it is written,

Rejoice, thou barren that bearest not;
Break forth and cry, thou that travailest not:
For more are the children of the desolate than of
her that hath the husband.

28 Now we, brethren, as Isaac was, are children of promise. 29 But as then he that was born after the flesh persecuted him that was born after the Spirit, so also it is now. 30 Howbeit what saith the scripture? Cast out the handmaid and her son; for the son of the handmaid shall not inherit with the son of the freewoman. 31 Wherefore, brethren, we are not children of a handmaid, but of the freewoman.

THE CHILDREN OF PROMISE.

This lesson is amply expounded in my commentary on the Epistle to the Galatians. It is unnecessary to repeat the exposition here, for it may be found and read there. He who desires further information on the subject may read the postils on the epistle lesson for the Sunday after Christmas and that for New Year's Day. There he will find all information. Thus will be obviated the necessity of repeating the discourse in various places.

Fifth Sunday In Lent

Text: Hebrews 9, 11-15.

11 But Christ having come a high priest of the good things to come, through the greater and more perfect tabernacle, not made with hands, that is to say, not of this creation, 12 nor yet through the blood of goats and calves, but through his own blood, entered in once for all into the holy place, having obtained eternal redemption. 13 For if the blood of goats and bulls, and the ashes of a heifer sprinkling them that have been defiled, sanctify unto the cleanness of the flesh: 14 how much more shall the blood of Christ, who through the eternal Spirit offered himself without blemish unto God, cleanse your conscience from dead works to serve the living God? 15 And for this cause he is the mediator of a new covenant, that a death having taken place for the redemption of the transgressions that were under the first covenant, they that have been called may receive the promise of the eternal inheritance.

CHRIST OUR GREAT HIGH PRIEST.

1. An understanding of practically all of the Epistle to the Hebrews is necessary before we can hope to make this text clear to ourselves. Briefly, the epistle treats of a twofold priesthood. The former priesthood was a material one, with material adornment, tabernacle, sacrifices and with pardon couched in ritual; material were all its appointments. The new order is a spiritual priesthood, with spiritual adornments, spiritual tabernacle and sacrifices—spiritual in all that pertains to it. Christ, in the exercise of his priestly office, in the sacrifice on the cross, was not adorned with silk

163

and gold and precious stones, but with divine love, wisdom, patience, obedience and all virtues. His adornment was apparent to none but God and possessors of the Spirit, for it was spiritual.

2. Christ sacrificed not goats nor calves nor birds; not bread; not blood nor flesh, as did Aaron and his posterity: he offered his own body and blood, and the manner of the sacrifice was spiritual; for it took place through the Holy Spirit, as here stated. Though the body and blood of Christ were visible the same as any other material object, the fact that he offered them as a sacrifice was not apparent. It was not a visible sacrifice, as in the case of offerings at the hands of Aaron. Then the goat or calf, the flesh and blood, were material sacrifices visibly offered, and recognized as sacrifices. But Christ offered himself in the heart before God. His sacrifice was perceptible to no mortal. Therefore, his bodily flesh and blood becomes a spiritual sacrifice. Similarly, we Christians, the posterity of Christ our Aaron, offer up our own bodies. Rom 12, 1. And our offering is likewise a spiritual sacrifice, or, as Paul has it, a "reasonable service"; for we make it in spirit, and it is beheld of God alone.

3. Again, in the new order, the tabernacle or house is spiritual; for it is heaven, or the presence of God. Christ hung upon a cross; he was not offered in a temple. He was offered before the eyes of God, and there he still abides. The cross is an altar in a spiritual sense. The material cross was indeed visible, but none knew it as Christ's altar. Again, his prayer, his sprinkled blood, his burnt incense, were all spiritual, for it was all wrought through his spirit.

4. Accordingly, the fruit and blessing of his office and sacrifice, the forgiveness of our sins and our justification, are likewise spiritual. In the Old Covenant, the priest with his sacrifices and sprinklings of blood effected merely as it were an external absolution, or pardon, corresponding to the childhood stage of the people. The recipient was permitted to move publicly among the people; he was externally holy and as one restored from excommunication. He who failed to obtain absolution from the priest was unholy, being de-

nied membership in the congregation and enjoyment of its privileges; in all respects he was separated like those in the ban today.

5. But such absolution rendered no one inwardly holy and just before God. Something beyond that was necessary to secure true forgiveness. It was the same principle which governs church discipline today. He who has received no more than the remission, or absolution, of the ecclesiastical judge will surely remain forever out of heaven. On the other hand, he who is in the ban of the Church is hellward bound only when the sentence is confirmed at a higher tribunal. I can make no better comparison than to say that it was the same in the old Jewish priesthood as now in the Papal priesthood, which, with its loosing and binding, can prohibit or permit only external communion among Christians. It is true, God required such measures in the time of the Jewish dispensation, that he might restrain by fear; just as now he sanctions church discipline when rightly employed, in order to punish and restrain the evil-doer, though it has no power in itself to raise people to holiness or to push them into wickedness.

6. But with the priesthood of Christ is true spiritual remission, sanctification and absolution. These avail before God—God grant that it be true of us—whether we be outwardly excommunicated, or holy, or not. Christ's blood has obtained for us pardon forever acceptable with God. God will forgive our sins for the sake of that blood so long as its power shall last and its intercession for grace in our behalf, which is forever. Therefore, we are forever holy and blessed before God. This is the substance of the text. Now that we shall find it easy to understand, we will briefly consider it.

"But Christ having come a high priest of the good things to come."

7. The adornment of Aaron and his descendants, the high priests, was of a material nature, and they obtained for the people a merely formal remission of sins, performing their office in a perishable temple, or tabernacle. It was

evident to men that their absolution and sanctification before the congregation was a temporal blessing confined to
the present. But when Christ came upon the cross no one
beheld him as he went before God in the Holy Spirit,
adorned with every grace and virtue, a true High Priest.
The blessings wrought by him are not temporal—a merely
formal pardon—but the "blessings to come"; namely, blessings which are spiritual and eternal. Paul speaks of them
as blessings to come, not that we are to await the life to
come before we can have forgiveness and all the blessings of
divine grace, but because now we possess them only in faith.
They are as yet hidden, to be revealed in the future life.
Again, the blessings we have in Christ were, from the standpoint of the Old Testament priesthood, blessings to come.

"Through the greater and more perfect tabernacle,
not made with hands, that is to say, not of this creation.

8. The apostle does not name the tabernacle he mentions; nor can he, so strange its nature! It exists only in
the sight of God, and is ours in faith, to be revealed hereafter. It is not made with hands, like the Jewish tabernacle; in other words, not of "this building." The old tabernacle, like all buildings of its nature, necessarily was made
of wood and other temporal materials created by God. God
says in Isaiah 66, 1-2: "What manner of house will ye
build unto me? . . . For all these things hath my hand
made, and so all these things came to be." But that greater
tabernacle has not yet form; it is not yet finished. God is
building it and he shall reveal it. Christ's words are (Jn
14, 3), "And if I go and prepare a place for you."

"Nor yet through the blood of goats and calves, but
through his own blood, entered in once for all into the
holy place, having obtained eternal redemption."

9. According to Leviticus 16, the high priest must once
a year enter into the holy place with the blood of rams and
other offerings, and with these make formal reconciliation
for the people. This ceremony typified that Christ, the true
Priest, should once die for us, to obtain for us the true atonement. But the former sacrifice, having to be repeated every

year, was but a temporary and imperfect atonement; it did not eternally suffice, as does the atonement of Christ. For though we fall and sin repeatedly, we have confidence that the blood of Christ does not fall, or sin; it remains steadfast before God, and the expiation is perpetual and eternal. Under its sway grace is perpetually renewed, without work or merit on our part, provided we do not stand aloof in unbelief.

"For if the blood of goats and bulls, and the ashes of a heifer," etc.

10. Concerning the water of separation and the ashes of the red heifer, read Numbers 19; and concerning the blood of bulls and goats, Leviticus 16, 14-15. According to Paul, these were formal and temporal purifications, as I stated above. But Christ, in God's sight, purifies the conscience of dead works; that is, of sins meriting death, and of works performed in sin and therefore dead. Christ purifies from these, that we may serve the living God by living works.

"And for this cause he is the mediator of a new covenant [testament]," etc.

11. Under the old law, which provided only for formal, or ritualistic, pardon, and restored to human fellowship, sin and transgressions remained, burdening the conscience. It—the old law—did not benefit the soul at all, inasmuch as God did not institute it to purify and safeguard the conscience, nor to bestow the Spirit. It existed merely for the purpose of outward discipline, restraint and correction. So Paul teaches that under the Old Testament dispensation man's transgressions remained, but now Christ is our Mediator through his blood; by it our conscience is freed from sin in the sight of God, inasmuch as God promises the Spirit through the blood of Christ. All, however, do not receive him. Only those called to be heirs eternal, the elect, receive the Spirit.

12. We find, then, in this excellent lesson, the comforting doctrine taught that Christ is he whom we should know as the Priest and Bishop of our souls; that no sin is forgiven, nor the Holy Spirit given, by reason of works or

merit on our part, but alone through the blood of Christ, and that to those for whom God has ordained it. This matter has been sufficiently set forth in the various postils.

Palm Sunday

Text: Philippians 2, 5-11.

5 Have this mind in you, which was also in Christ Jesus: 6 who, existing in the form of God, counted not the being on an equality with God a thing to be grasped, 7 but emptied himself, taking the form of a servant, being made in the likeness of men; 8 and being found in fashion as a man, he humbled himself, becoming obedient even unto death, yea, the death of the cross. 9 Wherefore also God highly exalted him, and gave unto him the name which is above every name; 10 that in the name of Jesus every knee should bow, of things in heaven and things on earth and things under the earth, 11 and that every tongue should confess that Jesus Christ is Lord, to the glory of God the Father.

CHRIST AN EXAMPLE OF LOVE.

1. Here Paul again presents to us as a powerful example of the celestial and eternal fire, the love of Christ, for the purpose of persuading us to exercise a loving concern for one another. The apostle employs fine words and precious admonitions, having perceived the indolence and negligence displayed by Christians in this matter of loving. For this the flesh is responsible. The flesh continually resists the willing spirit, seeking its own interest and causing sects and factions. Although a sermon on this same text went forth in my name a few years ago, entitled "The Twofold Righteousness," the text was not exhausted; therefore we will now examine it word by word.

169

"Have this mind in you, which was also in Christ Jesus."

2. You are Christians; you have Christ, and in him and through him all fullness of comfort for time and eternity: therefore nothing should appeal to your thought, your judgment, your pleasure, but that which was in the mind of Christ concerning you as the source of your welfare. For his motive throughout was not his own advantage; everything he did was done for your sake and in your interest. Let men therefore, in accord with his example, work every good thing for one another's benefit.

"Who, existing in the form of God, counted not the being on an equality with God a thing to be grasped, but emptied himself, taking the form of a servant."

["Who, being in the form of God, thought it not robbery to be equal with God; but made himself of no reputation, and took upon him the form of a servant."]

3. If Christ, who was true God by nature, has humbled himself to become servant of all, how much more should such action befit us who are of no worth, and are by nature children of sin, death and the devil! Were we similarly to humble ourselves, and even to go beyond Christ in humility —a thing, however, impossible—we should do nothing extraordinary. Our humility would still reek of sin in comparison with his. Suppose Christ to humble himself in the least degree—but a hair's breadth, so to speak—below the most exalted angels; and suppose we were to humble ourselves to a position a thousand times more abased than that of the devils in hell; yet our humility would not compare in the least with that of Christ. For he is an infinite blessing— God himself—and we are but miserable creatures whose existence and life are not for one moment secure.

4. What terrible judgment must come upon those who fail to imitate the ineffable example of Christ; who do not humble themselves below their neighbors and serve them, but rather exalt themselves above them! Indeed, the example of Christ may well terrify the exalted, and those high in authority; and still more the self-exalted. Who would

not shrink from occupying the uppermost seat and from lording it over others when he sees the Son of God humble and eliminate himself?

5.   The phrase "form of God" does not receive the same interpretation from all. Some understand Paul to refer to the divine essence and nature in Christ; meaning that Christ, though true God, humbled himself. While Christ is indeed true God, Paul is not speaking here of his divine essence, which is concealed. The word he uses—"morphe," or "forma"—he employs again where he tells of Christ taking upon himself the form of a servant. "Form of a servant" certainly cannot signify "essence of a real servant"—possessing by nature the qualities of a servant. For Christ is not our servant by nature; he has become our servant from good will and favor toward us. For the same reason "divine form" cannot properly mean "divine essence"; for divine essence is not visible, while the divine form was truly seen. Very well; then let us use the vernacular, and thus make the apostle's meaning clear.

6.   "Form of God," then, means the assumption of a divine attitude and bearing, or the manifestation of divinity in port and presence; and this not privately, but before others, who witness such form and bearing. To speak in the clearest possible manner: Divine bearing and attitude are in evidence when one manifests in word and deed that which pertains peculiarly to God and suggests divinity. Accordingly, "the form of a servant" implies the assumption of the attitude and bearing of a servant in relation to others. It might be better to render "Morphe tu dulu," by "the bearing of a servant," that means, manners of such character that whoever sees the person must take him for a servant. This should make it clear that the passage in question does not refer to the manifestation of divinity or servility as such, but to the characteristics and the expression of the same. For, as previously stated, the essence is concealed, but its manifestation is public. The essence implies a condition, while its expression implies action.

7.   As regards these forms, or manifestations, a threefold

aspect is suggested by the words of Paul. The essence may exist without the manifestation; there may be a manifestation without the corresponding essence; and finally, we may find the essence together with its proper manifestation. For instance, when God conceals himself and gives no indication of his presence, there is divinity, albeit not manifest. This is the case when he is grieved and withdraws his grace. On the other hand, when he discloses his grace, there is both the essence and its manifestation. But the third aspect is inconceivable for God, namely, a manifestation of divinity without the essence. This is rather a trick of the devil and his servants, who usurp the place of God and act as God, though they are anything but divine. An illustration of this we find in Ezekiel 28, 2, where the king of Tyre is recorded as representing his heart, which was certainly decidedly human, as that of a god.

8. Similarly, the form, or bearing, of a servant may be considered from a threefold aspect. One may be a servant and not deport himself as such, but as a lord, or as God; as in the instance just mentioned. Of such a one Solomon speaks (Prov 29, 21), saying: "He that delicately bringeth up his servant from a child shall have him become a son at the last." Such are all the children of Adam. We who are rightly God's servants would be God himself. This is what the devil taught Eve when he said, "Ye shall be as God." Gen 3, 5. Again, one may be a servant and conduct himself as one, as all just and faithful servants behave before the world; and as all true Christians conduct themselves in God's sight, being subject to him and serving all men. Thirdly, one may be not a servant and yet behave as one. For instance, a king might minister to his servants before the world. Before God, however, all men being servants, this situation is impossible with men; no one has so done but Christ. He says at the supper (Jn 13, 13-14): "Ye call me, Teacher, and, Lord: and ye say well; for so I am," and yet I am among you as a servant. And in another place (Mt 20, 28), "The Son of man came not to be ministered unto, but to minister."

9. From these explanations Paul's meaning must have become clear. His thought is: Christ was in the form of God; that is, both the essence and the bearing of Deity were his. He did not assume the divine form as he did that of a servant. He was, I repeat it; he was in the form of God. The little word "was" expresses that divinity was his both in essence and form. The meaning is: Many assume and display an appearance of divinity, but are not themselves actually divine; the devil, for instance, and Antichrist and Adam's children. This is sacrilege—the assumption of divinity by an act of robbery. See Rom 2, 22. Though the offender does not look upon such conduct as robbery, it is none the less robbing divine honor, and is so regarded by God and angels and saints, and even by his own conscience. But Christ, who had not come by divinity through arrogating it to himself, but was divine by nature according to his very essence, did not deem his divinity a thing he had grasped; nor could he, knowing divinity to be his very birthright, and holding it as his own natural possession from eternity.

10. So Paul's words commend Christ's essential divinity and his love toward us, and at the same time correct all who falsely assume a divine form. Such are we all so long as we are the devil's members. The thought is: The devil's members all would be God, would rob the divinity they do not possess; and they must admit their action to be robbery, for conscience testifies, indeed must testify, that they are not God. Though they may despise the testimony of conscience and fail to heed it, yet the testimony stands, steadfastly maintaining the act as not right—as a malicious robbery.

But the one man, Christ, who did not assume the divine form but was in it by right and had a claim upon it from eternity; who did not and could not hold it robbery to be equal with God; this man humbled himself, taking upon him the form of a servant—not his rightful form—that he by the power of his winning example, might induce them to assume the bearing of servants who possessed the form and character of servants, but who, refusing to own them, appropriated the appearance of divinity upon which they had no claim, since the essence of divinity was forever beyond them.

11. That some fail to understand readily this great text, is due to the fact that they do not accept Paul's words as spoken, but substitute their own ideas of what he should have said, namely: Christ was born true God and did not rob divinity, etc. The expression "who, existing in the form of God" sounds, in the Greek and Latin, almost as if Christ had merely borne himself as God, unless particular regard be given to the words "existing in," which Paul contrasts with the phrase "took upon him." Christ took upon himself the form of a servant, it is true, but in that form was no real servant. Just so, while dispensing with a divine appearance, behind the appearance chosen was God. And we likewise take upon ourselves the divine form, but in the form we are not divine; and we spurn the form of servants, though that is what we are irrespective of appearance. Christ disrobes himself of the divine form wherein he existed, to assume that of a servant, which did not express his essential character; but we lay aside the servant form of our real being and take upon ourselves, or arrogate to ourselves, the form of God to which we are not fitted by what we are in reality.

12. They are startled by this expression also: "Christ thought it not robbery to be equal with God." Now, at first sight these words do not seem to refer solely to Christ, since even the devil and his own, who continually aspire to equality with God, do not think their action robbery in spite of the testimony of their conscience to the contrary. But with Paul the little word "think," or "regard," possesses a powerful significance, having the force of "perfect assurance." Similarly he says (Rom 3, 28), "We reckon therefore that a man is justified by faith apart from the works of the law"; and (1 Cor 7, 40), "I think [deem] that I also have the spirit of God." But the wicked cannot boast it no robbery when they dare take upon themselves the form

of God; for they know, they are satisfied in themselves, that they are not God. Christ, however, did not, nor could he, think himself not equal to God; in other words, he was confident of his equality with God, and knew he had not stolen the honor.

Paul's words are chosen, not as an apology for Christ, but as a severe rebuke for those who arrogate to themselves the form of God against the protest of conscience that it is not their own but stolen. The apostle would show how infinitely Christ differs from them, and that the divine form they would take by theft is Christ's by right.

13. Paul does not use this expression, however, when he refers to Christ's assumption of the servant form which is his, not by nature, but by assumption. The words produce the impression that Christ took by force something not his own. Paul should be expected to say: "He held it not robbery to assume the form of a servant." Why should he rather have chosen that form of expression in the first instance, since Christ did not assume the divine form, but possessed it as his very own—yes, laid it aside and assumed a form foreign to his nature? The substance of the matter is that he who becomes a servant does not and cannot assume anything, but only gives, giving even himself. Hence there is no warrant here to speak of robbery or of a disposition to look upon the matter in this light.

On the other hand, assumption of the divine form necessarily involves taking, and altogether precludes giving. Hence there is warrant to speak of robbery in this connection, and of men who so view it. But this charge cannot be brought against Christ. He does not render himself guilty of robbery, nor does he so view his relation, as all others must do. Divinity is his by right, and so is its appropriate form a birthright.

14. Thus, it seems to me, this text very clearly teaches that to have divine form is simply to assume in regard to others, in word and deed, the bearing of God and Lord; and that Christ meets this test in the miraculous signs and life-giving words, as the Gospels contend. He does not rank

with the saints who lack the divine essence; he has, in addition to divine form, the divine essence and nature. On the other hand, the servant, or servile, form implies acting toward others, in word and deed, like a servant. Thus Christ did when he served the disciples and gave himself for us. But he served not as the saints, who are servants by nature. Service was, with him, something assumed for our benefit and as an example for us to follow, teaching us to act in like manner toward others, to disrobe ourselves of the appearance of divinity as he did, as we shall see.

15. Unquestionably, then, Paul proclaims Christ true God. Had he been mere man, what would have been the occasion for saying that he became like a man and was found in the fashion of other men? and that he assumed the form of a servant though he was in form divine? Where would be the sense in my saying to you, "You are like a man, are made in the fashion of a man, and take upon yourself the form of a servant"? You would think I was mocking you, and might appropriately reply: "I am glad you regard me as a man; I was wondering if I were an ox or a wolf. Are you mad or foolish?" Would not that be the natural rejoinder to such a foolish statement? Now, Paul not being foolish, nor being guilty of foolish speech, there truly must have been something exalted and divine about Christ. For when the apostle declares that he was made like unto other men, though the fact of his being human is undisputed, he simply means that the man Christ was God, and could, even in his humanity, have borne himself as divine. But this is precisely what he did not do; he refrained: he disrobed himself of his divinity and bore himself as a mere man like others.

16. What follows concerning Christ, now that we understand the meaning or "form of God" and "form of a servant," is surely plain. In fact, Paul himself tells us what he means by "form of a servant." First: He makes the explanation that Christ disrobed, or divested himself; that is, appeared to lay aside his divinity in that he divested himself of its benefit and glory. Not that he did, or could, divest himself

of his divine nature; but that he laid aside the form of divine majesty—did not act as the God he truly was. Nor did he divest himself of the divine form to the extent of making it unfelt and invisible; in that case there would have been no divine form left. He simply did not affect a divine appearance and dazzle us by its splendor; rather he served us with that divinity. He performed miracles. And during his suffering on the cross he, with divine power, gave to the murderer the promise of Paradise. Lk. 23, 43. And in the garden, similarly, he repelled the multitude by a word. Jn 18, 6.

Hence Paul does not say that Christ was divested by some outside power; he says Christ "made himself" of no repute. Just so the wise man does not in a literal way lay aside wisdom and the appearance of wisdom, but discards them for the purpose of serving the simple-minded who might fittingly serve him. Such man makes himself of no reputation when he divests himself of his wisdom and the appearance of wisdom.

17. Second: Christ assumed the form of a servant, even while remaining God and having the form of God; he was God, and his divine words and works were spoken and wrought for our benefit. As a servant, he served us with these. He did not require us to serve him in compensation for them, as in the capacity of a Lord he had a just right to do. He sought not honor or profit thereby, but our benefit and salvation. It was a willing service and gratuitously performed, for the good of men. It was a service unspeakably great, because of the ineffable greatness of the minister and servant—God eternal, whom all angels and creatures serve. He who is not by this example heartily constrained to serve his fellows, is justly condemned. He is harder than stone, darker than hell and utterly without excuse.

18. Third: "Being made in the likeness of men." Born of Mary, Christ's nature became human. But even in that humanity he might have exalted himself above all men and served none. But he forbore and became as other men.

And by "likeness of men" we must understand just ordinary humanity without special privilege whatever. Now, without special privilege there is no disparity among men. Understand, then, Paul says in effect: Christ was made as any other man who has neither riches, honor, power nor advantage above his fellows; for many inherit power, honor and property by birth. So lowly did Christ become, and with such humility did he conduct himself, that no mortal is too lowly to be his equal, even servants and the poor. At the same time, Christ was sound, without bodily infirmities, as man in his natural condition might be expected to be.

19. Fourth. "And being found in fashion as a man." That is, he followed the customs and habits of men, eating and drinking, sleeping and waking, walking and standing, hungering and thirsting, enduring cold and heat, knowing labor and weariness, needing clothing and shelter, feeling the necessity of prayer, and having the same experience as any other man in his relation to God and the world. He had power to avoid these conditions; as God he might have demeaned and borne himself quite differently. But in becoming man, as above stated, he fared as a human being, and be accepted the necessities of ordinary mortals while all the time he manifested the divine form which expressed his true self.

20. Fifth: "He humbled himself," or debased himself. In addition to manifesting his servant form in becoming man and faring as an ordinary human being, he went farther and made himself lower than any man. He abased himself to serve all men with the supreme service—the gift of his life in our behalf.

21. Sixth: He not only made himself subject to men, but also to sin, death and the devil, and bore it all for us. He accepted the most ignominious death, the death on the cross, dying not as a man but as a worm (Ps 22, 6); yes, as an arch-knave, a knave above all knaves, in that he lost even what favor, recognition and honor were due to the assumed servant form in which he had revealed himself, and perished altogether.

22. Seventh: All this Christ surely did not do because we were worthy of it. Who could be worthy such service from such a one? Obedience to the Father moved him. Here Paul with one word unlocks heaven and permits us to look into the unfathomable abyss of divine majesty and to behold the ineffable love of the Fatherly heart toward us —his gracious will for us. He shows us how from eternity it has been God's pleasure that Christ, the glorious one who has wrought all this, should do it for us. What human heart would not melt at the joy-inspiring thought? Who would not love, praise and thank God and in return for his goodness, not only be ready to serve the world, but gladly to embrace the extremity of humility? Who would not so do when he is aware that God himself has such precious regard for him, and points to the obedience of his Son as the pouring out and evidence of his Fatherly will. Oh, the significance of the words Paul here uses! such words as he uses in no other place! He must certainly have burned with joy and cheer. To gain such a glimpse of God—surely this must be coming to the Father through Christ. Here is truly illustrated the truth that no one comes to Christ except the Father draw him; and with what power, what delicious sweetness, the Father allures! How many are the preachers of the faith who imagine they know it all, when they have received not even an odor or taste of these things! How soon are they become masters who have never been disciples! Not having tasted God's love, they cannot impart it; hence they remain unprofitable babblers.

"Wherefore also God highly exalted him."

23. As Christ was cast to the lowest depths and subjected to all devils, in obeying God and serving us, so has God exalted him Lord over all angels and creatures, and over death and hell. Christ now has completely divested himself of the servant form—laid it aside. Henceforth he exists in the divine form, glorified, proclaimed, confessed, honored and recognized as God.

While it is not wholly apparent to us that "all things are put in subjection" to Christ, as Paul says (1 Cor 15, 27), the trouble is merely with our perception of the fact. It is true that Christ is thus exalted in person and seated on high in the fullness of power and might, executing everywhere his will; though few believe the order of events is for the sake of Christ. Freely the events order themselves, and the Lord sits enthroned free from all restrictions. But our eyes are as yet blinded. We do not perceive him there nor recognize that all things obey his will. The last day, however, will reveal it. Then we shall comprehend present mysteries; how Christ laid aside his divine form, was made man, and so on; how he also laid aside the form of a servant and resumed the divine likeness; how as God he appeared in glory; and how he is now Lord of life and death, and the King of Glory.

This must suffice on the text. For how we, too, should come down from our eminence and serve others has been sufficiently treated of in other postils. Remember, God desires us to serve one another with body, property, honor, spirit and soul, even as his Son served us.

SUMMER PART

Easter Sunday

Text: First Corinthians 5, 6-8.

6 Your glorying is not good. Know ye not that a little leaven leaveneth the whole lump? 7 Purge out the old leaven, that ye may be a new lump, even as ye are unleavened. For our passover also hath been sacrificed, even Christ: 8 wherefore let us keep the feast, not with old leaven, neither with the leaven of malice and wickedness, but with the unleavened bread of sincerity and truth.

EXHORTATION TO WALK AS CHRISTIANS.*

1. When God was about to lead the Israelites out of Egypt, he commanded, shortly before their departure, that they should eat the Passover the night they started; and as a perpetual memorial of their redemption, they were annually, on the recurrence of the season, to celebrate the feast of Easter for seven days. A specially urgent feature of the command was that on the first evening of the feast they must put out of their houses all leaven and leavened bread, and during the seven days eat none but the unleavened bread, or cakes. Hence the evangelists speak of the feast as the Feast (or Days) of Unleavened Bread. Mk. 14, 1; Lk. 22, 1.

2. Paul, in this lesson, explains the figure in brief but beautiful and expressive words. He is prompted to introduce the subject by the fact that in the preceding verses of this chapter he has been reproving the Corinthians for their

*This and all the following sermons on the Epistle Texts were first printed in 1540 and 1543 and included in the Epistle Postil.

181

disposition to boast of the Gospel and of Christ while abusing such liberty unto unchastity and other sins. He admon-

Foot Note. This and all the following sermons in the Epistle texts were first printed in 1540 and 1543 and included in the Epistle Postil.

ishes them that, possessing the Gospel and having become Christians, they ought, as becomes Christians, to live according to the Gospel, avoiding everything not consistent with the faith and with Christian character—everything not befitting them as new creatures.

3. So the apostle uses the figure of the Paschal lamb and unleavened bread requisite at the Jews' Feast of the Passover, in his effort to point the Corinthians to the true character and purpose of the New Testament made with us in the kingdom of Christ. He explains what is the true Paschal Lamb and what the unleavened bread, and how to observe the real Passover, wherein all must be new and spiritual. In the joy and wealth of his mind he presents this analogy to remind them that they are Christians and to consider what that means.

His meaning is: Being Christians and God's true people, and called upon to observe a Passover, you must go about it in the right way, putting away from you all remaining leaven until it shall have been purged out utterly.

What Paul means by "leaven" is told later in his phrase "neither with the leaven of malice and wickedness"; he means whatever is evil and wicked. Everything foreign to Christianity in both doctrine, or faith, and life, is "leaven." From all this Paul would have Christians purge themselves with the same throughness with which the leaven was to be put away from their Easter according to the law. And, holding to the figure, he would have us observe our Passover in the use of the sweet bread, which, in distinction from the leaven, signifies sincerity and truth, or a nature and life completely new.

4. The text, then, is but an admonition to upright Christian works, directed to those who have heard the Gospel and learned to know Christ. This is what Paul figuratively

calls partaking of the true unleavened bread—or wafers, or cakes. We Germans have borrowed our word "cakes" from the phraseology of the Jewish Church, abbreviating "oblaten," wafers, into "fladen," or cakes. How else should we gentiles get the idea of cakes on Easter, when at our Passover we, by faith, eat the Paschal Lamb, Christ? We are admonished to partake of the true unleavened bread, that life and conduct may accord with faith in Christ, whom we have learned to know. Paul's admonition begins:

> "Know ye not that a little leaven leaveneth the whole lump?"

5. This by way of introducing the succeeding admonitions. Leaven is a common figure with the apostle, one he uses frequently, almost proverbially; employing it, too, in his epistle to the Galatians (ch 5, 9). Christ, also, gives us a Scripture parable of the leaven. Mt 13, 33. It is the nature of leaven that a small quantity mixed with a lump of dough will pervade and fill the whole lump until its own acid nature has been inparted to it. This Paul makes a figure of spiritual things as regards both doctrine and life.

6. In Galatians 5, 9 he makes it more especially typify false doctrine. For it is just as true that the introduction of an error in an article of faith will soon work injury to the whole and result in the loss of Christ. Thus it was with the Galatians. The one thing insisted upon by the false apostles was circumcision, though they fully intended to preach the Gospel of Christ. Such innovation will pursue its course with destructive sweep until even the uncontaminated part becomes worthless; the once pure mass is wholly corrupted. The apostle writes to the Galatians (ch 5, 2): "Behold, I Paul say unto you, that, if ye receive circumcision, Christ wil profit you nothing." Again (verse 4), "Ye are severed from Christ—ye are fallen away from grace."

But in this text he has reference more particularly to an erroneous idea concerning life and conduct. In this instance it is likewise true that, once the flesh be allowed any license, and liberty be abused, and that under the name of the Gospel, there is introduced a leaven which will speedily corrupt faith and conscience, and continue its work until Christ and the Gospel are lost. Such would have been the fate of the Corinthians had not Paul saved them from it by this epistle admonishing and urging them to purge out the leaven of license; for they had begun to practice great wantonness, and had given rise to sects and factions which tended to subvert the one Gospel and the one faith.

7. This is, then, wise counsel and serious admonition, that faithful guard be maintained against the infusion or introduction into doctrine of what is false, whether it pertains to works or faith. The Word of God, faith and conscience are very delicate things. The old proverb says: "Non patitur jocum fama, fides, oculus;"—Good reputation, faith and the eye—these three will bear no jest.

Just as good wine or precious medicines are corrupted by a single drop of poison or other impurity, and the purer they are, the more readily defiled and poisoned; so, also, God's Word and his cause will bear absolutely no alloy. God's truth must be perfectly pure and clear, or else, it is corrupt and unprofitable. And the worst feature of the matter is, the sway and intrenchment of evil is so strong that it cannot be removed; just as leaven, however small the quantity, added to the lump of dough, soon penetrates and sours the whole lump, while it is impossible to arrest its influence or once more to sweeten the dough.

8. The proposal of certain wise minds to mediate, and effect a compromise, between us and our opponents of the Papacy, is wrong and useless. They would permit preaching of the Gospel but at the same time retain the Papistical abuses, advocating that these errors be not all censured and rejected, because of the weak; and that for the sake of peace and unity we should somehow moderate and restrict our demands, each party being ready to yield to the other and patiently bear with it. While in such case no perfect purity can be claimed to exist, the situation can be made endurable if discretion is used and trouble is taken to explain.

Nay, not so! For, as you hear, Paul would not mix even a small quantity of leaven with the pure lump, and God himself has urgently forbidden it. The slight alloy would thoroughly penetrate and corrupt the whole. Where human additions are made to the Gospel doctrine in but a single point, the injury is done; truth is obscured and souls are led astray. Therefore, such mixture, such patchwork, in doctrine is not to be tolerated. As Christ teaches (Mt 9, 16), we must not put new cloth upon an old garment.

9. Nor may we in our works and in our daily life tolerate the yielding to the wantonness of the flesh and at the same time boast the Gospel of Christ, as did the Corinthians, who stirred up among themselves divisions and disorder, even to the extent of one marrying his stepmother. In such matters as these, Paul says, a little leaven leavens and ruins the whole lump—the entire Christian life.

These two things are not consistent with each other: to hold to the Christian faith and to live after the wantonness of the flesh, in sins and vices condemned by the conscience. Paul elsewhere warns (1 Cor 6, 9-10): "Be not deceived: neither fornicators, nor idolaters, nor adulterers, nor effeminate, nor abusers of themselves with men, nor thieves, nor covetous, nor drunkards, nor revilers, nor extortioners, shall inherit the kingdom of God." Again (Gal 5, 19-21): "The works of the flesh are manifest . . . of which I forewarn you, even as I did forewarn you, that they who practice such things shall not inherit the kingdom of God."

10. Warrant is given here likewise for censuring and restraining the rash individuals who assert that men should not be terrified by the Law, nor surrendered to Satan. No! it is our duty to teach men to purge out the old leaven; we must tell them they are not Christians, but devoid of the faith, when they yield to the wantonness of the flesh and wilfully persevere in sin against the warning of conscience. We should teach that such sins are so much the more vicious and damnable when practiced under the name of the Gospel, under cover of Christian liberty; for that is despising and blaspheming the name of Christ and the Gospel: and therefore such conduct must be positively renounced and purged out, as irreconcilable with faith and a good conscience.

"Purge out the old leaven, that ye may be a new lump, even as ye are unleavened."

11. If we are to be a new, sweet lump, Paul says, we must purge out the old leaven. For, as stated, a nature renewed by faith and Christianity will not admit of our living as we did when devoid of faith and in sin, under the influence of an evil conscience. We cannot consistently be "a new lump" and partake of the Passover, and at the same time permit the old leaven to remain: for if the latter be not purged out, the whole lump will be leavened and corrupted; our previous sinful nature will again have supremacy and overthrow the faith, the holiness upon which we have entered and a good conscience.

12. Paul does not here speak of leaven in general; he commands to purge out the "old leaven," implying there may be good leaven. Doubtless he is influenced by respect for the words of the Lord Christ where (Mt 13, 33) he likens the kingdom of heaven also to leaven. In this latter case leaven cannot be bad in quality; rather, the object in mixing it with the lump is to produce good, new bread. Reference is to the Word of God, or the preaching of the Gospel, whereby we are incorporated into the kingdom of Christ, or the Christian Church. Though the Gospel appears to be mean, is despicable and objectionable to the world, yet such is its power that wherever introduced it spreads, finding disciples in whom it works; it transforms them, giving to them its own properties, even as leaven imparts its powers to the dough and causes it to rise.

..But Paul refers here to old, inactive and worthless leaven. He means teachings, views, or manner of life resulting from the Old Adam, from flesh and blood, and destructive of the pure, new doctrine, or a nature renewed by Christianity. Later on he terms it the "leaven of malice and wickedness," and in the verse under consideration bids the Corinthians be a new, pure lump.

13. Note the apostle's peculiar words. He enjoins purging out the old leaven, assigning as reason the fact: Ye are a new and unleavened lump. By a new unleavened lump he

means that faith which clings to Christ and believes in the forgiveness of sin through him; for he immediately speaks of our Passover: Christ, sacrificed for us. By this faith the Corinthians are now purified from the old leaven, the leaven of sin and an evil conscience, and have entered upon the new life; yet they are commanded to purge out the old leaven.

14. Now, how shall we explain the fact that he bids them purge out the old leaven that they may be a new lump, when at the same time he admits them to be unleavened and a new lump? How can these Corinthians be as true, unleavened wafers, or sweet dough, when they have yet to purge out the old leaven?

This is an instance of the Pauline and apostolic way of speaking concerning Christians and the kingdom of Christ; it shows us what the condition really is. It is a discipline wherein a new, Christian life is entered upon through faith in Christ the true Passover; hence, Easter is celebrated with sweet, unleavened bread. But at the same time something of the old life remains, which must be swept out, or purged away. However, this latter is not imputed, because faith and Christ are there, constantly toiling and striving to thoroughly purge out whatever uncleanness remains.

15. Through faith we have Christ and his purity perfectly conferred upon ourselves, and we are thus regarded pure; yet in our own personal nature we are not immediately made wholly pure, without sin or weakness. Much of the old leaven still remains, but it will be forgiven, not be imputed to us, if only we continue in faith and are occupied with purging out that remaining impurity.

This is Christ's thought when he says to his disciples (Jn 15, 3), "Already ye are clean because of the word which I have spoken unto you," and in the same connection he declares that the branches in him must be purged that they may bring forth more fruit. And to Peter—and to others— he says (Jn 13, 10), "He that is bathed needeth not save to wash his feet, but is clean every whit: and ye are clean, but not all." These passages, as is also stated elsewhere,

teach that a Christian by faith lays hold upon the purity
of Christ, for which reason he is also regarded pure and begins to make progress in purity; for faith brings the Holy
Spirit, who works in man, enabling him to withstand and
to subdue sin.

16. They are to be censured according to whose repre-
sentations and views a Christian Church is to be advocated
which should be in all respects without infirmity and defect,
and who teach that, when perfection is not in evidence, there
is no such thing as the Church of Christ nor as true Christians. Many erring spirits, especially strong pretenders to
wisdom, and precocious, self-made saints, immediately become impatient at sight of any weakness in Christians who
profess the Gospel faith; for their own dreams are of a
Church without any imperfections, a thing impossible in
this earthly life, even they themselves not being perfect.

17. Such, we must know, is the nature of Christ's office
and dominion in his Church that though he really does instantaneously, through faith, confer upon us his purity, and
by the Spirit transforms our hearts, yet the work of transformation and purification is not at once completed. Daily
Christ works in us and purges us, to the end that we grow
in purity daily. This work he carries on in us through the
agency of the Word, admonishing, reproving, correcting and
strengthening; as in the case of the Corinthians through the
instrumentality of Paul. Christ also uses crosses and afflictions in effecting this end.

He did not come to toil, to suffer and to die because he
expected to find pure and holy people. Purity and holiness
for us he has acquired in his own person to perfection, inasmuch as he was without sin and perfectly pure from the moment he became man, and this purity and holiness he com-
municates to us in their flawless perfection in so far our
faith clings to him. But to attain personal purity of such
perfection requires a daily effort on the part of Christ, until
the time shall have come that he has wrought in us a flawless perfection like his own.

So he has given us his Word and his Spirit to aid us in

purging out the remaining old leaven, and in holding to our newly-begun purity instead of lapsing from it. We must retain the faith, the Spirit and Christ; and this, as before said, we cannot do if we give place to the old carnal disposition instead of resisting it.

18. Note, one thing the text teaches: Even the saints have weakness, uncleanness and sin yet to be purged out, but it is not imputed unto them because they are in Christ and occupied in purging out the old leaven.

19. Another thing, it teaches what constitutes the difference between the saints and the unholy, for both are sinful; it tells the nature of sins despite the presence of which saints and believers are holy, retaining grace and the Holy Spirit, and also what sins are inconsistent with faith and grace.

20. The sins remaining in saints after conversion are various evil inclinations, lusts and desires natural to man and contrary to the Law of God. The saints, as well as others, are conscious of these sins, but with this difference: they do not permit themselves to be overcome thereby so as to obey the sins, allowing them free course; they do not yield to, but resist, such sins, and, as Paul expresses it here, incessantly purge themselves therefrom. The sins of the saints, according to him, are the very ones which they purge out. Those who obey their lusts, however, do not do this, but give rein to the flesh, and sin against the protest of their own consciences.

They who resist their sinful lusts retain faith and a good conscience, a thing impossible with those who fail to resist sin and thus violate their conscience and overthrow their faith. If you persist in that which is evil regardless of the voice of conscience, you cannot say, nor believe, that you have God's favor. So then, the Christian necessarily must not yield to sinful lusts.

21. The Holy Spirit is given for the very purpose of opposing sin and preventing its reign. Paul says (Gal 5, 17): "For the flesh lusteth against the Spirit, and the Spirit against the flesh . . . that ye may not do the

things that ye would." And again (Rom 8, 13): "If by the Spirit ye put to death the deeds of the body, ye shall live." Also (Rom 6, 12): "Let not sin therefore reign in your mortal body, that ye should obey the lusts thereof."

"For our passover also hath been sacrificed, even Christ."

["For even Christ our Passover is sacrificed for us."]

22. Here Paul assigns his reason for the statement just made—"Ye are unleavened." They are a new, unleavened or sweet lump, not because of any merit on their part, not because of their own holiness or worthiness, but because they have faith in Christ as the Passover sacrificed for them. This sacrifice makes them pure and holy before God. They are no more the old leaven they were when out of Christ. By this sacrifice they are reconciled with God and purified from sin.

23. Likewise for us God institutes a new ordinance, a new festival. The old has given place to something wholly new. A different and better Passover sacrifice succeeds that of the Jews. The Jews had annually to partake of their offered sacrifice, but they were not thereby made holy nor pure from sin. Theirs was a sign or earnest of the true Passover to come, the Passover promised by God, in the shed blood of which we are washed from sin and wholly healed—a Passover the partaking whereof we must enjoy by faith. We have now one perpetual and eternal Easter festival, wherein faith is nourished, satisfied and gladdened; in other words, we receive remission of sins and comfort and strength through this our Passover, Christ.

24. The meaning of the phrase "sacrificed for us" has been explained in the sermon on the Passion of Christ. Two thoughts are there presented: First, necessity of considering the greatness and terror of the wrath of God against sin in that it could be appeased and a ransom effected in no other way than through the one sacrifice of the Son of God. Only his death and the shedding of his blood could make satisfaction. And we must consider also that we by our sinfulness had incurred that wrath of God and therefore

were responsible for the offering of the Son of God upon the cross and the shedding of his blood.

Well may we be terrified because of our sins, for God's wrath cannot be trivial when we are told no sacrifice save alone the Son of God can brave such wrath and avail for sin. Do you imagine yourself able to endure that wrath of God, or to withstand it if you will not consider this and accept it?

25. The second thought presented in the sermon mentioned is, the necessity of recognizing the inexpressible love and grace of God toward us. Only so can the terrified heart of man regain comfort. It must be made aware why God spared not his own Son but offered him a sacrifice upon the cross, delivered him to death; namely, that his wrath might be lifted from us once more. What greater love and blessing could be shown? The sacrifice of Christ is presented to us to give us sure comfort against the terrors of sin. For we may perceive and be confident that we shall not be lost because of our sins when God makes such a sacrifice the precious pledge to us of his favor and promised salvation.

Therefore, though your sins are great and deserve the awful wrath of God, yet the sacrifice represented by the death of the Son of God is infinitely greater. And in this sacrifice God grants you a sure token of his grace and the forgiveness of your sins. But that forgiveness must be apprehended by the faith which holds fast the declaration, "Christ our Passover is sacrificed for us." By this promise must faith be comforted and strengthened.

"Wherefore let us keep the feast, not with old leaven, neither with the leaven of malice and wickedness, but with the unleavened bread of sincerity and truth."

26. Having, then, a Paschal Lamb and a true Easter, let us rightly value them. Let us observe the festival with the gladness it ought to inspire. Let us no longer eat the old leaven, but true wafers and paschal cakes. Where the Paschal Lamb is, there must be the unleavened bread. The former is Christ sacrificed for us. To this sacrifice we can

add nothing; we can only receive and enjoy it by faith, recognizing it as a gift to us.

However, possessing the Paschal Lamb, it is incumbent upon us to partake also of the sweet festal bread; in other words, while embracing the faith of the Passover, we are to maintain the true doctrine of the Gospel, illustrating it by the godly example of our own lives. We should live an eternal Easter life, as it were, to carry out Paul's analogy, a life wherein we, as justified, sanctified and purified people, continue in peace and the joy of the Holy Spirit, so long as we remain on earth.

27. In this verse, as in the preceding one, Paul contrasts the leaven and the unleavened bread. He makes leaven a general term for everything which proceeds from flesh and blood and an unrenewed sinful nature, but classifies it under two heads—the leaven of malice and the leaven of wickedness. By "malice" we understand the various open vices and sins which represent manifest wrong to God and our neighbor. "Wickedness" stands for those numerous evil tricks, those nimble, subtle, venomous artifices practiced upon Christian doctrine and the Word of God with intent to corrupt and pervert them, to mislead hearts from the true meaning thereof. Paul warns (2 Cor 11, 3): "But I fear, lest by any means, as the serpent beguiled Eve in his craftiness, your minds should be corrupted from the simplicity and the purity that is toward Christ." Under "wickedness" comes also such evils as hypocrisy and other false, deceptive dealing practiced in the name of God by way of adorning and covering the sin; false teaching and deceptive action passed off as right, proper and Christian. Such wickedness Christ terms "the leaven of the Pharisees and the leaven of Herod." Mk 8, 15. This sort of leaven, particularly, we have in the world to an unspeakable extent in this last and worst of times.

28. To the leaven of malice and of wickedness, Paul opposes the leaven of sincerity and truth. To be sincere is to live and act in an upright Christian way, prompted by a faithful, godly heart, a heart kindly disposed to all and medi-

tating wrong and injury to none; and to deal as you would be dealt with. To be true is to refrain from false and crafty dealing, from deceit and roguery, and to teach and live in probity and righteousness according to the pure Word of God. Truth and sincerity must prevail and be in evidence with Christians, who have entered upon a relation and life altogether new; they should celebrate the new Easter festival by bringing faith and doctrine and life into accord with it.

Easter Monday

Text: Acts 10, 34-43.

34 And Peter opened his mouth, and said: Of a truth I perceive that God is no respecter of persons: 35 but in every nation he that feareth him, and worketh righteousness, is acceptable to him. 36 The word which he sent unto the children of Israel, preaching good tidings of peace by Jesus Christ (he is Lord of all)—37 that saying ye yourselves know, which was published throughout all Judæa, beginning from Galilee, after the baptism which John preached; 38 even Jesus of Nazareth, how God anointed him with the Holy Spirit and with power: who went about doing good, and healing all that were oppressed of the devil; for God was with him. 39 And we are witnesses of all things which he did both in the country of the Jews, and in Jerusalem; whom also they slew, hanging him on a tree. 40 Him God raised up the third day, and gave him to be made manifest, 41 not to all the people, but unto witnesses that were chosen before of God, even to us, who ate and drank with him after he rose from the dead. 42 And he charged us to preach unto the people, and to testify that this is he who is ordained of God to be the Judge of the living and the dead. 43 To him bear all the prophets witness, that through his name every one that believeth on him shall receive remission of sins.

THE BLESSINGS OF CHRIST'S RESURRECTION.

1. This sermon Peter preached to Cornelius, the Cesarean centurion, a gentile but a believer, and to the centurion's assembled friends, Peter having been summoned by Cornelius and having responded to the call in obedience to a reve-

lation and to the Holy Spirit's command, as related in the preceding verses of the chapter. It is an excellent sermon and bears strong testimony to Christ's resurrection. As should ever be the case with the sermons of apostles and preachers of the Gospel, it is not only a historical record of Christ's life, death and resurrection, but portrays the power and blessing thereof. The entire sermon being easily understood without explanation—for it is itself an exposition of the article on Christ's resurrection—we will go over it but briefly.

2. First, Peter begins with the inception of the preaching of the Gospel of Christ, suggesting how it was promised in the Scriptures, being declared by the prophets, that Christ should come with a new doctrine, confirming it by miracles; also that he must suffer and die and rise from the dead, establishing thus a new kingdom; and how the promise was fulfilled. For confirmation of his words Peter appeals to his hearers, reminding them of their own knowledge that such was the promise of the Scriptures, and that the message has gone forth, not being uttered secretly, in a corner, but being proclaimed throughout all Judea; and how John the Baptist had shortly before testified he was sent as Christ's herald to prepare his way by directing and leading the people to Christ, etc.

THE GOSPEL A DOCTRINE OF PEACE.

3. Then Peter explains this new Gospel message as the doctrine of peace, the peace proclamation commanded of God; in other words, salvation and every good thing. The apostle portrays it as a comforting message, a Gospel of joy and grace, a message not accusing, threatening and terrifying with a vision of God's wrath for our sin, as did Moses with his doctrine of the Law. Peter offers to the hitherto terrified, God's favor, remission of sins and eternal life.

Similarly, of old did the prophets prophesy of this Gospel, calling it the message of peace. Peter's language is borrowed from them. For instance, Zechariah prophesies (ch 9, 10), "He shall speak peace unto the nations." And Isaiah

(ch 52, 7), "How beautiful upon the mountains are the
feet of him that bringeth good tidings, that publisheth
peace!" Paul offers the same thought (Eph 2, 17), "And
he came and preached peace to you that were far off, and
peace to them that were nigh." A delightful message is
this in which God recalls his wrath and, as Paul says (2
Cor 5, 18-20), reconciles us unto himself, having commanded
the Gospel to be preached to the world for that very purpose, and the office of preaching to be called the ministry
of reconciliation; and God admonishes us to be reconciled
unto himself, to be his friends, that we may from him receive grace and every good thing.

,4. Second: Peter declares what the Gospel message records concerning Christ: what he has wrought and the nature of his office—how he preached and worked miracles
in the service, and for the relief, of all men; what thanks
and reward his own people accorded him, in that they nailed
him to the cross and put him to death; that nevertheless
Christ was not destroyed by the power of the world nor
overcome by death, but even retained his freedom, showing
himself after death and letting his voice be heard; and that
he is now exalted Lord and Judge over all.

THE ARTICLE OF FAITH ON THE RESURRECTION.

5. Here are comprised in a few words the entire history
of the Gospel, and the articles of the Christian faith; but
particularly does Peter deal with the article of the resurrection, the fact that Christ has, in his own person, completely overcome death and reigns eternal King and Lord
of life. In proof of the truth of this article, the apostle ad-
duces the fact of Christ's manifesting himself alive to his
disciples, eating and drinking with them and appointing
them special witnesses to these things as men to whom the
doctrine had been proven, had been established by actual
sight of the miracles.

6. Third: Peter states the item of chief importance in
the article, the blessing resulting to us. He explains
first why Christ suffered all these things, and how the
Gospel was to be published and received; Christ's motive

in it all was not his advantage but our good. Before we could know the truth and be blessed, it was necessary that the message be preached. God commanded the apostles, Peter says, to preach the Gospel in all the world that all men might know it; and thus the blessing is brought to men through the public office of the ministry.

7. Fourth: Our obligation concerning the message brought to us, and what it works in ourselves, is indicated in these concluding words of Peter's sermon:

> "To him bear all the prophets witness, that through his name every one that believeth on him shall receive remission of sins."

8. This verse constitutes the principal theme of the sermon. It is one of the greatest in the writings of the apostles. It contains the vital element of the Gospel message, teaching how we may appropriate its blessing, how obtain what it offers, namely, by faith; faith lays hold of what is offered us in the Gospel. The message is preached that we may receive and retain it. Through the Word the blessing is pronounced our own—it is offered to, or given, us; but by faith we receive it, make it our own, permit it to work in us.

9. This power and work in us is called by Peter "remission of sins." This is the blessing, the possession, conferred through the preaching of the doctrine of Christ, or the articles of faith, particularly the articles of the resurrection. The meaning of the new message of comfort, the new declaration of peace, is that Christ, through his resurrection, has in himself conquered our sin and death, has turned away the wrath of God and procured grace and salvation; that he has commanded forgiveness to be preached unto us, desiring us to believe he gives it and confidently to receive it through faith.

10. Faith must be of such character as to apprehend and hold fast the truth Peter declares in this verse. It must say "in his name." That is, must ascribe to Christ alone the entire agency, merit and power responsible for remission of sins; must believe we have forgiveness, not through our

own worthiness, but for Christ's sake alone; must believe
that by virtue of Christ's resurrection we obtain remission
of sins, every namable element not from Christ being completely excluded, and the honor given to him alone.

What does the work, the ability, of all mankind amount
to when it comes to accomplishing or meriting a thing of
such magnitude as remission of sins and redemption from
death and eternal wrath? How will it compare with the
death and shed blood of the Son of God, with the power of
his resurrection? How will it divide honors with him in
having merit to secure remission of sin and redemption from
death? The efficacy of Christ's death and blood alone God
would have preached in all the world and accepted by mankind. Therein he rejects the boasting of the Jews and of
all aspirers to holiness through their own works, teaching
them they cannot obtain his favor through the Law, or by
their own efforts. In Christ's name alone is remission of
sins received, and that through faith.

11. Salvation through Christ, according to Peter, was
before that time proclaimed in the Scriptures, being declared by all the prophets. This is truly strong testimony
adduced by the apostle; the Jewish people certainly ought
to believe their own prophets unless they wilfully are hardened and lost. Much more should we gentiles have faith in
Christ's atonement, being obliged to confess that not in
any wise have we done aught that such grace should be
offered and given to us. We certainly ought to be honest
enough to honor Christ to the extent of believing the apostles, in fact the Scriptures entire. We ought to be ashamed
to doubt or question the fact of forgiveness of sins and
justification before God through Christ alone, to which all
Scripture testifies. If we are honest with ourselves, we
must confess it the truth, or secure forgiveness of sins or be
justified before God by our own works.

12. Now we have heard what is the substance, the chief
doctrine, of the Scriptures, the teaching to which all portions lead; namely, to teach and confirm the article of faith:
we have remission of sins for Christ's sake, through faith.

We have heard that such was the faith of the fathers, the prophets and all saints, from the beginning of the world, and later was the doctrine preached by Christ himself, and also the doctrine of the apostles, who were commanded to publish it to the world. To this day the same doctrine prevails, and it will until the end be unanimously accepted by the whole Christian Church, with the exception of our present opponents. The Christian Church has ever, as a unit, believed, confessed and contended for this article, the article maintaining that only in the name of the Lord Christ is remission of sin obtained; and in this faith its members have been justified before God and saved. Thus by such testimony is the foundation of our doctrine laid sufficiently firm; that article was with power contended for, defended and established long before our time.

13. He who inquires, who would know exactly, what the Christian Church ever holds and teaches, especially concerning the all-important article of justification before God, or the forgiveness of sins, over which there has always been contention, has it here plainly and exactly in this text. Here is the unwavering testimony of the entire Church from the beginning. It is not necessary, then, to dispute about the doctrine any more. No one can name any just reason, or have any excuse, for doubts on the subject; or reasonably wait for further determinations of investigating councils.

In this text we see that the reliability of the article of faith has long ago been proven, even in ancient time, by the Church of the primitive fathers, of the prophets and the apostles. A solid foundation is established, one all men are bound to believe and maintain at the risk of their eternal salvation, whatever councils may establish, or the world advance and determine, to the contrary. Indeed, the sentence has been declared to us; we are commanded to shun every other doctrine that may be believed, taught or ordained. Paul says (Gal 1, 8): "But though we, or an angel from heaven, should preach unto you any gospel other than that which we preached unto you, let him be anathema."

14. You see now against what the Papacy with all its

adherents blusters and rages, and how they are to be regarded who refuse to hear and to tolerate the article Peter here advances and confirms by the testimony of all the prophets and of the Scriptures entire; who cease not to persecute godly and innocent ones for their acceptance of this article of faith, under the pretense of being themselves the Church and of magnifying its name to the utmost while opposing us, though at the same time their doctrine, faith and deeds openly testify against them, proclaiming their belief and teaching to be contrary to the testimony of all the prophets and of the entire Church.

By no means can they be the Church who so rashly contradict Peter and the Scriptures, who even trample under foot, in his Word, Christ himself, the Head. Rather, they must be wicked devils, a miserable rabble, the worst enemies of the Christian Church; more wicked and pernicious than heathen or Turks.

15. Lastly: Peter, by way of proving conclusively to the world that this one Lord, as he names him, Jesus of Nazareth, is the true Messiah promised of old in the Scriptures, says: "To him bear all the prophets witness." The prophets plainly speak of such a person, one to be born of David's flesh and blood, in the city of Bethlehem, who should suffer, die and rise again, accomplishing just what this Jesus has accomplished and even proven by miraculous signs. Therefore, truly the Jews and the non-Christians have no reason to doubt concerning Christ, no reason to await the coming of another.

16. Further, Peter, citing the testimony of the prophets, indicates the nature of Christ's kingdom as not external power; not temporal dominion like that of earthly lords, kings, and emperors; not dominion over countries or control of people, property and temporal concerns; but a spiritual, eternal kingdom, a kingdom in the hearts of men, an authority over, and power opposed to, sin, everlasting death and hell, a power able to redeem us from those things and bestow upon us salvation. Salvation is ours, Peter teaches, through the preaching of the Gospel, and is received by

faith. Faith is the obedience every man must render unto the Lord. By faith he makes himself subject to Christ and partaker of his grace and blessings. Paul also (Rom 1, 5) uses the term "unto obedience of faith."

Easter Tuesday

Text: Acts 13, 26-39.

26 Brethren, children of the stock of Abraham, and those among you that fear God, to us is the word of this salvation sent forth. 27 For they that dwell in Jerusalem, and their rulers, because they knew him not, nor the voices of the prophets which are read every sabbath, fulfilled them by condemning him. 28 And though they found no cause of death in him, yet asked they of Pilate that he should be slain. 29 And when they had fulfilled all things that were written of him, they took him down from the tree, and laid him in a tomb. 30 But God raised him from the dead: 31 and he was seen for many days of them that came up with him from Galilee to Jerusalem, who are now his witnesses unto the people. 32 And we bring you good tidings of the promise made unto the fathers, 33 that God hath fulfilled the same unto our children, in that he raised up Jesus; as also it is written in the second psalm, Thou art my Son, this day have I begotten thee. 34 And as concerning that he raised him up from the dead, now no more to return to corruption, he hath spoken on this wise, I will give you the holy and sure blessings of David. 35 Because he saith also in another psalm, Thou wilt not give thy Holy One to see corruption. 36 For David, after he had in his own generation served the counsel of God, fell asleep, and was laid unto his fathers, and saw corruption: 37 but he whom God raised up saw no corruption. 38 Be it known unto you therefore, brethren, that through this man is proclaimed unto you remission of sins: 39 and by him every one that believeth is justified from all things, from which ye could not be justified by the law of Moses.

1. This sermon Paul preached in the synagogue at Antioch in Pisidia, to the assembled Jews and gentiles. Note, he says, "whosoever among you feareth God." It is a counterpart of the sermon in the preceding epistle lesson delivered by Peter at Cesarea. Here also the first part of the sermon is simply a narration of the historical facts of Christ's resurrection, and designed to prove Christ the true Messiah promised in the Scriptures. This is sufficiently demonstrated by the facts in the case that by his own divine power and strength Christ rescued himself from death and the grave, and rose from the dead and showed himself alive and talked with men, something no man but Christ alone had ever done or ever can do. Paul elsewhere (Rom 1, 3-4) says that this Jesus our Lord was born of the seed of David according to the flesh, and was declared to be the Son of God with power by the resurrection from the dead.

2. Not content with a mere narration of the history of the resurrection, Paul cites Scripture testimony incontestably proving that Christ necessarily must rise from the dead and set up his spiritual and eternal kingdom through the Word he commanded the apostles to publish world-wide. He also discloses the true meaning of Scripture from revelation itself, showing how to seek and find Christ therein, The preceding Gospel lesson also spoke of this.

3. Third, as was true of Peter, Paul does not fail to mention what is of surpassing importance, the use of the historical parts of Scripture and the blessing and benefit accruing to us from that which Scripture proclaims and witnesses; also the method of appropriating its power and blessing. And he concludes with a beautiful utterance of apostolic power, showing how we are to obtain remission of sins and be saved. He says: "Through this man is proclaimed unto you remission of sins: and by him every one that believeth is justified from all things, from which ye could not be justified by the law of Moses." This certainly is a powerful passage and so plain it needs no comment, no further explanation. It is a point most firmly established and emphasized everywhere in Paul's epistles. We should note

well and remember such clear passages, that we may gain strength and assurance as to the ground of Christian doctrine. Seeing how perfectly, as faithful, truthful and harmonious witnesses, these two apostles agree in their preaching, we are justified in confidently drawing the conclusion that any doctrine at variance with theirs, any teaching concerning the remission of sins and our salvation contrary to theirs, is not of the church, but of the devil's accursed teachers, a doctrine of Satan's own. Gal 1.

Easter Tuesday

Second Sermon. Same Text. Acts, 13, 26-39.

THE WORD AND THE RESURRECTION.*

1. This sermon was preached by Paul in the synagogue at Antioch of Pisidia, where were gathered with the Jews some Greek converts. Wherever in a city Jews were to be found, there also were their synagogues in which they taught and preached; and many gentiles, coming to hear, were converted to God through the preaching of his Word. Undoubtedly it was by God's wonderful direction that the Jews were dispersed throughout the world among the gentiles, after the first destruction of Jerusalem by the Assyrians. Inasmuch as this dispersion resulted in the spread of the Word, they were instrumental in securing salvation for the gentiles and in preparing the way for the world-wide preaching of the Gospel by the apostles. For wherever the apostles went they found Jewish synagogues and the opportunity to preach to a regular congregation, through whom their Gospel might be widely disseminated because of the many gentiles also in attendance. Had not these gentiles been already accustomed to the Jewish synagogues, they would not have listened to the apostles, nor even permitted them publicly to preach, strangers that they were.

2. Thus it is Paul comes into the synagogue on the Sabbath, a time when the congregation was wont to assemble

*This sermon appeared first in the Church Postil, the Explanation of the Epistle and Gospel Texts from Easter to Advent. Printed by Hans Lufft, Wittenberg, 1559.

and read the Scriptures. He and Barnabas being guests from the country of the Jews, Paul is besought to give an exhortation, or sermon, to the people, whereupon he rises and delivers a fine, lengthy discourse concerning Christ: how in the Scriptures he had been promised unto the fathers and to David the king, had been born of the seed of David and had received the public testimony of John the Baptist; how Christ was sacrificed by the Jews (Peter gives the same account in the preceding epistle lesson); how he rose from the dead and for some time showed himself alive; how he then commanded his apostles to publish to the world the new doctrine that God's promise to the Jews had been fulfilled; and how, by his resurrection, he brought to them the promised blessing, namely, the remission of sins unattainable through the Law of Moses and all their ordinances, but dispensed and imparted alone to faith in the Christ proclaimed.

3. As stated later in the text, there were, beside the Jews, many gentiles present at the preaching of this sermon, and at its conclusion they besought Paul to speak to them again between sabbaths. Accordingly, when he came to the synagogue the next sabbath, he found almost the whole city assembled.

But to return to the first sermon: Paul says, "Brethren, children of the stock of Abraham"—or, native Jews—"and those among you that fear God"—who are gentiles. Now, though this could not but be a discourse objectionable and highly offensive to the Jews, Paul opens with tender and nicely chosen words meant to conciliate and to secure their respectful attention. He highly honors them by addressing them as the people chosen by God in preference to all the gentiles; as children of the holy fathers who had a special claim to the promise of God. But, again, he vitiates his pleasing impression when he proclaims to the Jews naught else but the crucified and risen Christ, and concludes with the statement that with nothing but Moses' Law and ordinances they ranked no higher in the sight of God than the gentiles.

THE WORD OF SALVATION.

4. Paul's discourse is in perfect harmony with Peter's

sermon. Peter speaks of God having sent unto the Jews heralds proclaiming peace; and Paul here says, "To you [us] is the word of this salvation sent." Notwithstanding the joy and comfort wherewith these words are fraught, they could not please the Jews. The Jews disdained the idea—in fact, it was intolerable to them to hear it expressed—that after their long expectation of a Messiah to be lord and king of the world, they should receive a mere message, and at that a message rendering of no significance at all that Law and government for which they had expected, through that Messiah, exaltation and world-wide acceptance. Indeed, such an issue could only mean to them having entertained a vain hope.

5. Paul makes his teaching yet more offensive by not referring to the Gospel simply as the word of peace, as Peter does, but by giving it the greater and grander title, "the word of salvation"; in other words, a doctrine calculated to heal and save. No grander name could be found for the Gospel; for a message of salvation is an expression of God's grace, forgiveness of sins, abiding peace and life eternal. Moreover, these blessings were not to be bestowed upon the Jews alone; they were to be equally shared with the gentiles, who had no knowledge of God, of the Law, or of divine worship. The gentiles were thus to be made the equals of the Jews, leaving the latter without preference or special merit before God, and without advantage and lordship over the former in the world.

6. Thus early in his discourse Paul grows blunt and severe, kneading Jews and gentiles into one lump. Indeed, he plainly tells the Jews that the Law of Moses did not secure to them the favor of God in the past and would be equally profitless in the future; that through the Gospel message, and only so, they, and all gentiles as well, were to be delivered from sin, death and the power of the devil, and to become God's people, with power over all. Yet he presents no other tangible token of the great boon he calls salvation and blessedness than his preaching alone.

Now, one may say: "The word I hear, and Paul I see, a

poor human being; but this salvation—grace, life and peace —I behold not. On the contrary, I daily see and experience sin, terror, adversity, suffering and death, until it seems as if in all humanity none are so utterly forsaken by God as the Christians, who hear this message."

7. But this is precisely the precious doctrine to be learned if we are to be God's children and sensible of his kingdom within us, a doctrine beyond the knowledge and experience of the Jews with their Law and of the gentiles with their wisdom drawn from reason—this it is: our salvation stands in the word Paul here declares of Christ, a word which, in name and reality, is a word of salvation and peace; for salvation and peace are the blessings which it offers and imparts.

8. God has sent this word, Paul says. Its origin and conception is not with man. It is not the edict of the Roman emperor, nor the command of the high-priest at Jerusalem. It is the Word of the God of heaven. In it he speaks. He will have the message preached by poor human beings as a power unto happiness and salvation, both in name and reality. Such the Law never was. Paul says (Rom 1, 16): "I am not ashamed of the Gospel: for it is the power of God unto salvation to every one that believeth." And God himself has bound up with it our salvation when he manifests himself in the voice heard from heaven at Jordan, saying of Christ, "This is my beloved Son"—who is to be heard.

9. God desires Christ's Word to be heard. Otherwise expressed, his command is: "Here ye have the Word of peace and salvation. Not elsewhere may you seek and find these blessings. Cling to this Word if you desire peace, happiness and salvation. Let befall what may, crosses, afflictions, discord, death—whether you be beheaded, or fall victim to pest or stroke, or in whatever manner God may call you home—in it all, look only upon me, whose Word promises that you shall not die, what seems death being but a sweet sleep, ay, the entrance into life eternal. Christ says (Jn 8, 51): "Verily, verily, I say unto you, If a man keep my Word, he shall never see death."

Note, it is the keeping of the Word on which Christ lays stress. "Keeping" is holding fast to the promise, feeling and all senses to the contrary, doubting not the truth of the message heard. For he who promises is not man; it is the Lord of heaven and earth and all that in them is, who has to this moment controlled and preserved the same. One hundred years ago, what were you and I and all men now living but absolutely nothing? How and from what was creation effected when there was nothing to start with? "He spake and it was done"—that was created which before had not existence—declares Psalm 33, 9, quoting from Genesis 1; "he commanded, and it stood fast."

10. Being the Word of God, the Gospel is an entirely different thing from man's word, no matter though it be spoken by a mere man or even a donkey. Therefore, let there be, now or henceforth, discord, terror of sin; the menace of death and hell, of the grave and corruption: come upon you what may—only press to your heart this Word that Christ has sent you a message of salvation—of redemption, of triumph over all things; and that he commands you to believe it. Then you will perceive that he, as your God and Creator, will not deceive you. What are death, the devil and all creatures as a match for Christ?

11. The glory of Christ's message, then, here called by Paul "the word of salvation," is much greater and higher than would have been the promise of all the kingdoms, all the riches and splendors of the world, yes, of both heaven and earth. For what could they benefit if one possessed not the Word of salvation and eternal life? With all these, when assailed by sins, or by the distress and danger of death, one must still say, "Away with all the blessings and joys of the world, so that I may hear and have altogether the message of salvation sent by Christ." You must hold fast to it and know that it alone gives eternal peace and joy; that it must receive your faith in spite of all apparent contradiction; that you must not be governed by your reason or your feelings, but must regard that as divine, unchangeable and eternal truth which God has spoken and commands to be proclaimed. Such is Paul's exhortation addressed primarily to

the Jews to accept this message as sent by God and as being the bearer of wondrous blessings.

12. Next, he proceeds to remove their chief stumbling-block, the thing of greatest offense to them. He warns them against the course adopted by them of Jerusalem, who had the Word of salvation from Christ himself, who read it in the prophets every day, who should have had no trouble perceiving that the prophets testified to Christ and that there was complete harmony between their teaching and that of Christ and the apostles, yet would not understand. Because Christ came not in the manner they desired, they condemned the very One whom they read of in the Scriptures as appearing with this Word of salvation, the time of whose coming had been pointed out, leaving them to know it had long since arrived and they had no reason to wait for another. They understood not the Scriptures because their minds were completely hardened and dominated by the fixed idea that Christ should reign as a temporal king. So thoroughly was the whole Jewish nation impressed with this belief that the very apostles had no other conception of Christ's kingdom, even after his resurrection. As John says (ch. 12, 16), they did not understand the Scriptures until Christ ascended to heaven and the Holy Spirit came.

So long as there hangs before one's eyes this curtain—the carnal fancy of a temporal kingdom for Christ, an earthly government for his Church—the Scriptures cannot be understood. As Paul says of the Jews (2 Cor 3, 14), the veil remaineth in the reading of the Scriptures. But this lack of understanding is inexcusable. That is gross and wilful blindness which will not receive the instruction and direction imparted by the apostles. The Jews continue to rave against the Gospel; they will hear nothing of the Christ, though even after crucifying him they receive the offer of repentance and remission of sins at the hands of the apostles.

13. That Paul should make bold to tell the most prominent men and rulers of the whole Jewish nation—the heads of God's people, pillars of the Church, as we would say—that not only the common rabble, but likewise they them-

selves did not know and understand the Scriptures committed to them; ay, that, not content with such ignorance and
error, they had themselves become the individuals of whom
they read, the murderers and crucifiers of the Son of God,
their Saviour—this was a matter of grave offense indeed!

Offensive indeed was it to have this accusation brought
against them, a people among whom God had ordained his
worship, his temple and priesthood, and for whom he had
instituted a peculiar government, giving the high-priest
power to say, Do so or you will be put to death. Deut 17,
12. And of them were the glorious and great council of
the seventy-two elders originally ordained through Moses
(Ex 18, 25-26), the council called the Sanhedrim. They
ruled the entire people and certainly knew right and wrong
according to their law.

Was there not reason here to tear Paul to pieces with
red-hot pinchers as a seditious character, a public blasphemer,
speaking not only against the Jewish government but against
the honor of God himself; daring to accuse all the princes of
the nation of being in error, of knowing nothing of the
Scriptures, even of being murderers of the Son of God? The
Pope and his crowd lack the credentials of such glory and
endorsement by God. They have merely reared a system
of self-devised doctrine and idolatry, which they still defend.
Hence, whatever censure and condemnation we heap upon
the Pope and his crowd is small in comparison to the thrust
Paul dealt the Jewish leaders.

14. Note, Paul does not stand back for anything. He
teaches men utterly to disregard the hue and cry of the
offended Jews that they were the high-priests, teachers,
rulers in a government ordained by God and commanding the obedience of the people; that teaching disobedience to them was equivalent to teaching disobedience to
parents and to civil government, yes, to God himself—something in the nature of the case not to be tolerated. Yet Paul
fearlessly does so teach, as an apostle of God and in fulfilment of God's command. How much more would Paul oppose our popish deceivers who, without the authority of

God's Word, boast themselves heads of the Church and of
the people of God, at the same time neither teaching nor
understanding the Scriptures, but offering their own drivel
as God's commands!

15. But what cause has Paul at heart that he dares so
boldly condemn the judgment of these exalted officials? It
is this, according to his own statement: There is One called
Jesus Christ, of whom the prophets, in fact the entire Scriptures, speak. Him the Jews refuse to know. He is higher
and greater than the high-priests and the rulers, greater than
the temple or the whole city of Jerusalem. And the Jews
know his coming means their passing, and their obedience to
him as Lord and Supreme Ruler. Therefore, they are inexcusable in their rejection of Christ. Of no avail is their eva-
sion, "God has given us the dominion and the supreme
power, and has commanded obedience to us in equal degree
with obedience to parents."

16. The fact that an individual is a lord or a prince, a
father or a mother, a child or a subject, administers authority
or obeys it, will not excuse him from being baptized and believing in Christ. For Christ is sole and supreme Lord over
all kings, princes and governors. True, we should be obedient to parents and to civil authority, but not to the extent
of disobeying the Lord, him who has created and subjected
to himself emperors and magistrates equally with the low-
liest of men.

But the gentlemen and lords at Jerusalem, like those of
our day, were unwilling to permit obedience to any but
themselves. From such conditions arises the present dispute about ecclesiastical authority. To go counter to it in
obeying God's command—this the ecclesiasts unjustly call
disobedience and sedition. But such must be our course if
we are to be loyal to our Lord and theirs, whom they deny.

17. In the matter of salvation, Caiaphas or Pope, Cæsar
or king, avails naught; none avails but Jesus Christ. "Him,"
says Paul, "the rulers of Jerusalem, the Holy City, have
killed. Though ye were ordained by God and given authority, God no longer regards you, because ye reject Christ.

Ye have become great blockheads, blind leaders, understanding not at all the Scriptures. Yet ye should and would teach others, just as Moses and the prophets have pointed to this Christ promised to you and to all the world for salvation and solace. Persisting in your blindness, ye have brought him to the cross, though finding in him no cause for condemnation. Surely, he did you no injury; he deprived you of naught, neither money, goods, honor nor power, but has brought you all good—even salvation—if ye will but receive him. But ye made yourselves the very ones who fulfilled the Scriptures ye daily read—those who put Christ to death and brought to pass the fact that he rose from the dead (though without thanks to you or to Satan) and became a Lord commanding the obedience of all creatures.

"We shall no longer regard what ye, or all the world, have to say of our preaching Christ; it is all the same to us whether you rage or smile. For we boast the Lord, the Son of God, made Lord over all the fathers through his resurrection. It is his will that we preach of him, and that all men believe. Since ye refuse him, your God-given privilege ceases, which, however, was granted only until the advent of the Messiah. We must withdraw from you, renouncing your authority and priesthood, and Jerusalem itself. We tell you plainly that we cannot and will not obey you in opposition to the will of the Lord."

18. Mark you, in order to make the Jews Christians, Paul had to preach that Christ was already come; that he was no longer to be looked for. He was obliged to bring home to them what they had done to Christ, they the rulers and chief of those bearing the name of God's people and entrusted with the Law and the order of divine worship—he was forced to do so that they might perceive their sin and quit their boast of having the true Law and worship, having nothing whatever wherein to glory before God. For, though possessing the Law of Moses and having heard often enough the Word of God, they would not recognize and receive the Messiah sent by God in accordance with his promise, but condemned him and became his murderers.

In view of this fact, what .does their boast about being Abraham's children, God's people, possessors of the prophets and the Law and the priesthood, amount to? These privileges only magnify their sins, only make their guilt the more grievous, before God. Not as blind, ignorant heathen, but as a people who have, and should know, the Word of God, they wilfully put to death God's Son. Thus we have the first part of Paul's sermon.

THE RESURRECTION AND FAITH.

19. The second part deals with the resurrection of Christ and its power through faith. This is the goal Paul has in view when he tells them that they have slain the Christ, thus effecting their condemnation by God and forfeiting whatever glory they possessed as Jews, gaining shame and wrath before God in its stead. To be still delivered from such condemnation, and to obtain justification and salvation, as he expresses himself toward the end, it is necessary to hear and believe the word concerning the selfsame Christ. Moreover, inasmuch as they with their leaders have refused to receive and recognize this Messiah when he preached and wrought miracles in person; now, that he is invisible and absent in the body, they are called upon to receive him whom they themselves have crucified unto death, and to believe that he is risen from the dead as Lord over all, according to the testimony of the apostles.

The dreams of the past they are now utterly to forsake, and their expectations of a Messiah still to come and elevate them with their Law and manner of worship to fame, riches and position, and to spread abroad their Moses and their priesthood in all the earth. They must now thank God for being placed on the same footing with the gentiles, in that they may come with them to the Word of salvation for the purpose of obtaining God's favor, remission of sins and life eternal.

OLD TESTAMENT TESTIMONY.

20. Paul supports his discourse on the resurrection of Christ with many strong Scripture texts. There is no doubt that he dwelt on these at length and preached quite a ser-

mon, which, however, has not been recorded here in full, but only in part. The apostle's purpose was to point us to the Old Testament Scriptures, that we might there make diligent study for ourselves of how forcibly the prophets have spoken concerning Christ, his works and his kingdom.

21. The first text Paul cites is from the Second Psalm, which treats throughout of the Messiah and his reign, as even the Jews at the time when wisdom still prevailed had to admit. Christ's own words are: "I will tell of the decree: Jehovah said unto me, Thou art my Son; this day have I begotten thee.". Paul says he is here quoting from the First Psalm, though in all editions, old and new, this psalm comes second in order.* But the apostle does not have reference to the technical arrangement of the psalms in a book, but to the order of his quotations. The thought is: "First, I will prove it from the psalm," or, "First, as written in the psalm." Just as the preacher of today says, "I observe, first," or, "It is written, first, in the psalm," whether the psalm be the first, second, twentieth or thirtieth, he not having reference to the order of the psalm but to the order in which he cites it.

22. But how does Paul make this text prove the resurrection of Christ? It is truly a strong statement, and no doubt the apostle fully explained it, amplifying it beautifully and well. The psalm refers to that Messiah, or King, who shall reign in the Jewish nation, among the people; for the writer says plainly, "I have set my king upon my holy hill of Zion," or Jerusalem. The King, then, must be true man like other men. Indeed, the psalmist adds that the kings and rulers of earth shall rage and persecute him, which could not be unless he reigned upon earth.

23. But this verse also makes the King true God, for here God calls him his own Son, begotten of himself in his divine, eternal essence and majesty. He is, then, not an adopted Son, but the true Son of God by birth. Being man, however, just like others, he must, in accord with his human

*Since Luther's time this discrepancy has been removed by allowing the change, "second psalm."

nature, die; indeed, he must suffer crucifixion and death at the hands of the lords of the world. But, again, if he be also the begotten Son of God and therefore true God, he cannot, even according to his human nature, remain in death; he must come forth from it, must triumph over it, becoming Lord of life and death forever. Here is an indivisible Being, at the same time a Son of the virgin of the house of David and of God. Such cannot remain in death. If he enter death, it must be to overcome and conquer it, yes, to slay it, to destroy it; and to bring to pass that in him as Lord shall reign naught but life, life for all who receive him. This subject is elsewhere more fully expounded.

24. But the succeeding text cited on the resurrection— from Isaiah 55, 3—reads yet more strangely: "I will give you the holy and sure blessings of David," which in the Hebrew is: "I will make an everlasting covenant with you, even the sure mercies of David." The prophet has reference to the promise made to David in Second Samuel 7, concerning Christ. In the preceding verses of the chapter, Isaiah most tenderly entreats and invites the whole world to receive the promises of salvation, for thereby shall the poor, the wretched and the afflicted obtain the great treasures of joy and salvation. And immediately following the verse quoted, he speaks of the Messiah, the promised seed of David, as given to the Levites for a "witness"—in other words, a preacher sent by God—and for "a leader and commander to the peoples." The thought is of a King and Ruler differing from Moses and his priests and exponents of the Law; a ruler differing from every other lord, ruler and king, from David and all worldly rulers whatever, subjecting everything to himself. Not that this Leader should set up a new temporal government, or extend Jewish authority among the gentiles, but that both Jews and gentiles should receive him and believe in him, obtaining the fulfilment of that promise he here terms a covenant of the sure mercies of David. This covenant, God says, he enters into and keeps, a divine, sure covenant: through Christ shall be given whatever blessings God's mercy shall bestow, with remission or

blotting out of sins, redemption from death and life eternal.

25.   Now, if the Christ of this covenant is true man and, as the promise to David is, of David's flesh and blood; and if he is to bring eternal mercy, he must likewise be God, such gift being in the province and power of God alone. This being true, he cannot remain in death, although he may suffer death by reason of his human nature; he must of his own power rise from the dead.   Only so can he raise others and give them everlasting life; only so can he truly be called eternal King of grace, righteousness and life, according to the sure promise of God.

26.   Therefore, wherever the Scriptures speak of Christ's eternal kingdom, and of everlasting grace, they point out this article of the resurrection of Christ.   No doubt, the apostle in explanation of the text from the Second Psalm quoted other Old Testament passages; for instance, Psalm 110, 1: "Jehovah saith unto my lord, Sit thou at my right hand, until I make thine enemies thy footstool"; also verse 4: "Jehovah hath sworn, and will not repent: Thou art a priest for ever."   In these passages God has promised to give us Christ, him who was to sit at his right hand—that is, have the omnipotent, divine power possible only to an eternal Lord and King—and at the same time to have his kingdom on earth, at Zion—or Jerusalem; and who was, moreover, to be a priest forever, being taken from among men and like unto them, even in his ability to die, yet at the same time continuing a priest forever, thereby forestalling the necessity of remaining in death and grave.

27.   The third passage cited by Paul is taken from the Sixteenth Psalm, which is in reality one of the Messianic psalms.   This is the psalm Peter in his first sermon on the day of Pentecost more fully explains, drawing from it the irresistible conclusion, so apparent in his own words, that Christ indeed has died; not, however, to become victim to decay in the tomb, but, proof against mortal destruction and hurt, to arise on the third day.

Easter Wednesday

ALSO SUITED TO EASTER TUESDAY.

Text: Colossians 3, 1-7.

1 If then ye were raised together with Christ, seek the things that are above, where Christ is, seated on the right hand of God. 2 Set your mind on the things that are above, not on the things that are upon the earth. 3 For ye died, and your life is hid with Christ in God. 4 When Christ, who is our life, shall be manifested, then shall ye also with him be manifested in glory. 5 Put to death therefore your members which are upon the earth; fornication, uncleanness, passion, evil desire, and covetousness, which is idolatry; 6 for which things' sake cometh the wrath of God upon the sons of disobedience: 7 wherein ye also once walked, when ye lived in these things.

EXHORTATION TO TRULY GOOD WORKS.

1. We have been hearing of the glorious message of Christ's resurrection, how that resurrection took place and how we must believe, for our own blessing, comfort and salvation. Now, that we may be sincerely thankful to God for this inestimable blessing, and that our attitude toward the doctrine of the resurrection may be one to truly honor and glorify it, we must hear also, and practice, the apostles' teaching of its essential fruits, and must manifest them in our lives. Therefore, we will select Paul's admonition to the Colossians (ch. 3), which has to do with this topic par‹ ticularly.

Observe here, Paul exhorts Christians to be incited by the resurrection of Christ unto works truly good and becoming; the text declares unto us the supreme blessing and happiness the resurrection brings within our reach—remission of sins and salvation from eternal death. Lest, however, our wanton, indolent nature deceive itself by imagining the work is instantaneously wrought in ourselves, and that simply to receive the message is to exhaust the blessing, Paul always adds the injunction to examine our hearts to ascertain whether we rightly apprehend the resurrection truth.

HOW WE ARE RISEN WITH CHRIST.

2. By no means are we simply to assent to the words of the doctrine. Christ does not design that we be able merely to accept and speak intelligently of it, but that its influence be manifest in our lives. How is a dead man profited, however much life may be preached to him, if that preaching does not make him live? Or of what use is it to preach righteousness to a sinner if he remain in sin? or to an erring, factious individual if he forsake not his error and his darkness? Even so, it is not only useless but detrimental, even pernicious in effect, to listen to the glorious, comforting and saving doctrine of the resurrection. if the heart has no experience of its truth; if it means naught but a sound in the ears, a transitory word upon the tongue, with no more effect upon the hearer than as if he had never heard.

According to Paul in the text, this nobly-wrought and precious resurrection of Christ essentially must be, not an idle tale of fancy, futile as a dead hewn-stone or painted-paper image, but a powerful energy working in us a resurrection through faith—an experience he calls being risen with Christ; in other words, it is dying unto sin, being snatched from the power of death and hell and having life and happiness in Christ. In the second chapter (verse 12), the apostle puts it plainly, "buried with him in baptism, wherein ye were also raised with him through faith in the working of God, who raised him from the dead."

3. If, Paul says, ye have apprehended by faith the resurrection of Christ and have received its power and consolation, and so are risen with him, that resurrection will surely

be manifest in you; you will feel its power, will be conscious of its working within. The doctrine will be something more than words; it will be truth and life. For them who do not thus apprehend the resurrection, Christ is not yet risen, although his rising is none the less a fact; for there is not within them the power represented by the words "being risen with Christ," the power which renders them truly dead and truly risen men.

So Paul's intent is to make us aware that before we can become Christians, this power must operate within us; otherwise, though we may boast and fancy ourselves believing Christians, it will not be true. The test is, are we risen in Christ—is his resurrection effective in us? Is it merely a doctrine of words, or one of life and operating power?

4. Now, what is the process of the life and death mentioned? How can we be dead and at the same time risen? If we are Christians we must have suffered death; yet the very fact that we are Christians implies that we live. How is this paradox to be explained? Indeed, certain false teachers of the apostles' time understood and explained the words in a narrow sense making them mean that the resurrection of the dead is a thing of the past according to Paul's words in Second Timothy 1, 10, and that there is no future resurrection from temporal death. The believer in Christ, they said, is already risen to life; in all Christians the resurrection is accomplished in this earthly life. They sought to prove their position by Paul's own words, thus assailing the article of the resurrection.

5. But we will ignore these teachers as being condemned by Paul, and interpret the words as he meant them, his remarks both preceding and following making it clear and unquestionable that he refers to the spiritual resurrection. This fact is certain: If we are, at the last day, to rise bodily, in our flesh and blood, to eternal life, we must have had a previous spiritual resurrection here on earth. Paul's words in Romans 8, 11 are: "But if the Spirit of him that raised up Jesus from the dead dwelleth in you, he that raised up Christ Jesus from the dead shall give life also to your mortal

bodies through his Spirit that dwelleth in you." In other words: God having quickened, justified and saved you spiritually, he will not forget the body, the building or tabernacle of the living spirit; the spirit being in this life risen from sin and death, the tabernacle, or the corruptible flesh-and-blood garment, must also be raised; it must emerge from the dust of earth, since it is the dwelling-place of the saved and risen spirit, that the two may be reunited unto life eternal.

6. The apostle, then, is not in this text referring to the future resurrection of the body, but to the spiritual rising which entails the former. He regards as one fact the resurrection of the Lord Christ, who brought his body again from the grave and entered into life eternal, and the resurrection of ourselves, who, by virtue of his rising, shall likewise be raised: first, the soul, from a trivial and guilty life shall rise into a true, divine and happy existence; and second, from this sinful and mortal body shall rise out of the grave an immortal, glorious one.

So Paul terms believing Christians both "dead" and "alive." They are spiritually dead in this life and also spiritually alive. Nevertheless, this sinful temporal life must yet come to an end in physical death, for the destruction of the sin and death inherent therein, that body and spirit may live forever. Therefore he says:

> "If then ye were raised together with Christ, seek the things that are above, where Christ is, seated on the right hand of God."

7. In other words: Seek and strive after what is above—the things divine, heavenly and eternal; not the terrestrial, perishable, worldly. Make manifest the fact that you are now spiritually raised and by the same power will later be raised bodily.

8. But does this mean that we, as Christians, are no more to eat and drink, to till the ground, to attend to domestic or public duties, or to engage in any kind of labor? Are we to live utterly idle, practically dead? Is that what you mean, Paul, when you say we are not to seek the things of earth,

though all these are essentially incident to life? What can you say to the fact that Christ the Lord is, himself, with us on earth? for he said before his ascension to heaven (Mt 28, 20): "Lo, I am with you always, even unto the end of the world"; and also the baptism which he commands, the sacrament and the office of Gospel ministry whereby he governs his Church here—these are things of earth.

9. Paul, however, explains in the succeeding verse what he means by "things that are upon the earth" and "things that are above." He is not telling us to despise earthly objects. He does not refer to God's created things, all which are good, as God himself considered them; nor has he reference to the Christian who, in his earthly life, must deal with the things of creation. He has in mind the individual without knowledge of God; who knows no more, and aims no further, than reason teaches, that reason received from parents at physical birth; who is an unbeliever, ignorant of God and the future life and caring not for them; who follows only natural understanding and human desire and seeks merely personal benefit, honor, pride and pleasure. The apostle calls that a worldly life where the Word of God is lacking, or at least is disregarded, and where the devil has rule, impelling to all vices.

Paul would say: Ye must be dead to a worldly life of this sort, a life striven after by the heathen, who disregard God's Word and suffer the devil to have his way with them. Ye must prove the resurrection of Christ in you to be something more than vain words. Ye must show there is a living power manifest in you because ye are risen, a power which makes you lead a different life, one in obedience to the Word and will of God, and called the divine, heavenly life. Where this change does not take place, it is a sign ye are not yet Christians but are deceiving yourselves with vain fancies.

10. Under the phrase "things that are upon the earth"— worldly things—Paul includes not only gross, outward vices, sins censurable in the eyes of the world, but also greater immoralities; everything, in fact, not in accordance with the pure Word of God, faith and true Christian character.

SPIRITUAL AND CARNAL WORLDLINESS.

11. In order to a better understanding of the text, we shall adopt Paul's customary classification of life as spiritual and carnal. Life on earth is characterized as of the spirit, or spiritual; and of the flesh, or carnal. But the spiritual life may be worldly. The worldly spiritual life is represented by the vices of false and self-devised doctrine wherein the soul lives without the Word of God, in unbelief and in contempt of God; or, still worse, abuses the Word of God and the name of Christ in false doctrine, making them a cover and ornament for wicked fraud, using them falsely under a show of truth, under pretense of Christian love.

This is worldly conduct of the spiritual kind. It is always the worst, ever the most injurious, since it is not only personal sin, but deceives others into like transgression. Paul refers, in the epistle lesson for Easter, to this evil as the "old leaven" and the "leaven of wickedness." And in Second Corinthians 7, 1, he makes the same classification of spiritual and carnal sin, saying, "Let us cleanse ourselves from all defilement of flesh and spirit." By defilement of the spirit he means those secret, subtle vices wherewith man pollutes and corrupts his inner life in the sight of God; his sins not being manifest to the world, but deceiving human reason and wisdom.

12. If we would be Christians we must, first of all, be dead to conduct of this sort. We must not receive nor tolerate the worldly doctrine and corrupt inventions originating with ourselves, whether in the nature of reason, philosophy or law, theories ignoring the Word of God or else falsely passing under its name. For such are wholly of the world; under their influence man has no regard to God's will and seeks not his kingdom and eternal life. They are meant merely to further the individual's own honor, pride, renown, wisdom, holiness or something else. Though boast is made of the Gospel and of faith in Christ, yet it is not serious, and the individual continues without power and without fruit.

13. If we are risen with Christ through faith, we must set our affections upon things not earthly, corruptible, perishable, but upon things above—the heavenly, divine, eternal;

in other words, upon doctrine right, pure and true, and whatever is pleasing to God, that his honor and Christ's kingdom may be preserved. Thus shall we guard ourselves against abuse of God's name, against false worship and false trust and that presumption of self-holiness which pollutes and defrauds the spirit.

14. Under carnal worldliness Paul includes the gross vices, enumerating in particular here, fornication, uncleanness, covetousness, and so on, things which reason knows to be wicked and condemns as such. The spiritual sins take reason captive and deceive it, leaving it powerless to guard against them. They are termed spiritual sins not simply because of their spirit-polluting character, for all vices pollute the spirit, the carnal vices among them; but because they are too subtle for flesh and blood to discern. The sins of the flesh, however, are called carnal, or body-polluting, because committed by the body, in its members.

Now, as we are to be dead unto spiritual sins, so are we to be dead unto carnal sins, or at least to make continual progress toward that end, striving ever to turn away from all such earthly things and to look toward the heavenly and divine. He who continues to seek carnal things and to be occupied with them, has not as yet with Christ died unto the world. Not having died, he is not risen; the resurrection of Christ effects nothing in him. Christ is dead unto him and he unto Christ.

15. Paul's admonition is particularly necessary at the present time. We see a large and constantly-increasing number who, despite their boast of the Gospel and their certain knowledge of the polluting and condemning power of spiritual and carnal sins, continue in their evil course, forgetful of God's wrath, or endeavoring to trust in false security. Indeed, it is a very common thing for men to do just as they please and yet pretend innocence and seek to avoid censure. Some would represent themselves guileless as lambs and blameless; no act of theirs may be regarded evil or even wrong. They pretend great virtue and Christian love. Yet they carry on their insidious, malicious frauds, imposing falsehoods upon men. They ingeniously contrive to make

their conduct appear good, imagining that to pass as fault-
less before men and to escape public censure means to deceive God also.   But they will learn how God looks upon
the matter.   Paul tells us (Gal 6, 7) God will not, like men,
be mocked.   To conceal and palliate will not avail.   Nothing
will answer but dying to vice and then striving after what is
virtuous, divine and becoming the Christian character.

16.   Paul enumerates some gross and unpardonable vices
—fornication, or unchastity, and covetousness.   He speaks
also of these in Ephesians 5, 3-5 and in First Thessalonians
4, 3-7, as we have heard in the epistle lessons for the second
and third Sundays in Lent.   He enjoins Christians to guard
against these sins, to be utterly dead to them.   For they are
sensual, acknowledged such even among the gentiles; while
we strive after the perfect purity becoming souls who belong to Christ and in heaven.   It is incumbent upon the
Christian to preserve his body modest, and holy or chaste;
to refrain from polluting himself by fornication and other
unchastity, after the manner of the world.

17.   Similarly does the apostle forbid covetousness, to
which he gives the infamous name of idolatry in the effort
to make it more hideous in the Christian's eyes, to induce
him to shun it as an abominable vice intensely hated of God.
It is a vice calculated to turn a man wholly from faith and
from divine worship, until he regards not, nor seeks after,
God and his Word and heavenly treasures, but follows only
after the treasures of earth and seeks a god that will give
him enough of earthly good.

18.   Much might be said on this topic were we to consider
it relative to all orders and trades in succession.   For plainly
the world, particularly in our day, is completely submerged
in the vice of covetousness.   It is impossible to enumerate
the subtle arts it can invent, and the good and beautiful
things it knows how to pass off whereunder it masks itself
as a thing not to be considered sinful, but rather extremely
virtuous and indicative of uprightness.   And so idolatry ever
does.   While before God it is the worst abomination, before
the world its appearance and reputation are superior.   So

far from being recognized as sin, it is considered supreme holiness and divine worship.

The very worship of Mammon wears an imposing mask. It must not be called covetousness or dishonest striving after property, but must be known as upright, legitimate endeavor to obtain a livelihood, a seeking to acquire property honestly. It ingeniously clothes itself with the Word of God, saying God commands man to seek his bread by labor, by his own exertions, and that every man is bound to provide for his own household. No civil government, no, nor a preacher even, can censure covetousness under that guise unless it be betrayed in gross robbing and stealing.

19. Let every man know that his covetousness will be laid to the charge of his own conscience, that he will have to answer for it, for God will not be deceived. It is evident the vice is gaining ground. With its false appearance and ostentation, and its world-wide prevalence, it is commonly accepted as legal. Without censure or restraint, men are engrossed in coveting and accumulating to the utmost. Those having position and power think they have the right to acquire by violence as much as they can, daily making assessments and imposts, and new oppressions and impositions upon the poor. And the common rabble seek gain by raising prices, by extortion, fraud, and so on. Yet all desire not to be charged with wrong-doing; they would not they should be called unchristian on account of their conduct. Indeed, such excess of covetousness obtains that the public robbing and stealing, and the faithlessness and fraud, of the meanest hirelings, servants and maids everywhere can no longer be restrained.

20. But who would care to recount the full extent of this vice in all dealings and interests of the world between man and man? Enough has been said to induce every one who aims to be a Christian to examine his own heart and, if he find himself guilty of such vice, to refrain; if not, to know how to guard against it. Every individual can readily perceive for himself what is consistent with Christian character in this respect, what can be allowed with a good conscience;

for he has Christ's rule of dealing as we would be dealt with, which insures equality and justice. Where unfairness exists, covetousness must obtain to some extent.

21. If you will not desist from the vice of covetousness, then know you are not a Christian, not a believer, but, as Paul calls you, a base, detestable idolater, having no part in God's kingdom; for you are living wholly to the world and without intent to rise with Christ. You will receive no blessing from the joy-inspiring and gracious revelation that Christ died and rose for sinners. You cannot say, "Therefore he died for me, I trust." Truly, Christ died for you, but if you continue in your wickedness, using this revelation as a cloak for your mean covetousness, do not—such is the declaration of the text—by any means apply that comforting promise to yourself. Although Christ indeed died and rose for all, yet unto you he is not risen; you have not apprehended his resurrection by faith. You have seen the smoke but have not felt the fire; you have heard the words but have received nothing of their power.

THE NEW LIFE IN CHRIST.

22. If you would be able honestly to boast of this revelation as unto you, if you would have the comfort of knowing that Christ, through his death and resurrection, has blessed you, you must not continue in your old sinful life, but put on a new character. For Christ died and rose for the very purpose of effecting your eventual death with him and your participation in his resurrection: in other words, he died that you might be made a new man, beginning even now, a man like unto himself in heaven, a man having no covetous desire or ambition for advantage over a neighbor, a man satisfied with what God grants him as the result of his labor, and kind and beneficent to the needy.

23. In his desire to arouse Christians to the necessity of guarding against such vices as he mentions, Paul strengthens his admonition, in conclusion, by grave threats and visions of divine wrath, saying, "for which things' sake cometh the wrath of God upon the sons of disobedience"; that is, upon the unbelieving world, which regards not the Word

of God, does not fear or believe in it nor strive to obey it, and yet is unwilling to be charged with idolatry and other unchristian principles, desiring rather to be considered righteous and God's own people.

In the last quoted clause Paul also implies that worldly conduct, the life of worldly lusts such as covetousness and other vices, is inconsistent and impossible with faith, and that the power of Christ's resurrection cannot reach it. For this reason he terms them "sons of disobedience," who have not faith and who, by their unchristian conduct, bring God's wrath upon themselves and are cast out from the kingdom of God. God seriously passes sentence against such conduct, declaring he will reveal his wrath against it in bodily punishment in this world and eternal punishment in the world hereafter. Elsewhere Paul says practically the same thing (Eph 5, 6): "For because of these things cometh the wrath of God upon the sons of disobedience." See also Rom 1, 18.

24. Such is the admonition of Paul unto all who would be called Christians. He reminds them whereunto the Gospel of Christ calls them and what his resurrection should work in them—death to all life and doctrine not in harmony with God's Word and God's will—and that if they believe in the risen and living Christ, they, as risen with him, should seek after the same heavenly life where he sits at the right hand of God, a life where is no sin nor worldly error, but eternal life and imperishable treasures to be possessed and enjoyed with Christ forever.

25. But the revelation of Christ's resurrection can be apprehended by nothing but faith. The things Paul here tells us of life and glory for Christians in the risen Christ are not apparent to the world; in fact, Christians themselves do not perceive them by external sense. Notice, he says, "Ye died, and your life is hid with Christ in God." The world does not understand the Christian life and has no word of praise for it; it is hostile to the faith and cannot tolerate the fact that you believe in Christ and refuse to join hands with it in love for worldly lusts. A hidden life indeed is the Christian's; not only hidden to the world, but, so far

as external perception goes, to the Christian himself. Nevertheless, it is a life sure and in safe keeping, and in the hereafter its glory shall be manifest to all the world. For Paul says:

> "When Christ, who is our life, shall be manifested, then shall ye also with him be manifested in glory."

26. Here is comfort for Christians in this earthly life where, though they receive the doctrine of Christ and apprehend him by faith, their resurrection seems to the world and to their own perceptions untrue; where they must contend with sin and infirmities and moreover are subject to much affliction and adversity; and where consequently they are extremely sensible of death and terror when they would experience joy and life. In this verse Paul comforts them, showing them where to seek and surely apprehend their life.

27. Be of good cheer, he would say, for ye are dead to the worldly life. This life ye must renounce, but in so doing ye make a precious exchange. Dying unto the world is a blessed experience, for which ye will obtain a life far more glorious. Ye are now, through Christ's death, redeemed from sin and from death eternal and are made imperishable. Upon you is conferred everlasting glory. But this risen life ye cannot yet perceive in yourselves; ye have it in Christ, through faith.

Christ is spoken of as "our life." Though the life is still unrevealed to you, it is certain, insured to you beyond the power of any to deprive you of it. By faith in Christ's life, then, are ye to be preserved and to obtain victory over the terrors and torments of sin, death and the devil, until that life shall be revealed in you and made manifest to men.

In Christ ye surely possess eternal life. Nothing is lacking to a perfect realization except that the veil whereby it is hidden so long as we are in mortal flesh and blood, is yet to be removed. Then will eternal life be revealed. Then all worldly, terrestrial things, all sin and death, will be abolished. In every Christian shall be manifest only glory. Christians, then, believing in Christ, and knowing him risen, should comfort themselves with the expectation of living

with him in eternal glory; the inevitable condition is that
they have first, in the world, died with him.

28. Paul does not forget to recognize the earthly environ-
ment of Christians and saints, for he says: "Put to death
therefore your members which are upon the earth." Though
acknowledging Christians dead with Christ unto worldly
things and possessing life in Christ, he yet tells them to
mortify their members on earth, and enumerates the sins of
fornication, covetousness, etc.

This is truly a strange idea, that it should be necessary
for men who have died and risen with Christ and hence have
been made really holy, to mortify worldly inclinations in
their bodily members. The apostle refers to this subject in
Romans 7: 5, 8, 23, and elsewhere, frequently explaining
how, in the saints, there continue to remain various lusts of
original sin, which constantly rise in the effort to break out,
even gross external vices. These have to be resisted. They
are strong enough utterly to enslave a man, to subject him
to the deepest guilt, as Paul complains (Rom 7, 23); and
they will surely do it unless the individual, by faith and the
aid of the Holy Spirit, oppose and conquer them.

29. Therefore, saints must, by a vigorous and unceasing
warfare, subdue their sinful lusts if they would not lose
God's grace and their faith. Paul says in Romans 8, 13:
"If ye live after the flesh, ye must die; but if by the Spirit ye
put to death the deeds of the body, ye shall live." In order,
then, to retain the Spirit and the incipient divine life, the
Christian must contend against himself.

This cannot be accomplished by the monastic hypocrisies
wherewith some expect to resist sin. For the pollution of
sin is not merely something adhering to the clothing, or to
the skin externally, and easily washed off. It is not something to be discharged from the body by fasting and casti-
gation. No, it penetrates the flesh and blood and is diffused
through the whole man. Positive mortification is necessary
or it will destroy one. And this is how to mortify sin: It
must be perceived with serious displeasure and repented of;
and through faith Christ's forgiveness must be sought and

found. Thus shall sinful inclinations be resisted, defeated
and restrained from triumphing over you. More has been
said on this topic elsewhere.

Sunday After Easter

Text: 1 John 5, 4-12.

4 For whatsoever is begotten of God overcometh the world: and this is the victory that hath overcome the world, even our faith. 5 And who is he that overcometh the world, but he that believeth that Jesus is the Son of God? 6 This is he that came by water and blood, even Jesus Christ; not with the water only, but with the water and with the blood. 7 And it is the Spirit that beareth witness, because the Spirit is the truth. 8 For there are three who bear witness, the Spirit, and the water, and the blood: and the three agree in one. 9 If we receive the witness of men, the witness of God is greater: for the witness of God is this, that he hath borne witness concerning his Son. 10 He that believeth on the Son of God hath the witness in him: he that believeth not God hath made him a liar; because he hath not believed in the witness that God hath borne concerning his Son. 11 And the witness is this, that God gave unto us eternal life, and this life is in his Son. 12 He that hath the Son hath the life; he that hath not the Son of God hath not the life.

VICTORIOUS FAITH.

1. This epistle selection was primarily arranged for this particular Sunday because it treats of baptism and of the new birth of the believing Christian. It was in former time customary in the Church to baptize immediately after Easter those who had accepted the Christian faith and had been instructed in its precepts. This day is also called "Dominicam in albis," and by us Germans "Weiszer Sonntag" (White Sunday), because the candidates for baptism were

231

clad in white linen as indicative of their cleansing and new birth; just as today children to be baptized are arrayed in a white christening-robe.

THE NEW BIRTH.

2. While this lesson does not treat of the resurrection of Christ, it has reference to its fruits: faith, the very essence of Christianity, here expressed as being born of God; and the evidence of the Holy Spirit, received through baptism, which assures us we are children of God and have, through Christ, eternal life and all blessings.

3. Though John's language is, as usual, plain and simple, yet, in the ears of men generally, it is unusual and unintelligible. The world estimates it as similar to the prattle of children or fools. What, according to the world's construction, is implied by the statement, "Whatsoever is begotten [born] of God overcometh the world?" Overcoming the world, the unconverted would understand to mean bringing into subjection to oneself every earthly thing and assuming the position of sovereign of the world. Yet more absurd in the ears of this class is the saying that we must be born of God. "Did one ever hear of such a thing," they might exclaim, "as children born of God? It would be less ridiculous to say we must be born of stones, after the idea of the heathen poets." To the world there is no birth but physical birth. Hence such doctrine as our lesson sets forth will ever be strange, unintelligible, incomprehensible, to all but Christains. But the latter speak with new tongues, as Christ in the last chapter of Mark (verse 17) says they shall, for they are taught and enlightened by the Holy Spirit.

4. Clearly, then, when the Scriptures speak of being born of God, it is not in a human sense; the reference is not to the conditions of our temporal lives, but to those exalted ones of a future existence. To say we must be born of God is equivalent to saying that if man is to be redeemed from sin and eternal death, to enter into the kingdom of God and into happiness, his physical birth will not suffice; all which nature, reason, free-will and human endeavor may afford is inadequate. Physical birth, it is true, answers for every-

thing in the way of temporal possession and achievement, everything great, powerful, noble, rich, wise, learned; in short, every exalted and desirable thing of earth. But all such possession and achievement serves only the physical existence; it is swept away by death, to which event it is ever subject.

Hence becomes necessary a new and different birth, a birth more significant than that of the natural man even in the case of emperors, kings, or the wisest and most influential of earth. For as Isaiah says (ch. 40, 6): "All flesh is grass, and all the goodliness thereof is as the flower of the field. The grass withereth, the flower fadeth." The demand is for a divine birth, a birth in which parentage is wholly of God; a birth signifying the operation of God's divine power in man, a power achieving something beyond the attainment of his natural capacities and effecting in him new understanding and a new heart.

5. The process is this: When the individual hears the Gospel message of Christ—a message revealed and proclaimed not by the wisdom and will of man, but through the Holy Spirit—and sincerely believes it, he is justly recognized as conceived and born of God. John in his gospel (ch. 1, 12) says: "As many as received him, to them gave he the right to become children of God, even to them that believe on his name." And in the first verse of the chapter including our text, he tells us: "Whosoever believeth that Jesus is the Christ is begotten of God." Through that faith, for the sake of his Son, God accepts us as his children, pleasing to him and heirs of eternal life; and the Holy Spirit will be sent into our hearts, as is explained later.

6. This doctrine condemns those arrogant teachers who presumptuously expect to be justified before God by their own merits and works. They imagine that their wisdom, learning, good judgment, intelligence, fair reputation and morality entitle them, because of the good they are thus enabled to do, to the favor of God and to reception up into heaven. But the Scriptures clearly teach the very reverse, that all these things are nothing in the eyes of God. It is

sheer human effort; it is not being born of God. However wise and powerful you might be, if even the noblest, most beautiful, fruit human nature can produce, you could not see the kingdom of God unless you became a wholly differ-ent person, unless you were born anew, according to Christ's words in John 3, 3. And this is something impossible to your natural powers. You certainly cannot make yourself of other parentage than you are. God must begin the work in you, communicating his seed—his Word—by virtue of which the Holy Spirit operates in you, enabling you, by faith, to cling to the promise, as said before.

7. Now, he who is thus born of God, John declares, over-comes the world. Verily, this is a significant and forcible assertion the Holy Spirit makes; it represents a tremendous power, a great work. The child of God must, indeed, at-tempt and accomplish great things. The birth effected through the Word and faith makes men true sovereigns, above all earthly rulers; it gives them power even to over-come the world, something impossible to any Roman or Turkish potentate. They effect not their victory by phys-ical force or temporal power, but by the spiritual birth, through faith. As John says immediately after the clause we are discussing, "This is the victory that hath overcome the world, even our faith." Here is his own explanation of what he means by being born of God.

THE TWO KINGDOMS.

8. Now, in order to understand the nature of the spir-itual victory and how it is effected, we must know just what John means by the term "world." The reference is not to dominion over territory, to property or money. He implies the existence of two kingdoms. In one, the kingdom of God, the heavenly kingdom of Christ, is included, first, the angels in heaven, who are the chief lords, the inner circle of counselors; second, the entire Christian Church on earth, under one head, Christ the Lord and King. In the other kingdom, the hellish kingdom, the devil is prince, and his mighty counselors and servants are the angels who with him fell from heaven; it also includes the world, those on earth

who teach, believe and live contrary to Christ, who represent the heathen, the Jews, the Turks and false Christians.

By the heavenly kingdom of God we must understand, not only spiritual life and godly people, but the lord and regent of that kingdom—Christ with his angels, and his saints both living and dead. Thus, too, the kingdom of the world represents not only the earthly life with its worldly interests, but particularly its lord and regent—the devil and his angels, and all unchristian, godless, wicked people on earth. So, when John says, "Whatsoever is begotten of God overcometh the world," he means by "world" the devil and his whole earthly dominion.

9. Now, the workings of these two kingdoms are plainly evident, though the leaders—Christ the Lord, and the devil —are not visible to mortal eyes. Christ rules direct and effectually, in his own power, through the Word and through the Holy Spirit in the hearts of believers, maintaining them in the faith and in the knowledge of his Word, and protecting from the devil's wrath and subtlety; further, he rules through his angels, who guard his followers; again, he rules through his people themselves, who exercise authority one over another in loving service, each teaching, instructing, comforting and admonishing a noble little band of godly, obedient, patient, chaste, kind, tractable, benevolent souls.

The nature of the devil's kingdom, the manner of life the world leads, is easily apparent. This kingdom is simply a huge booth filled with faithless, shameless, wicked individuals, impelled by their god to every sort of disobedience, ingratitude and contempt of God and his Word; to idolatry, false doctrine, persecution of Christians and the practice of all wantonness, mischief, wickedness and vice.

10. These two kingdoms are opposed. They continually contend for the crown; they war with each other for supremacy. Christians are brought into the conflict to hold the field against God's enemy, whose rule of the world is one of falsehood and murder; they must contend with the enemy's servants, his horde of factious spirits and basely

wicked individuals, in an effort to restrain evil and promote
good. Christians must be equipped for the fray; they must
know how to meet and successfully resist the enemy, how
to carry the field unto victory, and hold it.

FAITH THE VICTOR.

11. Therefore, when John says, "Whatsoever is begotten of God overcometh the world: and this is the victory
that hath overcome the world, even our faith," his purpose
is to admonish Christians that believers must manifest the
power and working of faith in life and deed. In fact, his
chief aim in writing this text was to reprove false Christians
who are pleased to hear the doctrine that we are saved
through Christ alone, our works and merits not earning our
salvation; and who imagine the hearing of this doctrine constitutes them Christians and that there is no necessity for
any effort or contention on their part. They forget that
they must, through faith, become new persons fitted to overcome the world and the devil.

12. Victory over the devil is the sign of the true Christian. Thereby we may know men are born of God, may
distinguish them from the false children who enjoy but the
semblance of God's Word and never experience its power.
Such are mere "mondkinder" (moon-children)—still-born,
destitute of real divine life, or divine power. It cannot be
said we have been born of God when we continue in our
old dead and worldly course, and as before lie and live in sin
at the devil's pleasure. No, as children of God we must
resist the devil and his entire kingdom. If, then, instead
of overcoming the world you allow it to overcome you, then,
boast as you may of faith and Christ, your own conduct
testifies that you are not a child of God.

To illustrate, beginning with some of the lower and gross-
er sins: If you boast of being a child of God, but still live
in fornication, adultery, and such vices, the devil has already
overcome you and wrested you from the kingdom of God.
If you are miserly, injuring your neighbor by usury, by
overcharging, by false wares and fraudulent business, you
have permitted the world and your own flesh to overcome

you for a penny." If you entertain envy and hatred toward your neighbor, you are at once thereby a captive servant of the devil. The same principle holds in the case of sins more subtile and refined, where the malicious knavery of the devil must be resisted. For instance, the devil deceives with misleading doctrines, impelling men to idolatry, false faith, presumption, despair, blasphemy, and so on. Now, if you yield to him, suffering yourself to be seduced, what will it profit you to boast of the Gospel faith? for you have not properly grasped God's Word, you have not rightly recognized God in Christ, but continue in error, in false fancies, captivated and deceived by the devil.

13. It requires something more than mere human wisdom and skill, more than human power, to withstand and overcome an enemy so formidable as the devil. As said before, the Christian must be fortified with the knowledge of how to guard against his wiles and deceptions and how to withstand him. Hence a Christian is called a person who is born of God. He must be different from an intelligent heathen and a skillful worldling to rightly understand God's Word and apprehend Christ through faith, and must use such knowledge as weapons of offense and defense in the conflict. Thus will he be able to withstand the devil and the world and to gain the victory. God's Word and faith are the power which will bring him through; he cannot be overcome so long as he adheres to them.

In this connection are John's words immediately preceding our text: "This is the love of God, that we keep his commandments; and his commandments are not grievous." Then he goes on, "For whatsoever is begotten of God overcometh the world," etc. Such is the power represented by genuine new birth, that therein the devil, the world and all evil are overcome. Just as, in physical birth, a normal child fully born into the world may overcome a slight offensive disease, while an abnormal or still-born child perishes of its own weakness.

14. For example, if I have faith and am born of God, I will not pollute myself with unchastity and fornication, I

will not bring disgrace upon another's spouse or child. The new birth will indeed teach me not to reject shamefully the treasure I have in Christ, not to lose it willingly, and not to drive from me the indwelling Holy Spirit. Faith, if it truly dwells in me, will not permit me to do aught in violation of my conscience and of the Word and the will of God.

Should I be tempted by avarice to deceive and defraud my neighbor, or to close my hand when I should give him aid, if I am a Christian and born anew my faith will protest and turn me from such action. Can I injure my neighbor or permit him to suffer want when I might contribute to his relief, if I am aware that Christ has given his body and shed his blood for me? How can there enter into the heart of the Christian who believes he has received ineffable and eternal treasures through the Son of God, the inclination to permit his neighbor to suffer a trivial want when he can easily extend relief? Much less would it be possible for the Christian to injure or to do injustice to his neighbor for the sake of shamefully gaining some small advantage. Rather he would reflect: "If I am, through Christ, a child of God and an heir of heaven, the sum of this world's goods is far too insignificant to induce me, for the sake of a penny, to deceive or defraud anyone."

Then, too, if the devil tempt you by his tyrannical, factious spirits, or even by your own thoughts, to forsake your pure doctrine for his deceptions, you as a Christian are to resist the temptation, remembering the blessings you have through faith received from Christ in the Gospel; you have been liberated from darkness, blindness and error; have learned rightly to know God; and have obtained the sure consolation of grace and salvation, being aware upon what you must depend in life and death. Why, then, yield to the devil, allowing yourself to be robbed of salvation and eternal life? Why not much rather let go every earthly thing than to deny the Word of God or to permit this blessed consolation to be perverted, falsified and wrested from you?

15. So, then, John says, "This is the victory that hath

overcome the world, even our faith." It is, indeed, saying very much for the Christian faith to attribute to it such power over the devil and the world—a power transcending all human ability. It requires an agency greater and higher than human strength to triumph over the devil, especially in the perplexing conflicts of conscience, when he vexes and tortures the heart with terror of God's wrath in the attempt to drive us to despair. At such times all our works must immediately sink out of sight, leaving no help or victory except the faith that clings to the word of Christ the Lord, believing that, for the sake of his beloved Son, God will be merciful and will not condemn us for our sins and unworthiness if we believe in him. Such faith as this stands fast and gains the victory; neither the devil nor the gates of hell can prevail against it.

16. The same is true in all temptations. Before we can resist and overcome, we must have faith to believe that through Christ we have remission of sins and the favor of God; that God gives us help and strength to enable us to stand in the conflict and successfully resist the devil, the world, the flesh and death; that we obtain the victory by the divine power of the Holy Spirit, lacking whose help we all would be far too weak to win. Without faith, we are under the power of the devil and sin, being subject to them by natural birth. We can be liberated in no other way than through faith in Christ.

17. That John has reference to faith in Christ is plainly evident from his query, "Who is he that overcometh the world, but he that believeth that Jesus is the Son of God?" The apostle's purpose therein is to make plain just what the true Scriptural faith is and what it implies. For there are other beliefs which the world calls faith. The Jews, the Turks, the Papists, claim they also believe in God who created heaven and earth. That such belief is not the true faith, however, is proved by the fact of its ineffectiveness. It does not contend and overcome, and it permits the believer to remain as he is, in his natural birth and under the power of the devil and sin.

But the faith which believes Jesus is the Son of God is the true, triumphant sort. It is an invincible power wrought in the hearts of Christians by the Holy Spirit. It is a sure knowledge, that does not gaze and vacillate hither and thither according to its own thoughts. It apprehends God in Christ the Son sent from heaven, through whom God reveals his will and his love and transfers us from sin to grace, from death to a new and eternal life; a refuge and trust that relies not upon its own merit or worthiness, but upon Christ the Son of God, and in his might and power battles against the world and the devil. Therefore, the Christian faith is not the cold, ineffective, empty, lifeless conception which Papists and others imagine it to be; no, it is a living, active power, ever followed by victories and other appropriate fruits. Where such fruits are lacking, faith and the new birth are not there.

THE SOURCE OF FAITH.

18. Thus we have the first part of our sermon on the new birth and faith. For the second part, John shows whence and by what means comes the faith productive of victory; he says: "This is he that came by water and blood, even Jesus Christ; not with the water only, but with the water and with the blood. And it is the Spirit that beareth witness, because the Spirit is the truth. For there are three who bear witness [in earth], the Spirit, and the water, and the blood," etc.

19. John speaks of Christ's kingdom, and of the office the Holy Spirit bears outwardly and visibly in the Christian Church, represented in the ministerial office and the sacraments. He says: "There are three who bear witness [in earth]." John, as usual, employs the word "witness" in connection with the thought of preaching; it is a word he frequently uses. For instance, in the beginning of his gospel, where he speaks of John the Baptist, he says (ch. 1, 7): "The same came for a witness, that he might bear witness of the light." So, in his use of the phrase "witness" or "bearing witness," we are to understand simply the public preaching of God's Word. Again, Christ says (John

16, 9-14), that the Holy Spirit shall bear witness of him; that is, he shall publicly fill the ministerial office. This is God's own witness to his Son. And here John tells us we have the victory over the devil and the world, through faith, for the sake of Christ the Son of God.

20. This witness Christ himself ordains shall ever go forth, and remain, in the Church. To this end Christ sent the Holy Spirit; to this end Christ himself called and gave the Holy Spirit to the apostles and their successors, ministers, preachers and teachers, as Paul tells us (Eph 4, 11-13), who are to exercise the Word, that the Word may resound always and everywhere in the world, reaching to children's children, and on down to future generations. Were the witness not in the Church, the pulpit—in fact, the entire outward administration of the Church—would be useless, for every man could read the Scriptures for himself. But for the sake of the uninstructed masses and the constantly rising young who, as yet in ignorance of the Word, need admonition— for the sake of these, the Spirit must bear public witness or administer the preaching office that they, too, may learn to know the grace of God manifest and given to us through Christ, and that God's wondrous works may be publicly recognized and extolled by us in opposition to the devil and the world.

21. Wherever such witness is borne, there certainly will be some fruit. The witness never fails of effect. Some surely will be reached; some will accept and believe it. Since it is the witness of the Holy Spirit, and the apostle says here, the Spirit beareth witness, he will be effective, producing in us that to which John refers when he says we are children of God, and have the victory and eternal life. So the Word—or the Gospel message accompanied by the witness of the Spirit—and faith are vitally related. In the last analysis they are inseparable. Without faith, preaching will be fruitless; and faith has origin in the Word alone. Therefore, we should gladly hear and handle the Word. Where it is, there is also the Holy Spirit; and where the Spirit is, there must be at least some believers.

Even if you have already heard the Word and obtained faith, it will always continue to strengthen you as you hear it. One knows not at what hour God may touch and illumine his or another's heart. It may be in a time when we least look for it, or in the individual of whom we have least expectation. For the Spirit, as Christ says, breathes where he will, and touches hearts when and where he knows them to be receptive.

22. It is relative to the power and energy wrought by the Holy Spirit that John speaks, indicating the source and means of the power of this witness, when he says of Christ, "This is he that came by water and blood," etc. In this sentence is included all we possess in the kingdom of Christ, and here is extolled the efficacy of our beloved baptism and the blood or sufferings of Christ. Here John unites all the elements in one bundle, so to speak, making a triune witness. They bear joint witness to our faith and confirm it—these three: the water, the blood and the Spirit.

BAPTISM BY WATER AND BLOOD.

23. Christ comes, first, "by water"; that is, by holy baptism. He employs baptism as an outward sign of his work in the new birth of man and in man's sanctification. This water by which Christ comes cannot be a mere, empty sign; for he comes not merely to cleanse or bathe the body with water, but to purify the whole man from all pollution and blemishes inherent in him from Adam. Christ has instituted a cleansing wholly unlike the Mosaic ablutions under the Old Testament dispensation. Moses came with various laws relating to washings and purifications, but they were only cleansings of the body or of the flesh and had daily to be repeated. Now, since these ceremonials contributed nothing to man's purification in God's sight—a thing to be effected by nothing short of a new birth—Christ came with a new order of cleansing, namely, baptism, which is not a mere external ablution from physical impurities, but a washing effective in man's purification from the inward pollution of his old sinful birth and from an evil conscience, and bringing remission of sin and a good conscience

toward God, as Peter says. 1 Pet 3, 21. Paul, also (Tit 3, 5), calls baptism the "washing of regeneration and renewing of the Holy Spirit."

24. Christ first instituted baptism through John the Baptist. To distinguish it from the Mosaic baptism, the old Jewish rite of washings, Christ styles it "a baptism unto repentance and the remission of sins." He designs that therein man shall perceive his inner impurities and know them to be, in God's sight, beyond the power of outward Mosaic ablutions to reach; shall know also that purification of the conscience and remission of sins must be sought and obtained through the power of Christ the Lord, who instituted baptism.

25. Secondly, that this cleansing of sin may be effected in us through baptism, something more than mere water must be present. Mere water could effect no more than do ordinary washings, and no more than Jewish and Turkish baptisms and washings effect. There must be a power and force accompanying the water effective to work inward purification, the purification of the soul. Therefore, John says, Christ came, not by water alone, but also by blood; not the blood of bulls, or of calves, or of goats, those Old Testament sacrifices, but his own blood, as Paul declares. Heb 9, 12. He comes through the preaching office of the New Testament, which is his rule upon earth, imparts to us the effective power of his shed blood, his sacrifice for our sins, and thus applies to us the treasure wherewith he purchased our redemption.

26. Hence there is now in baptism this efficacy of the blood of Christ. That is the true caustic soap which not only removes the uncleanness of the outer man, but penetrates to the inner nature, consuming its impurities and cleansing them away, that the heart may become pure in God's sight. Thus, the blood of Christ is so effectively mingled with the baptismal water that we must not regard it as mere water, but water beautifully dyed with the precious crimson blood of our dear Saviour, Christ. Baptism, then, cannot rightly be regarded a physical cleansing, like the

Mosaic ablutions, or like the cleansing the bathhouse affords; it is a healing baptism, a baptism or washing with blood, instituted by none but Christ, the Son of God, and that through his own death.

27. In the record of Christ's passion, careful note is made of the fact that blood and water flowed immediately from the spear-thrust in Christ's side as he hung upon the cross; it is pointed out as a special miracle. The design there is to teach that Christ's shed blood is not without significance, but stands for a washing or bath whose efficacy is present in the baptism with water; and that from the slain body of Christ issues an unceasing stream of water and blood, flowing on down through the entire Christian Church, wherein we must all be cleansed from our sins. What makes baptism so precious, so holy and essential is the mingling and union of the water with the blood of Christ; to be baptized into Christ with water is really to be washed and cleansed with the blood of Christ.

THE SPIRIT.

28. To these two John adds a third witness, "the Spirit." The Spirit bears witness with the water and the blood; in fact, through these other two he operates. It is the Holy Spirit himself; not as he is invisible up in heaven in his divine essence, but the Spirit who publicly manifests himself through his external office and permits himself to be heard through his Word. As John here asserts, the Spirit bears witness on earth with both the water and the blood.

29. Neither Moses nor any other teacher in his doctrines of personal effort and external purifications, his washings and his sprinklings of the blood of sheep and goats—no such teacher brings and gives the Spirit. With them is no Spirit, no divine power, no regeneration of man. Any unbelieving, spiritless, wicked knave can exercise human effort and practice physical cleansing. But Christ alone brings with him the power and presence of the Holy Spirit, who sanctifies us through the blood and water issuing from the divine side. The Spirit makes us partakers of its cleansing influence through the external office of preaching and

through the sacraments, which are called the office and gifts of the Holy Spirit. Through these the Spirit works in the Christian Church just as he did at first, among the apostles on the Day of Pentecost, and will continue to do in the whole world, unto the last day. Without his ministration we would never obtain, nor know anything about, the saving power of Christ's blood in baptism.

30. Such is the kingdom Christ unceasingly develops through the Christian Church. In him we have eternal purification when to the water is added the Spirit, who through the Word enkindles the heart and purifies it, not with the cleansing qualities of the water alone, but with the healing efficacy of the blood of Christ, whereby sins are exterminated and God's wrath appeased. Although the work of our redemption was wrought once for all in Christ's blood shed upon the cross and is sufficient to cancel the sins of the entire world, yet Christ so instituted it that the same efficacy should remain forever, and be daily distributed and offered to us through the Holy Spirit.

31. This work of the Holy Spirit is neither received nor perceived except through faith in this witness, the preached word of Christ—when with the heart man grasps it and confidently believes it is fulfilled in himself as the Word declares. Thus is the heart really cleansed, the individual born anew, through the Holy Spirit present in the sacred cleansing of water and of the blood of Christ.

Peter (1 Pet 1, 2) speaks of the sanctification of Christians as the "sprinkling of the blood of Jesus Christ" upon us by the Holy Spirit through the public preaching of the Gospel. This sprinkling radically differs from the Jewish sprinkling of water, or of the ashes of a red heifer, or of the blood of a dead lamb or goat, round about the altar and upon the applicants for purification. In the sanctification of Christians, the true consecrated water and the sprinkled blood of Christ are combined; that is, the message concerning the shed blood of our Lord Jesus Christ is "sprinkled," so to speak, upon the soul, and wherever that Word touches the soul it is effective. The blood in this case is not the inef-

fective, lifeless blood of a slain animal, but the potent, living blood of the Son of God. Under its application the soul
cannot remain impure. Christ's blood purifies and heals
from sin and death; it strikes at their very foundation, and
entirely releases us from their power and grants us eternal
life for soul and body.

32. Note, this text is a grand sermon on the witness
Christians have here on earth, which the apostle in concluding explains and extols in beautiful and comforting words.
He calls it a witness that God himself bears to his Son and
that serves to assure us of being the children of God and possessors of eternal life. For he says: "And the witness is
this, that God gave unto us eternal life," etc. This is indeed
an excellent witness, which God himself witnesses and declares to you, and the Holy Spirit brings and reveals to you.
God cannot lie nor deceive, he is the eternal, unchangeable
truth, as already mentioned. If you believe this witness, you
certainly have received and possess it, as John again says:
"He that believeth on the Son of God hath the witness in
him."

FAITH TO BE IMPLICIT.

33. The true, saving doctrine of the Christian faith is
this: There must be witness and confidence of heart so absolute as to leave no room for doubt that, through Christ,
we are God's children and have remision of sins and eternal
life. By way of showing us how God earnestly enjoins such
faith upon us and forbids us to have any doubts on the
subject, John says, "He that believeth not God hath made
him a liar; because he hath not believed in the witness that
God hath borne concerning his Son."

34. This passage annihilates the pernicious, damnable,
diabolical doctrine of the Papists, who shamelessly claim it
is right to doubt and that a Christian should doubt his title to
grace. This doctrine is equivalent to teaching the propriety
of disbelieving the testimony of God. It is charging God
with falsehood, dishonoring and blaspheming the Lord
Christ, openly affronting the Holy Spirit, knowingly plung-
ing people into unpardonable sins and blasphemies and con-

sequently sending them to the devil without hope or comfort of salvation.

35.   Such is the beautiful fruit of papistical doctrine; such is papistical holiness.   This is what they who would be the Christian Church recommend to us.   They would have us, with them, openly and fearlessly charge God with falsehood, trample his Word under foot and worship the devil in his stead.   Further, they require us to praise and honor them and render them thanks, rejoicing to be offered their stipulated terms of friendship.   At the same time they have not in a single instance repented of their abominable idolatry or acknowledged their error; rather they plume themselves on having in their purity taught no wrong.   If we will not accede to their demands, we must be persecuted, put to death, exterminated everywhere in the world with fire and sword.   But the devil and death may accede in our stead.   Let the godly Christian desire and pray that God may hurl such accursed doctrine into the abyss of hell and punish as they deserve the impenitent blasphemers since they will not cease.   And let all the people say, Amen, amen.

36.   Note particularly the consolation of Paul's concluding words.   Here he embraces in one clear word the whole substance of the Gospel when he says: "He that hath the Son hath the life; he that hath not the Son of God hath not the life."   How could he speak plainer and more forcibly?   What is the need of further inquiry and investigation or discussion of this theme?   Do you wish to have assurance of eternal life?   According to this verse, you have it truly if you possess Christ the Son of God; and you have Christ when you believe this witness and preaching as John says, and you should confidently rely upon it in life and in death as the divine, eternal truth.   But if you believe not, you have not life; and all effort and suffering on your part, yes, combined with the effort and suffering of the whole world, will profit you nothing.   You have not the Son of God if you do not believe God's witness of him but charge God with falsehood.

Second Sunday After Easter

Text: 1 Peter 2, 20-25.

20 For what glory is it, if, when ye sin, and are buffeted for it, ye shall take it patiently? but if, when ye do well, and suffer for it, ye shall take it patiently, this is acceptable with God. 21 For hereunto were ye called: because Christ also suffered for you, leaving you an example, that ye should follow his steps: 22 who did no sin, neither was guile found in his mouth: 23 who, when he was reviled, reviled not again; when he suffered, threatened not; but committed himself to him that judgeth righteously: 24 who his own self bare our sins in his body upon the tree, that we, having died unto sins, might live unto righteousness; by whose stripes ye were healed. 25 For ye were going astray like sheep; but are now returned unto the Shepherd and Bishop of your souls.

PATIENCE UNDER TRIBULATION.

1. This epistle lesson is a beautiful selection from apostolic teaching. Doubtless it was intentionally arranged for this Sunday; for Peter's concluding words, "For ye were going astray like sheep; but are now returned unto the Shepherd and Bishop of your souls," accord with the gospel selection about the Good Shepherd. Yet it might also properly serve in part for the text of a sermon on the passion of Christ; for the sufferings of Christ are here presented as an example unto us. In the preceding part of the chapter, Peter taught the Christians how, having obtained faith, they are to exhibit its fruits—good works in the various stations of

248.

life. Particularly does he admonish them to manifest the fruit of patience under crosses and afflictions.

2. When the individual accepts Christ and begins to profess his faith in word and life, invariably—it cannot be otherwise—the world, that eternal enemy of Christ and faithfully-obedient servant of the devil, will be dissatisfied. The world regards it contemptible, disgraceful, to live any life but one pleasing to itself, to do and speak aught but as it desires. Its rage is excited toward the Christian and it proceeds to persecute, to torture, even to murder him when possible. We often hear the wiseacre scoffers say that Christ could have enjoyed peace had he desired to. The same may be said of Christians; they could have peace and pleasure if they would but take advice and conform to the world.

3. What are we to do? It is a fact that to maintain and obey the truth is to stir up wrath and hatred. Even the heathen assert as much. But the fault lies not with the advocate of truth but with its rejecters. Is the truth not to be preached at all? Must we be silent and permit all mankind to go direct to hell? Who could or would heap upon himself the guilt of such negligence? The godly Christian, who looks for eternal life after the present one and who aims to help others to attain unto the same happy goal, assuredly must act the part he professes, must assert his belief and show the world how it travels the broad road to hell and eternal death. And to do so is to antagonize the world and incur the displeasure of the devil.

4. Now, since there is no escaping the fact that he who would confess Christ and make the world better must, in return for his service and benefactions, heap upon himself the enmity of the devil and his adherents, as Peter says— since this is the case, we must remember that it is incumbent upon us to have patience when the world manifests its bitterest, most hateful enmity toward our doctrine and toward our very lives, when it reviles and slanders and persecutes us to the utmost for our principles. Peter here admonishes and persuades Christians unto patience under these circum-

stances, and at the same time seeks to comfort them with tender and impressive words.

5. First, Peter reminds the believers of their calling—of their reason and purpose in embracing Christianity. He says, in effect: "Remember, belief in Christ necessitates confession of him, and the entire Christian Church is numbered in the holy, divine calling that stands for the praise of God and the promotion of his kingdom." An essential feature of this calling is the suffering of evil in return for good. It seems inevitable that Christians be condemned in the eyes of the world and incur its highest displeasures; that they be destined to take up the gauntlet against the devil and the world. It is said (Ps 44, 22): "For thy sake are we killed all the day long; we are accounted as sheep for the slaughter," or for the sacrifice. Sacrificial sheep were kept in an enclosure, not permitted to go to pasture with the others. They were not kept for breeding, but to be daily, one after another, slaughtered.

6. Paul would say: "What will you do, beloved Christians? Will you live in the world and not encounter any persecution because of your good deeds? Will you rage at the wickedness of the world, and in your rage become wicked yourself and commit evil? Understand, you are called to suffer persecutions; they are a consequence of your baptism, your Christianity. For these you renounced the devil and professed Christ. You are baptized unto the suffering of every sort of misfortune, unto the enduring of the world and the devil." You cannot escape the smoke when compelled to live in the inn where the devil is host and the whole house is filled with it. Again, if you would have fire, you must have smoke as a consequence; if you would be a Christian and a child of God, you must endure the resultant evils that befall you.

7. In short, the Christian, because he is a Christian, is subjected to the holy and precious cross. He must suffer at the hands of men and of the devil, who plague and provoke him; outwardly with misery, persecution, poverty and illness, or inwardly—in heart—with their poisonous darts.

The cross is the Christian's sign and watchword in his holy, precious, noble and happy calling unto eternal life. To such a calling must we render full dues and regard as good whatever it brings. And why should we complain? Do not even wicked knaves and opposers of Christians often suffer at the hands of one another what they are not pleased to endure? And every man must frequently suffer injuries and misfortunes relative to body, property, wife and children.

8. Then, if you would be a Christian and live justly in your calling, be not so terribly alarmed, so filled with hostile rage, so extremely impatient, at the torments of the world and the devil. If you are unwilling to suffer and to be reviled and slandered, if you prefer honor and ease, then deny Christ and embrace the delights of the world and the devil. You will not, even then, be wholly free from suffering and sorrow, though it will be your prerogative not to suffer as a Christian and for the sake of Christ. At the same time, you will discover that even though you enjoy only pleasure on earth, it will be but for a brief time and ultimately you will find the bitter end of the pleasure sought.

CHRIST OUR PATTERN.

9. In the second place, by way of rendering more impressive his admonition, Peter holds up the example of our real Master, our Leader and Lord, Christ, who endured persecutions similar to ours, and himself suffered more than any. The apostle refers to him in a truly scriptural way— as of a twin or dual character. He presents him not as an example of a saint in the ordinary sense, but as the real Shepherd and Bishop of our souls, who suffered for us, making sacrifice for our sins in his own body on the cross. In this capacity, he is our treasure, comfort and salvation.

10. The apostle beautifully and strikingly points out the sublime perfections of our Pattern, in his suffering, by way of gently urging us to patience. He presents the chief points of Christ's endurance, examples of real patience; all our sufferings, when compared with those of Christ, are cast into the shade. "The passion of Christ," Peter would say,

"the suffering of the Lord, is a surpassing, a preëminent and sublimely glorious thing, transcending every other instance of suffering; first, because it was for an example to us; second, because he suffered to save us; third, because he suffered innocently in all respects, never having committed any sin." In these three points we must leave to him alone the distinction, humbling ourselves before them; even had we suffered death in its every form, we must cry that all our suffering is nothing in comparison with his.

Even if we could attain to the sublimest, the supreme, the most glorious degree of suffering, it would be but walking in his footprints, following his example; it would be but to fall far short of his suffering. He would stand preeminent—the Master. He would maintain immeasurable superiority and we would still be left to follow as best we could. The extent of his agony, the intensity and bitterness of his sufferings, no one on earth can comprehend. And if it be beyond our comprehension, how much more is it beyond our power to imitate or experience. We may thank God we have it before us for an example to behold and follow. True, we fall far short of perfect following, but we may approach it in proportion to our sufferings, faith and patience; for one may exceed another in these things.

Christ is an example, Peter says, for all saints; not for a certain few. Contrasted with Christ, all saints must with downcast eyes confess: "Intense, bitter, grievous as our sufferings truly are, when the sufferings of Christ our Lord are mentioned we will willingly keep silent; for no human example of suffering will compare with that of Christ."

11. Now, this one fact, that one so exalted as Christ himself, the only and eternal Son of God, has trod the path of suffering before us, enduring unlimited distress, agony transcending the power of humanity to experience—this alone should be enough to admonish and urge anyone to patiently endure affliction. Why, then, should we disciples, we who are so insignificant and inexperienced in comparison with our Master—why should we be at all troubled at any suffering for his sake? especially when all he asks of

us is to follow him, to learn of him and to remain his disciples. Here, mark you, is the example set before the entire
Christian Church, the pattern she is to follow to the extent
of at least walking in Christ's steps, at the same time, however, remembering that her most intense sufferings are
naught in comparison to a single drop of his shed blood, as
we shall hear later.

12. Again, this example assumes its ineffable and inimitable character from the fact that Christ suffered not for himself, nor yet merely as an example, but in our stead. This
act, to say the least, transcends all human ability. No saint
can boast of equaling this example, can say he suffered for
another as Christ suffered for our sins. No, here all boasting is summarily disposed of. In respect to atonement,
Christ left us no example, for none can imitate him in that.
He stands alone there. He alone was called to suffer for all
men; for those individuals now called and holy, and for the
still uncalled and sinners.

13. The atonement is the chief, the most exalted, article
of the Christian doctrine. Faith alone apprehends it as the
highest good, the greatest blessing, of our salvation, and
recognizes that we cannot, by our works or our sufferings,
do or merit anything in atoning for sin. The manner in
which this subject is scripturally presented prohibits us from
adding to it anything of human origin. But so the accursed
popedom has done in the teachings of its pillars and sup-
porters the monks, who regard the sufferings of Christ as
merely an example to us. They pervert and render imma-
terial the fact that he suffered for us; they place the entire
responsibility upon ourselves, as if we, by our own works or
our suffering are to make satisfaction for our sins, to ap-
pease God's wrath and to merit grace. This is a doctrine
not found in the Word of God, but is of their own trivial,
self-selected, self-devised and false human teachings.

14. They have carried their untruthful, worthless inventions to the extent of claiming for the saints not only sufficient acquired merit for their own salvation, but a large
accumulated surplus available for others, which they have

bequeathed to the Pope, thus furnishing him with an abundant treasury. The Pope, through indulgences, is to distribute this excess, these superfluous merits, as he feels disposed, at the same time dipping out for himself and his shorn fat swine the riches of the world; indeed, the ecclesiasts distribute their own merits and works. This is the refined monastic chastity, poverty and rigid obedience of the orders—nothing but shameless falsehood and scandalous vice, practiced under that covering, both privately and publicly, with the exception of a few who were sincere in their desire to be monks, of whom I was one. These falsehoods the orders readily sold to the laity on deathbeds and under other circumstances.

Indeed, wretched mortals who had incurred a death penalty and were about to be publicly executed, they referred not to Christ for comfort, but counseled patience in their own well-deserved suffering and death; as if God would accept their pain as atonement for their sins if only they suffered patiently. Purchasing of merit was the ecclesiasts' chief doctrine, their strongest point. They fearlessly proclaimed it in public, and through its influence erected numerous churches and cloisters and satiated the avarice and cupidity of the Pope. And I too, alas, was one of these knaves until God delivered me. And now, God be praised, I am execrated and condemned by the hellish seat of the Roman dragon with its scales because I assailed this papal doctrine and would not justify it.

15. Oh, the shameful abomination, that in the temple of God and in the Christian Church must be taught and received things which make wholly insignificant the sufferings and death of Christ! Gracious God! what can be said for human merit—for superfluity of human merit—when not one saint on earth has, with all his pains, suffered enough to cancel his own obligations; much less to be entitled to the honor of making his sufferings avail anything before God's judgment-seat, by way of remuneration or satisfaction for the mortal sins of others in the face of divine wrath? Note, Peter says Christ left us an example that we

should follow his steps; which is but concluding that no saint ever wrought or suffered enough to warrant the claim: "I have accomplished the measure—reached the limit; Christ is no more an example and pattern for me." No; the saint ought to be ashamed to boast of his sufferings in comparison to those of Christ, and ought to rejoice in the privilege of being partaker of the divine pain, of sharing it so far as he can, and thus be found in the footsteps of Christ.

16. The theme of Christ's passion, then, must far outrank every other. His sufferings are like pure and precious gold, compared to which ours are as nothing. No one but Christ has suffered for the sins of another. No man has ever paid the price of his own sins, great or small. Even if man's suffering could avail aught for sin, the individual could not go beyond expiating his own sins. But Christ had no need at all to suffer for himself; for, as follows in the text, he had committed no sin. He suffered to leave us an example, but yet also to bring to man the great blessing of being able to say, "My sins and the sins of the whole world were atoned for upon the cross, blotted out, through Christ's death." Peter, Mary, John the Baptist, and every soul born of woman must include himself or herself in this statement, "Christ also suffered for you."

17. In the third place, Christ stands preëminent, above all others, in the affirmation of Peter, quoted from Isaiah 53,9:

"Who did no sin, neither was guile found in his mouth."

18. You may draw your own conclusions as to the eminence of such a one; for certainly there is to be found no other human being who has not at some time sinned in word or deed. "If any man stumbleth not in word, the same is a perfect man," says James 3, 2. But where is this perfect man, and what is his name? It is this Christ, he alone of all, James should have added. For Peter excludes all other individuals, in one class, saying, "Ye were going astray like sheep." And later on (ch. 3, 18) he tells us plainly, "Christ also suffered for sins once, the righteous for the unrighteous." This statement leaves no man innocent of

sin, either in word or deed; and in word and deed is included man's whole life. Speech and action are associated in various Scripture references; as in Psalm 34, 13-14: "Keep thy tongue from evil, and thy lips from speaking guile. Depart from evil, and do good." But in speech is the greatest liability to error. In teaching, counseling, admonishing, consoling and censuring, and in confessing the truth, no one indeed will be found so perfect in his utterances as never to commit a blunder.

19. But Christ is the one perfect example in this respect. It is impossible for saints to attain to his faultlessness. Surely no man—unless he desires to be a liar and a true disciple of the devil instead of a child of God and a faithful Christian—will be presumptuous enough to put himself on an equality with Christ, will dare boast himself without sin in word and act. Christ alone has suffered, the righteous for the unrighteous; that prerogative can honorably and truthfully be ascribed only to Christ the Lord, and is his perpetually. No man is just and innocent in word and act. All must confess their sufferings, of whatever nature, to be the result of their own sins, and well deserved chastisement. For the fact of having escaped the eternal wrath, condemnation and punishment of God, they must thank this just one alone, he who, being himself blameless, voluntarily suffered to make satisfaction for the unrighteous, and appeased God's wrath. The sufferings of all saints, then, must be rated far below those of Christ the Lord. The saints must clothe and adorn themselves with his innocence, and with the entire Christian Church pray, "Forgive us our trespasses"; and they must confess the article, "I believe in the forgiveness of sins."

20. Now, let us sum up the three arguments Peter uses in admonishing Christians to patience in suffering. First: He says, "Hereunto were ye called." Though you do have to suffer much and severely, you have ever before you the example of Christ, to the limit of whose sufferings you can never attain. You dare not boast even if you have suffered everything. Moreover, you are under obligation to suffer

for God's sake. Second: Christ did not suffer for his own sake, nor of necessity; he suffered for your sake, and all from good will toward you. Third: He was wholly innocent—free from sin; internally—in heart—and externally —in word and deed. For where evil dwells in the heart, it cannot long remain concealed. It must manifest itself in words, at least. Christ says (Mt 12, 34), "Out of the abundance of the heart the mouth speaketh."

21. Why, then, should you complain of your suffering or refuse to suffer what your sins really deserve? Indeed, you deserve much more than you receive—even eternal suffering. But God forgives you and remits the eternal punishment for the sake of Christ the Lord, desiring that you patiently endure the lesser suffering for the utter mortification of the sins inherent in your flesh and blood. To make such lot the less grievous to you, Christ has gone before and left you an example of perfect patience under the most intense suffering, an example equaled nowhere in the world. The Supreme Majesty, God's own Son, suffered in the most ignominious manner the extremity of torture, pain and anguish in body and soul, something intolerable to mere human nature; and that innocently, and for us condemned sinners—suffering for the sins of strangers.

"Who, when he was reviled, reviled not again; when he suffered threatened not."

22. To further emphasize and make effectual in us the example of Christ's patience, Peter proceeds to analyze it, to show it in its true colors, to mention the details and make plain how it differs from any other example of suffering. He has told us before that Christ did no sin, neither was guile found in his mouth. Why, then, did the Jews persecute and crucify him—put him to death? Inquire into his entire life history and you will find that no one could justly impeach, nor could convict, him for any sin. He himself appealed to his enemies to prove aught of sin in him. No one could show an injury he had ever done to anyone, or a wrong he had ever taught or practiced. On the contrary, he had gone about to bring to the Jewish nation the grace

and salvation of God. He had revealed God's Word, opened the eyes of the blind, healed the sick, cast out devils, fed great multitudes when hungry and lacking food. In short, in all his life, there was nothing in word or act but truth, goodness, beneficence and a disposition to aid. In return for the good he wrought, he was compelled to receive the ungrateful reward of man's hatred and condemnation. His enemies were moved solely by obdurate, diabolical hatred, and could not cease their persecutions until they brought him to the cross, where he was disgracefully hung up nude between two murderers, being lifted up as unworthy to touch the earth and to live among men.

23. Christ was under no obligation to endure disgrace and ill-treatment. He might have refrained from his benevolent ministrations when he saw the futility of his efforts with the Jews. But he did not so; even in his sufferings upon the cross he charitably prayed for his enemies. He had authority, he had power enough, and he would have been justified in the action, had he revenged himself on his furious enemies, invoked evil upon them, and execrated them as they deserved to be execrated; for they had treated him with gross injustice before all the world, as even the testimony of his betrayer and his judge and all creatures admitted, and had bitterly reviled him when he hung upon the cross. But he did none of these things. He bore with ineffable meekness and patience all the ill-treatment his enemies could heap upon him. Even in his extremity of anguish, he benevolently interceded for them to his Heavenly Father, to which act the prophet Isaiah (ch. 53) offers a tribute of high praise.

24. Notice, we have here in all respects a perfect and inimitable example of patience—patience of the most exalted kind. In this example we may behold as in a glass what we have yet to learn of calm endurance, and thus be impelled to imitate that example in some small measure at least.

25. Not without reason does Peter applaud the fact that when Christ was reviled he reviled not again, and when he suffered he threatened not. Though to endure undeserved

violence and injustice is hard enough, that which more than aught else naturally renders suffering grievous and makes men impatient is to experience the monstrous unfairness of receiving the mean and vexatious reward of ingratitude from individuals who have enjoyed one's favors and greatest benefactions. Base ingratitude is extremely painful for human nature to endure. It makes the heart flutter and the blood boil with a spirit of revenge. When no alternative presents, an outburst of reviling, execration and threatening follows. Flesh and blood has not the power of restraint to enable it to remain calm when evil is returned for favors and benevolence, and to say, "God be thanked."

26. Mark the example of Christ, however, and there learn to censure yourself. Beloved, how can you complain when you see how infinitely greater was the grief and how much more painful the anxiety endured by your beloved Lord and faithful Saviour, the Son of God himself, who yet bore all patiently and submissively and, more than that, prayed for those instrumental in causing that agony? Who with a single drop of Christian blood in his heart would not blush with shame to be guilty of murmuring at his sufferings when, before God, he is so sinful and is deserving of much more affliction? Wicked, unprofitable and condemned servant must he be who does not follow his Lord's example of endurance but presumes to think himself better and nobler than Christ; who with inimical spirit murmurs, complaining of great injustice, when he really deserves affliction, and when he suffers infinitely less than did his dear, righteous, innocent Lord. Beloved, if Christ so suffered in return for the great blessing he conferred, be not too indolent to imitate him in some degree by suffering without anger and reproaches. Less reason have you to be angry and reproachful from the fact that you, too, were one whose sins brought Christ to the cross.

27. But you may say: "What? Did not Christ revile when (Mt 23) he called the scribes and pharisees hypocrites, murderers, serpents, a generation of vipers, and even more severely rebuked them?" I reply: Oh yes, we would

gladly follow Christ's example here; we could cheerfully
revile and accuse. It is much easier than being patient.
We would need no Master to help us in this. But note
what Peter says: When Christ was about to suffer death,
having fulfilled the obligation of his ministry—having proclaimed the truth, rebuked falsehood and been brought to
the cross therefor—and being about to conclude his mission
'by suffering, he reviled not; as a sheep for the slaughter,
he permitted himself to be executed and opened not his
mouth against his calumniators and murderers. See Isaiah
53, 7.

28. It is necessary, then, to make a distinction here. Reviling—or pronouncing execrations and threats—is of two
kinds. In one case it is official and pronounced of God; in
the other, without authority and comes from man. It was
one of the duties of Christ's office on earth, and one now
incumbent upon those called to bear that office after him,
to assert the truth and censure the evil. Such a course is
essential to the honor of God and the salvation of souls;
for if the truth were to be ignored, who would come to God?
Official chastisement is a work of divine, Christian love. It
is a parental duty imposed of God. God has implanted in
the parent nature intense love for the child; at the same
time, if parents are godly and have proper affection for their
children they will not connive at, or let pass unpunished,
the disobedience of the latter. They must chastise, both
with reproof and with keen rods. These are official strokes
—love stripes—enjoined of God, and their infliction is our
duty. They are not injurious, but beneficial. Solomon says
(Prov 13, 24): "He that spareth his rod hateth his son;
but he that loveth him chasteneth him betimes." And Jesus
the son of Sirach says in Ecclesiasticus: "He that loveth
his son causeth him oft to feel the rod, that he may have
joy of him in the end."

29. So everyone may, and should, reprove when official
duty or his neighbor's case requires; it serves to reform
the subject. To quote Solomon again (Prov 27, 6): "Faithful are the wounds of a friend; but the kisses of an enemy

are profuse [deceitful]." Reproofs and stripes prompted by love and a faithful heart are beneficial. On the other hand, an enemy may use fair and flattering words when he has enmity and deceit at heart, preferring to let you go on to ruin rather than by gentle reproof to warn of danger and rescue you from destruction. The faithful, conscientious physician must often, of necessity and with great pain to the patient, amputate a limb in order to save the body.

Paul, too, commands pious bishops to be urgent in season, out of season; to reprove, rebuke, exhort, with all longsuffering. 2 Tim 4, 2; Tit 2, 15. By our silence to commend or to encourage to evil the wrong-doer would not be to manifest one's love to the offender, but rather to give him over wholly to death and the devil.

30. It was this love and sincerity of heart which prompted Christ in his office to censure and rebuke, for which he merited only wrath and hatred; as we say, he sought his stripes. But the duty of his office required such action on his part. His motive was to turn the transgressors from their blindness and malice, and to rescue them from perdition; and he could not be deterred by the consequent persecution, cross and death which awaited. But having fulfilled his official duties, and the hour of his suffering having arrived, he suffered patiently, permitting his enemies to heap upon him all possible evil in return for his manifested love and blessings. Instead of angrily reviling and execrating while, suspended from the cross, he endured the most shameful calumnies, he, with strong cries and with tears, prayed, "Father, forgive them." It was, indeed, a heart of unfathomable love that, in the midst of extreme suffering, had compassion on its persecutors and blessed them in greater measure than parent can bless child or one individual bless another.

31. Observe, then, the distinction between official and unofficial censure and rebuke; the former is prompted by love, and the latter by wrath and hatred. The world, however, is artful and cunning enough when it hears this distinction, to pervert and confuse the two, exercising its own

revenge under the name of official zeal and reproof. For
instance, if a preacher is disposed to act the knave, he can
easily give vent to his personal anger and vengeance in his
pulpit utterances, censuring and rebuking as he pleases, and
then claim it is all in obedience to the demand of office and
for the good of the people.

Again, a judge, a mayor, or other prominent official, desiring revengefully to satisfy a personal grudge, can more
successfully accomplish his object under the title of the
office he bears and the obligations imposed upon him for
the punishment of the wicked than in any other way. This
practice now frequently obtains since the world has learned
to use the Gospel to conceal its malice and knavery, to
adorn it with the name of a divinely appointed office. It
ever uses the name and Word of God to cloak its infamy.
But who is vigilant enough to elude such knavery and to
make the children of the devil honest? Let him who would
be a Christian, then, take heed how he shall answer such
accusation. Assuredly God will not allow himself to be
deceived. He will, in due time, relieve the innocent victim
of injustice, and his punishment will seek out the wicked.
Peter says, further:

"But committed himself to him that judgeth righteously."

32. Who revealed to Peter the nature of Christ's thoughts
upon the cross? The apostle has just been saying that
Christ reviled not nor thought of revenge, but rather manifested love and good-will toward his virulent enemies. How
could Christ approve such malice? Truly he could not en-
dorse it. Nor could he commend his enemies for crucifying
him and puting him to death upon the cross without cause.
No such conclusion may be drawn. The devil and his adherents must not construe the passage to mean license to
heap all manner of torture and distress upon Christ and
his saints as upon those who must not only patiently bear
these things, unmoved by revengeful desires, but must
render gratitude to their persecutors as if their acts were
praiseworthy. No; this can by no means be permitted.

Could I be said to suffer innocently if I am obliged to confess I am well treated? Several times in this epistle Peter admonishes Christians not to suffer as evil-doers, thieves, murderers. But if I suffer innocently and am unjustly treated, I am not to justify the ill-treatment and strengthen the enemy in his sins; for, so doing, I would approve his conduct and assume the guilt attributed. That principle would be pleasing to the Pope and the devil and to tyrants; they would willingly have it obtain. They are not wholly satisfied even to murder the innocent; they would prefer to be justified in their action—to have us confess to wrong-doing. But that is something no Christian heart will do; it may be left to the devil.

33. But the Papists will say: "However, it is written, You must suffer and not revile; you must thank God for persecution and pray for your enemies." That is true; but it is one thing to suffer patiently, the while wishing your enemies well and praying for them, and quite a different thing to justify them in their conduct. I must cease not to confess the truth and maintain my innocence, both in heart and with my lips. But if men will not accept my word, my heart must tell me I have suffered injustice. Rather should I endure ten deaths, could my enemies inflict them, than to condemn myself in violation of conscience. So, when Peter made this little statement about Christ not reviling nor threatening, which was true, he did not mean that Christ justified his persecutors in their treatment of him. But what are we to do? If we do not justify our enemies when they make us suffer, they will do even worse things to us; for they desire the name and the credit, in the eyes of the world, of having done right by us. Yes, as Christ has somewhere said, they would have it thought they do God great service by murdering us. Now, who is to judge and decide the question?

34. Peter declares that Christ committed the matter to him who judges righteously. How should he do otherwise, knowing that his persecutors treated him unjustly and yet maintained the contrary? There was for him no judge on

earth. He was compelled to commit the matter to that righteous judge, his Heavenly Father. Well he knew that such
sins and blasphemies could not go unpunished. No, the
sentence was already passed, the sword sharpened, the
angels given orders, for the overthrow of Jerusalem. Previous to his sufferings, on his way to Jerusalem, as Christ
beheld the city, he announced its coming doom and wept
over it. Therefore, he prays for his enemies, saying: "Dear
Father, I must commit the matter to thee, since they refuse
to hear or to see the wrong they do. Well I know they
are rushing into thy wrath and thy terrible punishment, but
I pray thee to forgive them what they do to me." And so
they would have been forgiven had they afterward repented
at the apostles' preaching, and had they not further sinned
in persecuting God's Word and thus brought upon their
unrepentant selves ultimate punishment.

CHRIST OUR EXAMPLE IN SUFFERING.

35. Observe, as Christ did, so should we conduct ourselves in our sufferings; not approving or assenting to whatever may be heaped upon us, but yet not seeking revenge.
We are to commit the matter to God, who will judge aright.
We cannot maintain our rights before the world; therefore
we must commit our cause to God, who judges righteously
and who will not allow calumniation of his Word and persecution of believers to pass unpunished. We must, however,
pray for our persecutors, that they may be converted and
escape future wrath and punishment; and so we do. If it is
possible for some of the bishops and other Gospel-persecut-
ing tyrants to be converted, we will heartily pray and desire
that their conversion may come to pass. But if it be impossible, as now, alas, is to be feared, since, after having
been much admonished and often prayed for and having
enjoyed the best advantages, they wittingly rage against the
known truth—if so, then we must commit them to God's
judgment. What more can we do?

I am persuaded that the intolerable persecution and calum-
niating of the Gospel prevalent today cannot be permitted
to pass with impunity. It must ultimately meet the com-

ing judgment upon the Papacy and Germany. Of this there can be no doubt. But it is ours to continue preaching, praying, admonishing and beseeching, in the hope of effecting repentance. Then, if our enemies still refuse to turn from their evil ways, if they perish in their impenitence, what can we do but say: "Dear God, we commit the matter to thee. Thou wilt punish them; thou canst, indeed, most terribly."

36. Such, mark you, is the example of Christ, presented to the entire Christian Church—set up as a pattern for her. Hence it is the duty of the Church, as Peter elsewhere tells us, to arm herself with the same mind which was Christ's, to suffer as Christ did and to think: If Christ, my Lord and Leader, has suffered for me with so great meekness and patience, how much more reason have I to submit to suffering! And what can it harm me to suffer when I know it is God's will? Not because the suffering in itself is so perfecting and precious, but for the sake of the dear Saviour who suffered for me. I know, too, that my persecutors thus commit most abominable sins against God and incur his wrath and punishment. Why, then, should I be impatient or desire revenge? I am already too highly honored of God in the fact that my sufferings meet his approbation and that he will perfectly avenge me of mine enemies. What can it advantage me for them to burn eternally in hell? I will rather pray and use my utmost efforts for their conversion. If I fail and they are determined to persist in their course, I must bring the matter home to God—must commit it to him.

> "Who his own self bare our sins in his body upon the tree, that we, having died unto sins, might live unto righteousness."

37. Peter's is the true preaching concerning the passion of Christ. He teaches not only the merit in Christ's sufferings, but introduces both themes—its efficacy and example. Such is Paul's custom, also. In this verse Peter presents Christ's sufferings in the light of a sacrifice for sin. They constitute a work acceptable to God as satisfaction for the

sins of the whole world and effective to reconcile him to
men. So great is God's wrath toward sin that none but that
eternal one, the Son of God, could avert it. He had himself to be the sacrifice, to allow his body to be nailed to the
cross. The cross was the altar whereupon the sacrifice was
consumed—wholly burned—in the fire of his unfathomable
love. He had to be his own high priest in this sacrifice:
for no earthly mortal, all being sinners and unclean, could
offer to God the sacrifice of his beloved and wholly sinless
Son; the boasting of the priests of Antichrist in regard to
their masses, to the contrary notwithstanding. Now, by
the single sacrifice of God's Son, our sins are remitted and
we obtain grace and forgiveness; and this fact can be
grasped in no other way than through faith.

38. Peter mentions the ultimate object of the divine sacrifice made for us, what it accomplished in us, the fruit
Christ's passion shall yield; for he would not have the
Christian Church overlook that point, or neglect to preach
it. Christ, he tells us, took upon himself our sins, suffering the penalty. Therefore, Christ alone is entitled to be
called a sacrifice for all our sins. It was not designed, however, that after the sacrifice we should remain as before; on
the contrary, the purpose was ultimately to work in us
freedom from sins, to have us live no longer unto sin but
unto righteousness. Now, if in Christ our sins are sacrificed, they are put to death, blotted out; for to sacrifice
means to slay, to kill. Under the Old Testament dispensation, all sacrifices had to be presented to God slain. Now,
if our sins are put to death, it is not meant that we are to
live in them.

39. Therefore, the saving doctrine of remission of sins
and of Christ's grace cannot be so construed as to admit
of our continuing in the old life and following our own desires. According to Paul (Rom 6, 1-8), enjoying grace
and remission of sins does not give license to live in sin.
How shall we who are dead to sin live any longer therein?
The very fact that we may be reckoned dead unto sins
means they may no longer live and reign in us. In Christ's

holy body were they throttled and slain expressly that they might also be slain in us.

40.   Be careful, then, what you believe and how you live, that the efficacy of Christ's sufferings may be manifestly fulfilled in you. If, through faith, you have rightly apprehended his sacrifice, its virtue will be indicated in the subduing and mortifying of your sins, even as they are already slain and dead through his death on the cross. But if you continue to live in sins, you cannot say they are dead in you. You but deceive yourself, and your own evidence is false when you boast of Christ in whom all sins are put to death, if sin remains vigorous in you. We naturally conclude it is inconsistent for sin to be dead in us and yet alive; for us to be free from sin and yet captive or fast therein. This fact has already been sufficiently pointed out.

41.   It is ours, Peter says, not only to believe that Christ has, through the sacrifice of his own body, put to death sin and liberated us therefrom—a thing the combined sacrifices of all mortal bodies could never have effected—but, sin being put to death by him, to endeavor to become ever more and more free from sin's sway in our bodies, and to live henceforth unto righteousness, until we shall be completely and finally released from sin through death. Therefore, if before you believed on Christ you were an adulterer, a miser, a coveter, a maligner, you ought now to regard all these sins as dead, throttled through Christ; the benefit is yours through faith in his sacrifice, and your sins should henceforth cease to reign in you. If you have not so received the sacrifice, you cannot boast of Christ and faith. Though Christ has died for you, though your sins have been put upon him and reckoned dead, still you are not rid of those sins if you do not desire to be, if you do not, through faith, apprehend Christ and his blessing, nor in your life and conduct follow his example.

42.   Now you will say: "But you teach that we are all sinners, that there is not even a saint on earth without sin. And surely we must confess the article, 'I believe in the remission of sins,' and must pray, 'Forgive us our debts.'" I

LUTHER'S EPISTLE SERMONS.

reply, most assuredly you never will attain sinless perfection here on earth; if such were the case you would have no further need for faith and Christ. At the same time, it is not designed that you should continue as you were before obtaining remission of sins through faith. I speak of known sins wittingly persisted in, in spite of the rebuke and condemnation of conscience. These should be dead in you; in other words, they are not to rule you, but you are to rule them, to resist them, to undertake their mortification. And if occasionally you fail, if you stumble, you should immediately rise again, embrace forgiveness and renew your endeavor to mortify your sins.

"By whose stripes ye were healed."

43. It seems as if Peter could not sufficiently exalt and make impressive Christ's sufferings. He brings in nearly the entire Fifty-third chapter of Isaiah in the attempt. Note how, in regard to the efficacy of works, he always significantly introduces the two themes at the same time—how he carefully distinguishes between performing human works in obedience to Christ's example, and receiving by faith the merit of Christ's work. First, we have, "Who his own self bare our sins in his body upon the tree . . . by whose stripes ye were healed." This is the vital part in our salvation. Christ alone could fully accomplish the work. This doctrine must be taught in its purity and simplicity, and must so be believed, in opposition to the devil and his factions. Only so can we maintain the honor and the office of Christ wherein is anchored our salvation. But the second part of the doctrine must not be overlooked. There are false Christians who accept only the first part and make no effort to reform themselves; but, being liberated from our sins and in a state of salvation, we may not again defile ourselves therewith. Where these two principals of the Christian doctrine are not maintained in their proper relation, injury must result to the truth in two respects: they who are occupied solely with their own works corrupt the true doctrine of faith; they who neglect to follow the example of Christ retard the efficacy and fruit of that faith.

"For ye were going astray like sheep."

44. Here Peter bluntly and clearly points out the fact I have stated, that liberation from sin and death was effected not by our works and merits, but by Christ's wounds and death alone. Forgiveness cost you nothing, Peter teaches; no blood, no wounds. You were powerless in this direction. You were but miserable, erring, lost sheep, separated from God, condemned to hell and unable to council or help yourselves. In just such condition are all they who are out of Christ. As Isaiah the prophet says more plainly in the chapter from which these words are taken (verse 6): "All we like sheep have gone astray; we have turned every one to his own way." That is, whatever our lives, whatever our intent, we but turned farther away from God. As it is written (Ps 14, 3): "They are all gone aside; they are together become filthy; there is none that doeth good, no, not one."

45. That men are prone to go astray like sheep is clearly exhibited in their conduct; history proves it. It has ever been the case that when mankind was divided into various idolatries or false services of God, into superstitions numerous and varied, even when God's people thought to have attained the perfection of holiness—then one ran here and another there, ever seeking and seeking to come upon the road to heaven but getting farther and farther from it. It was exactly the case of the sheep straying from the flock and lost to the shepherd: the farther it runs and the more it follows the voice of strangers, the farther astray it goes. It continues to wander and to flee until it finally perishes, unless it hears again the voice of the shepherd. Let no one, then, dare boast of having himself found the right way to heaven, of having merited God's grace and the remission of sins by his own manner of life. All men must confess the truth of Scripture testimony that we were but erring sheep, fleeing ever farther from our Shepherd and Saviour, until he turned us back to himself.

"But are now returned unto the Shepherd and Bishop of your souls."

46. You have now heard the voice of your Shepherd,

who has brought you back to himself, from your erring and idolatous ways. It was not your own effort that effected your return; it was accomplished at the cost of your Shepherd's wounds and shed blood. Be careful, then, Peter would say, to live not like erring and lost sheep; but, being converted—turned back—follow your beloved Saviour. In him you have a godly Shepherd who faithfully pastures and cares for you; and also a loyal Bishop who ever watches over and guards you, not permitting you to stray.

47. Immeasurably gracious and comforting are these words. But the meaning of the word "bishop" has been miserably obscured and perverted by our idolatrous priests and episcopal frauds. Likewise have they perverted and corrupted the terms "ecclesiasts," "Church," "divine service," "priest," etc., by their antichristian rule. Only those have right to the name "ecclesiast" who have been redeemed from their sins through Christ's wounds, and who live holy lives. But the Papists have taken the name away from true Christians and applied it to the Pope's besmeared, and shaven-headed ones. Again, when we hear the word "bishop" we think only of great, pointed caps and of silver staves. As if it were sufficient to place in the Church such masks, such carved and hewn idols! For they are nothing better; in fact, they do more harm.

According to the Scriptures, a true bishop is an overseer, a guardian, a watchman. He is like unto the householder, the warder of the city, or any judicial officer or regent who exercises constant oversight of state or municipal affairs. Formerly there were bishops in each parish, deriving their name from the fact that their office required oversight of the Church and the guarding against the devil, against false doctrines and all manner of offenses. Paul, too (Acts 20, 28), reminds the bishops of their office, saying: "Take heed unto yourselves, and to all the flock, in which the Holy Spirit hath made you bishops [overseers]." And overseers should bishops still be, as in fact all godly preachers and carers for souls are. But in all Popedom the office now is but a mere name, to the sin and shame of the entire Christian Church.

48. Now, Christ our Lord is that faithful Guardian, that true Bishop, who above all others is entitled to the name (with him office and name are identical), and who bears it with due honor, to our eternal happiness. For, standing at the right hand of God and showing his wounds, he unceasingly intercedes for us before the Father; and moreover, on earth he rules, sustains, nourishes and protects, through his Word, his sacraments and the efficacy of the Holy Spirit, the little flock that believe in him. Were he not present with and watching over us here, the devil would long ago have overthrown and destroyed us, and also the Word of God and the name of Christ. And such is the case when God in wrath turns away his eyes from the world to punish its ingratitude. Then immediately everything falls into the devil's power. Therefore, pure doctrine, faith, confession and the use of the sacraments are dependent for their perpetuity solely upon the vigilant guardianship of our beloved Shepherd and Bishop.

49. Comforting, indeed, is it to have in Christ a priest so faithful and righteous; though, alas, the worthy name of "priest" also has been subjected to shame and contempt because of the Pope's disgraceful, shaven, shallow-headed occupants of the office. Comforting, indeed, it is to be the happy lambs who have a welcome refuge in the Shepherd and find in him joy and comfort in every time of need, assured that his perfect faithfulness cares for and protects us from the devil and the gates of hell. Relative to this subject, the entire Twenty-third Psalm is a beautiful and joyous song, of which the refrain is, "The Lord is my Shepherd."

Third Sunday After Easter

Text, First Peter 2, 11-20.

"11 Beloved, I beseech you as sojourners and pilgrims, to abstain from fleshly lusts, which war against the soul; 12 having your behavior seemly among the Gentiles; that, wherein they speak against you as evildoers, they may by your good works, which they behold, glorify God in the day of visitation.

"13 Be subject to every ordinance of man for the Lord's sake: whether to the king, as supreme; 14 or unto governors, as sent by him for vengeance on evildoers and for praise to them that do well. 15 For so is the will of God, that by well-doing ye should put to silence the ignorance of foolish men: 16 as free, and not using your freedom for a cloak of wickedness, but as bondservants of God. 17 Honor all men. Love the brotherhood. Fear God. Honor the king.

"18 Servants, be in subjection to your masters with all fear; not only to the good and gentle, but also to the froward. 19 For this is acceptable, if for conscience toward God a man endureth griefs, suffering wrongfully. 20 For what glory is it, if, when ye sin, and are buffeted for it, ye shall take it patiently? but if, when ye do well, and suffer for it, ye shall take it patiently, this is acceptable with God."

OUR CHRISTIAN DUTIES.

1. This epistle selection, too, is an admonition to good works, or the fruits of faith. It touches upon nearly every condition of life, teaching how each individual should live and conduct himself. But first, Peter admonishes Christians in general that in their intercourse with gentiles, or

272

the unbelieving world, they give no real occasion for censure or reproach concerning their conduct. The admonition seems to hinge upon the fact that Christians, as the apostle reminds them in the first and second chapters, have been called to a lively, a never-dying, hope of an imperishable inheritance in heaven, and of eternal joy and salvation; that they are now redeemed, having obtained remission of sins through the precious blood of Christ; and again, that they are become a holy nation and royal priesthood, to show forth and magnify the grace of God, they who in time past were not God's people and had not obtained grace. "But now," Peter would say, "you have obtained grace through the divine calling of Christ, through the suffering of your Lord. Live, then, as a holy people of God and citizens of heaven."

2. We have already heard that in the Christian life are two essential principles, two principles upon which Christian teachers may lay emphasis. First, faith in the fact that through Christ's blood we are released from sin and have forgiveness; second, being forgiven, our natures are to be changed and we are to walk in newness of life. In baptism, when we first believe, we obtain not only remission of sins whereby we are of grace made children of God, but also the power to purge out, to mortify, the remaining sins. Our transgressions are not forgiven, Paul says (Rom 1, 6), with the privilege of continuing in them, as the insolent rejecters of grace imagine. It is this way: Our sins being blotted out through the blood of Christ, we need not to make remuneration or render satisfaction for them; we are children of grace and enjoy forgiveness. Nevertheless, inherent sin is not entirely purged out, or mortified.

REMISSION AND MORTIFICATION DEFINED.

3. There is difference between remission of sins and mortification of them. The distinction should be made clear for the sake of combating those who confound and pervert the two principles by their false doctrines. In regard to remission, the Pope and many others have taught that forgiveness of sins is obtained through the foolishness of men's own self-elected works, the satisfactions of their own devis-

ing. This error has ever prevailed in the world. Cain was
the first to make it, and it will continue to the end. And
where this error is refuted, false teachers are found who, on
the other hand, accept and boast of the doctrine of grace
without enjoying its happy results. They proceed as if mere
forgiveness were enough, and without further effect than
averting punishment; as if it leaves us where we were before, not ameliorating in any wise our moral condition; and
as if no more is to be known about Christ and the Gospel.

Therefore, they who claim to be Christians must learn
that, having obtained forgiveness without merit on their
part, they should henceforth give no place to sins, but rather
resist their former evil lusts and avoid and flee from the
fruits and works thereof. Such is the substance of this lesson.

4. But note from the apostle's words how his view has
changed since the time when, as a fisherman of Bethsaida,
he went about with the Lord previous to the Lord's death
and resurrection. At that time Peter and the other apostles,
in fact the entire Jewish nation, had no other conception of
Christ's kingdom—or the kingdom of God—than as an earthly one wherein they should know only happiness, figuring
as wealthy farmers, citizens, noblemen, counts and lords.
The sum of the world's goods should be theirs, and all the
gentiles their vassals. They were to be thenceforth undisturbed by enemies, wars, famine or misfortune, and to enjoy
the extremity of peace, leisure and happiness under their
supreme King, the Messiah. Such were their hopes, even
their expectations. With these pleasing fancies were their
minds filled. And just so today are the Jews full and
drunken with their visionary dreams.

THE NATURE OF CHRIST'S KINGDOM.

5. Observe here, however, Peter teaches that the lot of
the sharer in Christ's kingdom is quite the reverse of what
he once imagined. "O beloved Christians," he would say,
"who are called and baptized into the royal and priestly
kingdom of Christ, I have now to tell you things quite different from the ideas and dreams you and I used to enter-

tain. We are, it is true, citizens, counts and lords in the kingdom where Christ reigns supreme over all earthly kings and lords, and where is only eternal riches, peace and happiness in every form; but the life of that kingdom is unlike that of earthly kings and dominions. You are not, be it known, lords and noblemen in a worldly sense; neither is Christ a king as the world regards kingliness, and the kingdom of the world is not in harmony with his. Know, then, you must regard yourselves strangers and pilgrims in the kingdom of the world.

"Therefore, I admonish you that, having now become Christians—brothers in the eternal heavenly kingdom—your manner of life should be such as becomes them who are no longer of a worldly kingdom. Regard this earthly life only as the traveler or pilgrim regards the country wherein he journeys, the inn where he procures a night's lodging. He does not expect to remain in the city, to be mayor or even a citizen. He finds there his food, but his thoughts are cast beyond its gates, to the place where home is. So, Peter says, must you look upon your earthly course. You did not become Christians with the prospect of reigning here on earth, as the Jews fancy they shall reign and be established. The dwelling-place, the citizenship and the authority of Christians are to be found in another direction, not in this world. Therefore, think of yourselves as pilgrims on earth, directing your attention toward other possessions and another country, wherein you shall be lords forever, and where no discord nor misfortune such as you must endure in this earthly harbor shall ever enter."

CHRISTIAN USE OF THIS LIFE.

6. But how is indifference to this life to be accomplished? Peter goes on to say: "Be subject to every ordinance of man . . . whether to the king . . . or unto governors"; again, "Servants, be in subjection to your masters . . . also to the froward." How is it consistent with royal citizenship in a celestial country to be a pilgrim on earth? How can we live here with wives and children, houses and lands, and being citizens under a temporal gov-

ernment, and yet not be at home? There is a distinction here which, as before said, was at first difficult for the beloved apostles themselves to understand. But to Christians, especially those of today, it should be clear. Christ and the apostles do not, in this teaching, design the rejection of external government and human authority—what Peter here terms ordinances of men. No, they permit these to remain as they are; moreover, they enjoin us to submit to and make use of them.

7. This is the difference to be kept in mind: We are to conduct ourselves in our earthly stations and occupations as not regarding this life our true kingdom and best good. And we are not to think the life beyond holds nothing more nor better than what we possess here, as do the Jews and the Turks. Although they believe in the resurrection of the dead, they carnally imagine the future life will be like the present except for its perfect peace and happiness, its freedom from misfortune, persecution and all ills. It is the prerogative of the Pope and his holy epicures to believe nothing in any respect.

Every Christian, be he lord or servant, prince or subject, should conduct himself as befits his station, using in trust whatever God has given him—dominion and subjects, house and home, wife and children, money and property, meat and drink. He is to regard himself solely as a guest of earth, as one eating his morsel of bread or taking his lunch in an inn; he must conduct himself in this earthly harbor as a pious guest. Thus may he actually be a king reigning with fidelity, or a lord faithful to his office, and at the same time declare: "I count nothing on this life. I do not expect to remain here. This is but a strange country to me. True, I am seated in the uppermost place at table in this inn; but the occupant of the lowest seat has just as much as I, here or yonder. For we are alike guests. But he who assigned my duty, whose command I execute, gave me orders to conduct myself piously and honorably in this inn, as becomes a guest."

8. So should Christians in all stations of life—lords and

ladies, servants and maids—conduct themselves as guests of earth. Let them, in that capacity, eat and drink, make use of clothing and shoes, houses and lands, as long as God wills, yet be prepared to take up their journey when these things pass, and to move on out of life as the guest moves on out of the house or the city which is not his home. Let them conduct themselves as does the guest, with civility toward those with whom they come in contact, not infringing on the rights of any. For a visitor may not unrestrainedly follow his own pleasure and inclinations in the house of a stranger. The saying is: "If you would be a guest, you must behave civilly; otherwise you may promptly be shown the door or the dungeon."

9. Christians should be aware of their citizenship in a better country, that they may rightly adapt themselves to this world. Let them not occupy the present life as if intending to remain in it; nor as do the monks, who flee responsibility, avoiding civil office and trying to run out of the world. For Peter says rather that we are not to escape our fellows and live each for himself, but to remain in our several conditions in life, united with other mortals as God has bound us, and serving one another. At the same time, we are to regard this life as a journey through a country where we have no citizenship—where we are not at home; to think of ourselves as travelers or pilgrims occupying for a night the same inn, eating and drinking there and then leaving the place.

10. Let not the occupants of the humbler stations—servants and subjects—grumble: "Why should I vex myself with unpleasant household tasks, with farm work or heavy labor? This life is not my home anyway, and I may as well have it better. Therefore, I will abandon my station and enjoy myself; the monks and priests have, in their stations, withdrawn themselves from the world and yet drunk deeply, satisfying fleshly lusts." No, this is not the right way. If you are unwilling to put up with your lot, as the guest in a tavern and among strangers must do, you also may not eat and drink.

Similarly, they who are favored with loftier positions in life may not, upon this authority, abandon themselves to the idea of living in the sheer idleness and lustful pleasure their more favored station permits, as if they were to be here always. Let them reason thus: "This life, it is true, is transitory—a voyage, a pilgrimage, leading to our actual fatherland. But since it is God's will that everyone should serve his fellows here in his respective station, in the office committed to him, we will do whatever is enjoined upon us. We will serve our subjects, our neighbors, our wives and children so long as we can; we would not relax our service even if we knew we had to depart this very hour and leave all earthly things. For, God be praised, had we to die now we would know where we belong, where our home is. While we are here, however, on the way, it is ours to fulfill the obligations of our earthly citizenship. Therefore, we will live with our fellows in obedience to the law of our abiding-place, even unto the hour wherein we must cross the threshold outward, that we may depart in honor, leaving no occasion for complaint.

11. Thus, mark you, should every Christian conduct himself here on earth, according to Peter. In the first place, he should know where is his real home, his fatherland. We learn this through faith in Christ, whereby we become children of God, heirs of eternal life, citizens of heaven. Accordingly, we sing: "Now we pray thee, Holy Spirit, for true faith," etc., when we depart home from this wretchedness. This sentiment accords beautifully with the text here where Peter calls us "sojourners and pilgrims"—wayfarers in earthly wretchedness, desiring home and casting our thoughts beyond the gates of our sojourning-place. Second, though we must suffer this wretched condition in a foreign land, we are under obligation to render every honor to the host and to respect the inn, making the best of whatever may befall us.

12. The prophet Jeremiah found it necessary to give admonition of this sort to his wretched Jewish countrymen in Babylon who longed unspeakably to be home again and al-

most despaired because of having so long to suffer misery among strangers when many of their brethren were at home. Other prophets had encouraged them with the promise of soon being returned. Consequently many of them ceased to till the land and neglected to provide for a livelihood. To these Jeremiah writes (ch. 29, 10): "Ye must have patience, for ye are not so soon to return—not till seventy years be accomplished." Meanwhile, though in wretchedness and captivity, they were to do as he bids in verses 5-7: "Build ye houses, and dwell in them; and plant gardens, and eat the fruit of them. Take ye wives, and beget sons and daughters; and take wives for your sons, and give your daughters to husbands, that they may bear sons and daughters: and multiply ye there, and be not diminished. And seek the peace of the city whither I have caused you to be carried away captive, and pray unto Jehovah for it; for in the peace thereof shall ye have peace."

That there in their misery they should build houses and make themselves citizens of Babylon, should marry and rear children—yes, give their children in marriage—as if they were to remain there permanently—this injunction of the prophet was altogether disagreeable and annoying to them. And still more offensive was the command to pray for the city and kingdom wherein they were captives. Much rather would they have prayed for liberation; for, influenced by the other prophets, they hoped to return home the following year.

13. Now, how was it with them? The godly, faithful ones had reason to hope and trust in release and a return to their own kingdom. Surely there was no pleasure, no joy, for them in their present miserable condition, as in Psalm 137 they testify and complain by the rivers of Babylon. There they cried and wept and had not an hour of enjoyment when they thought of home. The long seventy years their hearts continually stood at the gate ready to depart, so that they had no inclination whatever to build houses, to cultivate farms, to make gardens, to take wives and rear children. Nevertheless, the prophet bids them meet all the

requirements of citizens of that country; and more than that, to pray for their hosts in the same spirit in which they would pray for their neighbors and fellow-citizens, asking God for peace and prosperity upon the city.

CHRISTIANS SUBJECTS OF TWO KINGDOMS.

14. So, too, Christians are subjects of two kingdoms— they have experience of two kinds of life. Here on earth where the world has its home and its heavenly kingdom, we surely are not citizens. According to Paul (Phil 3, 20), "our conversation"—our citizenship—"is with Christ in heaven"; that is, in yonder life, the life we await. As the Jews hoped to be released from Babylon, we hope to be released from this present life and to go where we shall be lordly citizens forever. But being obliged to continue in this wretched state—our Babylon—so long as God wills, we should do as the Jews were commanded to do—mingle with other mortals, eat and drink, make homes, till the soil, fill civil offices and show good will toward our fellows, even praying for them, until the hour arrives for us to depart unto our home.

15. He who is guided by these facts, who comprehends the distinction between the kingdom of heaven and the kingdom of the world, will know how to resist successfully all classes of fanatics. For these latter paint this life in a terrible aspect. They want to run out of the world entirely, and are unwilling to associate with anyone; or they proceed to disturb civil regulations and to overthrow all order; or again, as with the Pope, they interfere in secular rule, desiring temporal authority, wholly under the name and color of Christianity.

Having as Christians forgiveness of sins, and being now people of God, children of his kingdom, citizens no longer of Babylon but of heaven, let us know that during the period of our sojourn here among strangers, it is ours to live righteously, honorably and chastely, to further civil and domestic peace and to lend counsel and aid to benefit even the wicked and ungrateful, meanwhile constantly striving after our inheritance and keeping in mind the kingdom whither we are bound.

16. In short, a Christian must be one who, as Paul says (1 Cor 7, 29-31), uses this world as not abusing it, who buys and possesses as though he possessed not, who has wife and children as though he had them not and who builds as though not building. How is it possible to reconcile these seeming inconsistencies? By making the Christian faith distinct from the faith of the Jews and Turks—yes, of the Papists even: by accepting the fact that the Christian's attitude toward this earthly life is the attitude of the guest; that in such capacity is he to build, to buy, to have dealings and hold intercourse with his fellows, to join them in all temporal affairs—a guest who respects his host's wishes, the laws of the realm and of the city and the customs of the inn, but at the same time the Christian refrains from attesting his satisfaction with this life as if he intended to remain here and hoped for nothing better. Thus will the Christian pass through every temporal event in the right way— having every possession as though not having it, using and yet not cleaving to it; not so occupied with the temporal as to lose the eternal, but leaving behind—forgetting—the former while striving after the latter as the goal set before him.

17. Therefore, they who presume to run out of the world by going into the desert or the wilderness; who, unwilling to occupy the inn but finding it indispensable nevertheless, must become their own hosts—these are great and unreasonable fools. Surely they must eat and drink and have clothing and shelter. With these things they cannot dispense, even if they can withdraw from all society. Nor is their action forsaking and fleeing the world, as they imagine it to be. Whatever your station and condition, whatever your occupation in life, of necessity you must be somewhere on earth while mortal life is yours. Nor has God separated you from men; he has placed you in society. Each individual is created and born for the sake of other individuals. But observe, wherever you are and whatever your station, you are, I say, to flee the world.

HOW TO ESCAPE THE WORLD.

18. But how are we to flee the world? Not by donning

caps and creeping into a corner or going into the wilderness.
You cannot so escape the devil and sin. Satan will as easily
find you in the wilderness in a gray cap as he will in the
market in a red coat. It is the heart which must flee, and
that by keeping itself "unspotted from the world," as James
1, 27 says. In other words, you must not cling to temporal
things, but be guided by the doctrine of faith in Christ, and
await the eternal, heavenly inheritance; and in that faith
and that hope are you to execute the trust and work committed to you here, declaring the while: "That which I do
here is not the chief good, the thing of real value, for which
I live; though such is the case with the world, the Jews, the
Turks and the Papists. I hold this temporal life as a tavern,
valuing it no more than the guest values the inn where he
enjoys food and lodging, while heart and mind turn ever
to his own home."

What tolerance would there be for one foolish enough to
declare: "I will not eat nor drink here. I will behave
peculiarly, smashing windows and turning things upside
down, for this is not my abiding-place"? For the very purpose of advancing himself on his journey, the traveler should
make use of the inn, accepting whatever is offered.

19. Likewise should Christians use the world, constantly
casting their thoughts beyond this life, notwithstanding
they have here house and home, wife and children. These
are for the present life only, yet the Christian owes them
due consideration, the while he asserts: "Today we are
here, tomorrow elsewhere. Now we avail ourselves of this
inn, the next day of another. We do not expect to remain
here."

Relative to this subject, Peter in his beautiful Pentecostal
sermon says concerning David, who nevertheless was a holy
king, that he did not ascend into the heavens, but, having
fulfilled the will of God, fell asleep. Peter, so far from
being willing to disparage David's office and rule, to criticise him therein for wrong-doing, rather magnifies it in
glowing terms. David was a king, and cast not aside his
crown; no, he retained his royal glory. He held his office

as a God-intrusted one, in the execution whereof he served God. Similarly should the righteous ruler do—in fact, all men in their respective offices and stations. Let them remember they are not placed where they are to choose their own pleasure, but solely for the service of God. Such is their duty so long as they are here—transients, like the stranger at the inn with other guests, who conducts himself with respect to the needs and the pleasure of his fellows, doing as they do, and in case of danger and necessity uniting with them in the effort to help and protect.

20. King David did not regard his kingdom and his God-bestowed blessings as his real glory, but as his office, his opportunities for service in this earthly pilgrimage. In it all he remains a guest, expecting to leave this tarrying-place for a certain abode. Hence he says (Ps 39, 12): "I am a stranger with thee, a sojourner, as all my fathers were." How is that? Has a king of David's glorious rank occasion to speak thus? Is he a guest who occupies a royal throne, who is lord of landed estate and of more than twelve hundred thousand people according to his own calculation? This is David's meaning: In his kingdom he serves God as a transient here on earth, and set apart by God for that purpose; but at the same time as a citizen of God's kingdom in another life, another existence, which he regards more glorious than earthly glory, and as affording something better than a temporal crown.

REASONS TO ABSTAIN FROM CARNAL LUST.

21. Such is Peter's teaching. He admonishes Christians to Christlike lives and works in view of the fact that they are called to great glory, having become through Christ a royal priesthood, a people of God and citizens of heaven. He would have them occupy this temporal world as guests, striving after another and eternal kingdom; that is, to abstain from all carnal lusts and maintain a blameless walk, a life of good works. The apostle assigns two reasons for such self-denial: First, that we may not, through carnal, lustful habits, lose the spiritual and eternal; second, that God's name and the glory we have in Christ may not be

slandered among our heathen adversaries, but rather, because of our good works, honored. These are the chief
reasons for doing good works. They ought most forcibly to
urge us to the performance of our duties.

22. Peter admonishes, first, to "abstain from fleshly lusts,
which war against the soul." He implies that if we do not
resist carnal inclinations, but rather follow them, we shall
lose our priceless eternal inheritance. To be a stranger on
earth, striving after another and better life, is inconsistent
with living in fleshly lusts as if one's sole intent was to remain in the world forever. If you would have the things
of one life, Peter says, you must forsake the things of the
other. If you forget your fatherland and lie drunken with
this carnal life, as does the heathen world in living in unbelief and without hope of eternal life, you will never reach
yonder existence; for so you reject it.

It is necessary to strive if we are to withstand the lusts
of the flesh; for these, Peter says, war against the soul—
against faith and the good conscience in man. If lust tri-
umphs, our hold on the Spirit and on faith is lost. Now, if
you would not be defeated, you must valiantly contend
against carnal inclinations, being careful to overcome them
and to maintain your spiritual, eternal good. In this instance, our own welfare demands the conquest.

23. In the second place, God's honor calls for it. God's
honor here on earth is affected by our manner of life. We
are to avoid giving occasion for our enemies to open their
mouths in calumniation of God's name and his Word.
Rather must we magnify the name of God by our confession
and general conduct, and thus win others, who shall with us
confess and honor him. Christ commands (Mt 5, 16):
"Even so let your light shine before men; that they may
see your good works, and glorify your Father who is in
heaven."

24. Peter proceeds to enumerate certain good works appropriate to Christians in all stations of life, particularly
those Christians under authority, or in a state of servitude—
—men-servants and maid-servants. In the apostle's day,

Christians had to submit to heathen authority—to serve unbelieving masters. Peter admonishes Christians to glorify God by their conduct, patiently bearing the violence and injustice offered, and forbearing to return evil; as we heard in the epistle lesson for the preceding Sunday which follows today's text. But to take up all the good works Peter enumerates here would require too much time at present.

Third Sunday After Easter

Second Sermon.

Text: First Corinthians 15, 20-28.

20 But now hath Christ been raised from the dead, the firstfruits of them that are asleep. 21 For since by man came death, by man came also the resurrection of the dead. 22 For as in Adam all die, so also in Christ shall all be made alive. 23 But each in his own order: Christ the firstfruits; then they that are Christ's, at his coming. 24 Then cometh the end, when he shall deliver up the kingdom to God, even the Father; when he shall have abolished all rule and all authority and power. 25 For he must reign, till he hath put all his enemies under his feet. 26 The last enemy that shall be abolished is death. 27 For, He put all things in subjection under his feet. But when he saith, All things are put in subjection, it is evident that he is excepted who did subject all things unto him. 28 And when all things have been subjected unto him, then shall the Son also himself be subjected to him that did subject all things unto him, that God may be all in all.

We have no desire to reject the Sunday epistle readings in common use up to this time, particularly as some of them are excellent and profitable; nevertheless, a different order and selection might well have been made. For portions have been taken from James for the two Sundays following, the intent of the compilers having been to choose something from each of the apostles, among whom they regarded James one of the chief. These selections, however, seem not to have been written by an apostle; they do not at all compare with the selections from the other apostles. It were better for the instruction and comfort of the people, and as befitting this season, to handle the article of the resurrection—concerning the resurrection of both Christ and ourselves, or of all the dead—between Easter and Pentecost. It seems appropriate so to do, making selections from the preaching of the apostles; for instance, the entire fifteenth chapter of Paul's first epistle to the Corinthians, which treats throughout of the resurrection of the dead. Therefore, we shall arrange this chapter to the present and following Sundays. It is our intent to so use it hereafter, and they who feel disposed may adopt it likewise. But it is not our purpose in so doing to restrict those who prefer the old arrangement. The entire fifteenth chapter, however, being amply explained in special sermons, we would advise everyone to read those expositions.

Fourth Sunday After Easter

Text: First Corinthians 15, 35-50.

35 But some one will say, How are the dead raised? and with what manner of body do they come? 36 Thou foolish one, that which thou thyself sowest is not quickened except it die: 37 and that which thou sowest, thou sowest not the body that shall be, but a bare grain, it may chance of wheat, or of some other kind; 38 but God giveth it a body even as it pleased him, and to each seed a body of its own. 39 All flesh is not the same flesh; but there is one flesh of men, and another flesh of beasts, and another flesh of birds, and another of fishes. 40 There are also celestial bodies, and bodies terrestrial; but the glory of the celestial is one, and the glory of the terrestrial is another. 41 There is one glory of the sun, and another glory of the moon, and another glory of the stars; for one star differeth from another star in glory. 42 So also is the resurrection of the dead. It is sown in corruption; it is raised in incorruption: 43 it is sown in dishonor; it is raised in glory: it is sown in weakness; it is raised in power; 44 it is sown a natural body; it is raised a spiritual body. If there is a natural body, there is also a spiritual body. 45 So also it is written, The first man Adam became a living soul. The last Adam became a life-giving spirit. 46 Howbeit that is not first which is spiritual, but that which is natural; then that which is spiritual. 47 The first man is of the earth, earthy; the second man is of heaven. 48 As is the earthy, such are they also that are earthy: and as is the heavenly, such are they also that are heav-

enly. 49 And as we have borne the image of the earthy we shall also bear the image of the heavenly.

50 Now this I say, brethren, that flesh and blood cannot inherit the kingdom of God; neither doth corruption inherit incorruption.

This selection follows immediately after the one we have arranged for the preceding Sunday, concerning the resurrection of the dead. In the text Paul deals with the question, How are the dead raised, and with what body do they come? This passage likewise is treated fully enough in the sermons on the fifteenth chapter, and they who desire may read those discourses; they are too lengthy to insert here.

The selection from the first chapter of James, however, having commonly been read for this Sunday, and as it contains good instruction and admonition, we will, for the sake of some who may desire to retain it, allow it to remain; and we will make some explanation of it lest we be thought to desire its rejection altogether. It was not, however, written by an apostle. It does not bear the apostolic stamp in all particulars, and is not in every respect compatible with the true doctrine.

Fourth Sunday After Easter

Second Sermon.

Text: James 1, 16-21.

16 Be not deceived, my beloved brethren. 17 Every good gift and every perfect gift is from above, coming down from the Father of lights, with whom can be no variation, neither shadow that is cast by turning. 18 Of his own will he brought us forth by the word of truth, that we should be a kind of firstfruits of his creatures.

19 Ye know this, my beloved brethren. But let every man be swift to hear, slow to speak, slow to wrath: 20 for the wrath of man worketh not the righteousness of God. 21 Wherefore putting away all filthiness and overflowing of wickedness, receive with meekness the implanted word, which is able to save your souls.

1. This lesson was addressed to all Christians. Particularly was it meant for the time when they had to endure from the unbelieving world persecutions severe and oft; as James indicates at the outset, where he says (verses 2-4): "Count it all joy, my brethren, when ye fall into manifold temptations; knowing that the proving of your faith worketh patience. And let .patience have its perfect work, that ye may be perfect and entire." Again (verse 12): "Blessed is the man that endureth temptation."

WHY MEN REJECT THE GOSPEL.

2. Two things there are which part men from the Gospel:

*This sermon was printed first in the "Two Sermons on Anger," by Luther, Wittenberg, 1536.

one is angry impatience, and the other evil lust. Of these James speaks in this epistle. The former sin, he says, arises under persecution—when for the sake of Christ the Lord you must give up property and honor, and risk body and life; must be regarded as fools, as the drudges, yes, the footstool, of the world. Painful and intolerable to the point of discouragement and weariness is such a lot, particularly when it is apparent that your persecutors enjoy good fortune, having honor, power and wealth, while you suffer constantly. Peter, too, admonishes (1 Pet 3, 10), upon authority of Psalm 34, 12-14: He who would be a Christian must be prepared to avoid evil and do good, to seek peace, to refrain his tongue from evil and his lips from speaking guile, and must commit himself to God.

In the case of a great many people otherwise favorably disposed toward the Gospel, it is nothing but persecution which deters and repels them from it. They cannot endure the injuries and reproaches they must suffer for its sake. But for the precious holy cross which is laid upon Christians, and their inability to overcome indignation and impatience, the world would long ago have been crowded with Christians. But on account of trials men recoil, saying: "Rather than endure these, I will remain with the majority; as it is with them, so be it with me."

3. The second thing to which James refers is worldly lust—"filthiness," as James terms it. This, too, is a prevailing evil, particularly with the common people. When they once hear the Gospel they are prone to think right away that they know all about it. They cease to heed it and drown in lust, pride and covetousness of the world, being concerned entirely with accumulating wealth and seeking pleasure.

4. That these two evils prevail is apparent to the eyes of all men today. We fear that we shall fare no better than the prophets and the apostles; these things are likely to continue. Nevertheless, we must unceasingly exert ourselves in behalf of ourselves and others to guard diligently against both these evils. Particularly must we not impa-

tiently murmur and rage against God; we must also show meekness toward our fellowmen, to the end that wrath everywhere may be quelled and subdued, and only patience and meekness reign among Christians.

5. As I said before, such seems to be the trend of the whole text. The apostle gives a reason why we should be patient to the extent of not allowing ourselves to be vexed with them who injure us, especially ungrateful rejecters of the Word of God or persecutors of Christians. The reason he assigns is the debt of gratitude we owe: we are to remember the great good we receive from God in heaven— "Every good gift and every perfect gift is from above, coming down from the Father of lights."

OUR BLESSINGS OUTWEIGH OUR ILLS.

6. If you carefully balance our gifts and trials against each other and weigh them carefully, you will find the blessings conferred upon you so numerous and rich as far to outweigh the injuries and reproaches you must incur. Therefore, if you are assailed by the world, and are provoked to impatience by ingratitude, contempt and persecution, compare with your trials the blessings and consolations you have in Christ and his Gospel. You will soon find you have more reason to pity your enemies than you have to murmur and to rage against them.

7. Again, concerning them who live in worldly lusts— in "filthiness," as the apostle terms it: let not their conduct induce you to forsake the Gospel to be like them; for their portion is altogether paltry in comparison with your glorious blessings and divine riches. Take thought, then, and do not allow yourselves to be misled either by the wanton wickedness of the world, through the injury and pain it may inflict, or by the prosperity of the world's wealthy, who live riotously in all manner of voluptuousness. Look upon what you have from the Father in comparison—his divine blessings, his perfect gifts.

8. For the sake of distinction, we shall designate by "good gifts" the blessings we enjoy here in this life; by "perfect gifts" those awaiting us in the life to come. James

implies this distinction when he says: "Of his own will he brought us forth by the word of truth, that we should be a kind of first-fruits of his creatures." In the terms "good gifts" and "perfect gifts," the apostle comprehends all our blessings, those we have already received in the present life and those to be ours in the life to come.

9. I will not now speak particularly of earthly, transient and changeable blessings, such as temporal goods, honor, a healthy body and others, but could we only compare our blessings with these and weigh our treasures and surpassing blessings, we should presently conclude that ours transcend in value a hundred thousand times anything the world possesses and boasts. Many individuals there are who would give thousands of dollars to have the sight of both eyes. So much do they prize the blessing of sight, they would willingly suffer a year's illness or endure other great inconveniences to obtain it. Less sensible would they be to such discomforts than to the deprivation of the thing they desire.

Of physical blessings particularly, we shall not now speak, however, save to mention that they are never equaled by physical ills. Who can purchase or merit, even by enduring tenfold his present physical ills, the very least of God's gifts; as, for instance, the beholding of the light of the beautiful sun for a single day? And so long as mortal life itself remains, you have the greatest of blessings, one outweighing far all gold and silver and all the misfortunes you may endure.

OUR BLESSINGS IN CHRIST'S RESURRECTION.

But we shall speak now particularly of the blessings we have in Christ's resurrection, a subject appropriate to this Paschal season. The text says, Every good gift and every perfect gift cometh down from the Father of lights. For God has begun the work of edifying us, of building us up, and will constitute us his own children, his heirs. This work, James says, is wrought through the Gospel, or "the word of truth," as he terms it.

10. But what does the resurrection advantage us? It has

already brought us this gain: our hearts are enlightened and filled with joy, and we have passed from the darkness of sin, error and fear into the clear light; the Christian is able to judge all sects, all doctrines of devils, that may arise on earth. Is it not a thing of unspeakable value, a precious gift, to be enlightened and taught of God to the extent of being able to judge correctly every doctrine and every kind of conduct exhibited in this world, and to show all men how to live—what to do and what to avoid? "Well may we boast, then, of having here on earth also a Father—"the Father of lights"—from whom we receive blessings of such magnitude that man should willingly yield body and life for their attainment.

What would I in my darkness not have given to be liberated from the very dread which prompted the celebration of masses and other abominations, yes, from the torture and anguish of conscience which left me no rest? or to have instruction enabling me rightly to interpret a single psalm? I would, for such enlightenment, readily have crawled on the ground to the ends of the earth. Thank God, we now have the blessed treasure abundantly, the great and precious light, the gracious Word. What is the sum of all suffering and misfortune compared to this light?

11. Secondly, through Christ's resurrection we have a good, joyous conscience, one able to withstand every form of sin and temptation and to maintain a sure hope of eternal life. The great, glorious gifts and blessings of the resurrection are these: the Gospel, Holy Baptism, the power of the Holy Spirit, and comfort in all adversity. What is a slight injury or the loss of some temporal blessing in comparison with these? What reason has any man to murmur and to rage when such divine blessings are his, even here in this life, blessings which none can take away or abridge?

If, then, you are called to renounce money, possessions, honor and men's favor, remember you have a treasure more precious than all the honors and all the possessions of the world. Again, when you see one living in great splendor, in pleasure and presumption, following his own inclinations,

think thus: "What has he? A wretched portion, a beggarly
morsel. In contrast, I have divine grace enabling me to
know God's will and the work he would have me do, and
all in heaven and on earth is mine." Look, says James, upon
the treasure already obtained from the Father of lights—
his great and glorious gifts.

12. But these do not represent the consummation of resurrection blessings. We must yet await the real, the perfect, gifts. Our earthly condition does not admit of perfection; hence we cannot truly perceive, cannot comprehend,
our treasure. We are but "a kind of first-fruits of his creatures." God has only commenced to work in us, but he will
not leave us in that state. If we continue in faith, not allowing ourselves to be turned away through wrath and impatience, God will bring us to the real, eternal blessings, called
"perfect gifts," the possession of which excludes error, stumbling, anger, and any sin whatever.

THE FUTURE LIFE OF BLESSEDNESS.

13. That future existence, James goes on to say, will be
one wherein is "no variation, neither shadow that is cast
by turning"—no alternating of light and darkness. In other
words, there will not be the variation and instability characteristic of this world, even of the Christian life—today
joyous, tomorrow sad; now standing but soon tottering. It
is in the Christian life just as in the physical world: we find
variableness and continual change—light is succeeded by
darkness, day by night, cold by heat; here are mountains,
there valleys; today we are well, tomorrow ill; and so it
goes. But all this change shall be abolished. The present
life shall be succeeded by one wherein is no variation, but
a permanence and eternity of blessing. We shall unceasingly behold God in his majesty where dwells no darkness,
no death, plague nor infirmity, but pure light, joy and happiness. Look to this future life! call it to mind, when assailed by the world and enticed to anger or evil lust. Remember the great blessings of heaven assuredly promised
you, and whereof Christ your Head has already taken possession, that he may make sure your entrance into the same

blessings. These should be to you far more precious and desirable than the things of earth, which all men must leave behind.

14. To these things the Christian should direct his thoughts and efforts, that he may learn to prize his blessings, to recognize his treasures as great and glorious, and to thank God for the beginnings of his grace and blessing bestowed here below. Let us ever look and turn toward true knowledge and understanding, toward righteousness and life; so shall we attain that perfection wherein we are freed from the present imperfect, unstable existence, the yoke we now bear upon our necks and which continually weighs upon us and renders us liable to fall from the Gospel.

Impulse and aid for such pursuit we are to receive from the holy cross and persecution, as well as from the example of the world. With what ease the poor, wretched people are wrested from the Word and from faith, wherein they might enjoy unspeakable grace and blessings, by the sordid, beggarly pleasures to be sought for here!

15. Therefore, James says: "Why trouble yourselves about earthly blessings, which though God-given are transitory? Why not much rather rejoice in the comforting prospect of the great heavenly blessings already abundantly yours and which cannot be taken from you?" And by way of explanation he says further: "Of his own will he brought us forth by the word of truth."

GOD'S CHILDREN BEGOTTEN BY THE WORD.

16. The first, and in fact the best, thing Christ has sent us from on high is sonship. He brought us forth, made us his children, or heirs. We are truly called children born of God. But how are we born? Through "the Word of truth," or the true Word. By this statement James makes a wide thrust at all factions and sects. For they also have a word and boast much of their doctrine, but theirs is not the Word of truth whereby men are made children of God. They teach naught, and know naught, about how we are to be born God's children through faith. They prate much about the works done by us in the state derived from Adam.

But we have a Word whereby, as we are assured, God makes us his beloved children and justifies us—if we believe in that Word. He justifies us not through works or laws. The Christian must derive his sonship from his birth. All whittling and patching is to no purpose. The disciples of Moses, and all work-mongers, would effect it by commandments, extorting a work here and a work there, effecting nothing. New beings are needed, children of God by birth, as John 1, 12 says.

17. The children of God, John tells us, are they who believe on the name of Christ; that is, who sincerely cling to the Word. John extols the Word as the great, the mighty, gift. They are children who cleave to the message that through Christ God forgives their sins and receives them into his favor; who adhere to this promise in all temptations, afflictions and troubles. The Word here on earth is the ᵥjewel which secures sonship. Now, since God has so greatly blessed you as to make you his own begotten children, shall he not also give you every other good?

18. Whence, then, do you derive sonship? Not from your own will, not from your own powers or efforts. Were it so, I and other monks surely should have obtained it, independently of the Word; it would have been ours through the numerous works we performed in our monastic life. It is secured, James says, "of his will." For it never entered into the thought of any man that so should we be made children of God. The idea did not grow in our gardens; it did not spring up in our wells. But it came down from above, "from the Father of lights," by Word and Spirit revealed to us and given into our hearts through the agency of his apostles and their successors, by whom the Word has been transmitted to us. Hence we did not secure it through our efforts or merits. Of his Fatherly will and good pleasure was it conferred upon us; of pure grace and mercy he gave it.

CHRISTIANS THE FIRST-FRUITS.

19. James says, "That we should be a kind of first-fruits of his creatures"; that is, the newly-begun creature, or work,

of God. By this phrase the apostle distinguishes the creatures of God from the creatures of the world, or creatures of men. Likewise does Peter when he says (1 Pet 2, 13), "Be subject to every ordinance [or creature] of man"; that is, to everything commanded, ordained, instituted, made, by men. For instance, a prince constitutes men tax-gatherers, squires, secretaries, or anything he desires, within the limits of his power.

But new creatures are found with God. They are styled "creatures of God" because he has created them as his own work, independently of human effort or human power. And so the Christian is called a "new creature of God," a creature God himself has made, aside from all other creatures and higher than they. At the same time, such creation of God is only in its initial stage. He still daily operates upon it until it becomes perfect, a wholly divine creature, as the very sun in clearness and purity, without sin and imperfection, all aglow with love divine.

20. Take into careful consideration these facts. Keep before you the great blessing, honor and glory God has conferred upon you in making you heirs of the life to come, the life wherein shall be no imperfection nor variation, the life which shall be an existence in divine purity and protection like God's own. Do not, then, by any means allow yourselves to be provoked to anger by the wretched, sordid, beggar's wallet which the world craves. Rather, much rather, rejoice in the divine blessings, and thank God for having made you worthy of them. Whether sweet or bitter— in comparison with these let everything else be spurned. "For I reckon that the sufferings of this present time are not worthy to be compared with the glory which shall be revealed to us-ward"—to us the children of God—says Paul in Romans 8, 18.

IMPATIENT ANGER FORBIDDEN.

21. So James draws the conclusion: "Let every man be swift to hear, slow to speak, slow to wrath." In other words, in receiving counsel or comfort be swift; but do not permit yourselves readily to criticise, curse, or upbraid God

or men. James does not mean to prohibit reproof, censure, indignation and correction where the command of God or necessity requires; but he forbids rashness or hastiness on our part, despite our provocation in the premises. When we are provoked we should first hear what the Word of God says and be advised thereby. It is the right and true counsel, and we should ever permit ourselves to be led by it; according to its teaching should all our decisions, reproofs and censures be regulated. In immediate connection, James bids us receive the Word with meekness; we are not to be incensed when censured by its authority, or to become impatient and murmur when we have to suffer something because of it.

The reason James assigns for restraining our anger is: "For the wrath of man worketh not the righteousness of God." This is a truth admitted even by the heathen—"Ira furor brevis est," etc.—and verified by experience. Therefore, upon authority of Psalm 4, 4, when you feel your wrath rising, sin not, but go to your chamber and commune with yourself. Let not wrath take you by surprise and cause you to yield to it. When slander and reproach is heaped upon you, or curses given, do not rashly allow yourself to be immediately inflamed with anger. Rather, take heed to overcome the provocation and not to respond to it.

22. The apostle's first point, then, is: Christians should guard against yielding to wrath and impatience, and should remember the great blessings they enjoy—gifts wherewith all the advantages and favors of the world are unworthy of comparison.

23. Similarly, James says regarding the other point: "Wherefore putting away all filthiness and overflowing of wickedness," etc. By "filthiness" he means the impure life of the world—indulgence, voluptuousness and knavery of every sort. These things, he would say, should be far from you Christians who enjoy blessings so great and glorious. Could you rightly recognize and appreciate these blessings, you would regard all worldly pursuits and pleasures mere filth in comparison. Nor is this overdrawn; they are such

when contrasted with the good and perfect heavenly gifts and treasures.

24. "Receive with meekness the implanted word." You have the Word, James says, a Word which is yours not by your own fancy or effort, but which God, by grace, gave to you—implanted in you. It has free course—is preached, read and sung among you. (By the grace of God, it is free among us, too.) In this respect, God be praised, there is no lack. It is of the utmost importance, however, to receive it, to make profitable use of it; to handle it with meekness that we may hold it fast and not allow it to be effaced by anger under persecution or by the allurements of worldly lusts. Christ says (Lk 21, 19), "In your patience possess ye your souls [ye shall win your souls]."

MEEKNESS AND PATIENCE ENJOINED.

Meekness and patience are necessary to enable us to triumph over the devil and the world. Without them we shall not be able to hold fast the Word in our strife against those evil forces. We must fight and contend against sin, but if we essay to cool our wrath by grasping the devil and his followers by the hair and wreaking vengeance upon them, we will accomplish nothing and may thereby lose our treasure, the beloved Word. Therefore, lay hold of the Word planted or engrafted within you, that you may be able to retain it and have it bring forth its fruit in yourself.

THE POWER OF THE WORD.

25. It is a Word, says James in conclusion, "which is able to save your souls." What more could be desired? You have the Word, the promise of all divine blessings and gifts. It is able to save you if you but steadfastly cleave to it. Why, then, need you take any account of the world, and anything it may do, whether good or evil? What injury can the world render, what help can it offer, so long as you hold the treasure of the Word? Observe that the apostle ascribes to the spoken Word, the preached Gospel, the power to save souls. Similarly, Paul commends it to the Romans (ch. 1, 16), in almost the same words, as "the power of God unto salvation to every one that believeth."

26. Now, the Word is implanted within you in a way to give you the certain comfort and sure hope of your salvation. Be careful, then, not to permit yourselves to be wrested from it by the wrath or the filth of the world. Take heed to accept in purity and to maintain with patience the Word so graciously and richly given you by God without effort or merit on your part. Those who are without the Word, and yet endeavor to attain heaven, what efforts have they made in the past! what efforts are they making today! They might torment themselves to death; they might institute and celebrate every possible service—they would accomplish nothing. Is it not better to cling to the Word and maintain this treasure whereby you attain salvation and divine sonship than to permit the world to wrest you from it through persecution, passion or moral filth the source of its own ruin and perdition?

Fifth Sunday After Easter

Text: First Corinthians 15, 51-57.

51 Behold, I tell you a mystery: We all shall not sleep, but we shall all be changed, 52 in a moment, in the twinkling of an eye, at the last trump: for the trumpet shall sound, and the dead shall be raised incorruptible, and we shall be changed. 53 For this corruptible must put on incorruption, and this mortal must put on immortality. 54 But when this corruptible shall have put on incorruption, and this mortal shall have put on immortality, then shall come to pass the saying that is written, Death is swallowed up in victory. 55 O death, where is thy victory? O death, where is thy sting? 56 The sting of death is sin; and the power of sin is the law: 57 but thanks be to God, who giveth us the victory through our Lord Jesus Christ. 58 Wherefore, my beloved brethren, be ye stedfast, unmovable, always abounding in the work of the Lord, forasmuch as ye know that your labor is not vain in the Lord.

You will find this lesson explained in the special sermons on the same chapter.

Ascension Day

Text: Acts 1, 1-11.

The former treatise I made, O Theophilus, concerning all that Jesus began both to do and to teach, 2 until the day in which he was received up, after that he had given commandment through the Holy Spirit unto the apostles whom he had chosen: 3 to whom he also showed himself alive after his passion by many proofs, appearing unto them by the space of forty days, and speaking the things concerning the kingdom of God: 4 and being assembled together with them, he charged them not to depart from Jerusalem, but to wait for the promise of the Father, which, said he, ye heard from me: 5 for John indeed baptized with water; but ye shall be baptized in the Holy Spirit not many days hence.

6 They therefore, when they were come together, asked him, saying, Lord, dost thou at this time restore the kingdom to Israel? 7 And he said unto them, It is not for you to know times or seasons, which the Father hath set within his own authority. 8 But ye shall receive power, when the Holy Spirit is come upon you: and ye shall be my witnesses both in Jerusalem, and in all Judea and Samaria, and unto the uttermost part of the earth. 9 And when he had said these things, as they were looking, he was taken up; and a cloud received him out of their sight. 10 And while they were looking stedfastly into heaven as he went, behold two men stood by them in white apparel; 11 who also said, Ye men of Galilee, why stand ye looking into heaven? this Jesus, who was received up from you into heaven, shall so come in like manner as ye beheld him going into heaven.

This epistle text is simply a narrative concerning the visible ascension of Christ into heaven. It is in itself clear. Whatever it may be necessary to say relative to the article of Christ's ascension, we shall leave for the sermons on the Festivals of Christ as they occur at intervals during the year, at which times it is fitting to speak particularly of each article concerning Christ.

Sunday After Ascension Day

Text: First Peter 4, 7-11.*

7 But the end of all things is at hand: be ye therefore of sound mind, and be sober unto prayer: 8 above all things being fervent in your love among yourselves: for love covereth a multitude of sins: 9 using hopitality one to another without murmuring: 10 according as each hath received a gift, ministering it among your-selves, as good stewards of the manifold grace of God; 11 if any man speaketh, speaking as it were oracles of God; if any man ministereth, ministering as of the strength which God supplieth: that in all things God may be glorified through Jesus Christ, whose is the glory and the dominion for ever and ever. Amen.

EXHORTATION TO CHRISTIAN LIVING.

1. This text, too, is an admonition to Christian living, a discourse concerning the fruits of a good tree, a figure ap-plied to the Christian; in other words, concerning the fruits of the one who, through faith, has obtained redemption from sin and death and has a place in the kingdom of grace and of eternal life. Such a one is exhorted to live henceforth in a manner indicative of the fact that he has apprehended the treasure of salvation and is become a new man.

EXHORTATION TO SOBERNESS.

2. Certain good works are also introduced, and in the first part of our text Peter makes an especially emphatic continuation of the admonition in the foregoing part of the chapter, warning Christians to abstain from gross vices—carnal lusts—which in the world lead to obscenity, and

*This sermon appeared as early as 1525 in pamphlet form.
303

from the wild, disorderly, swinish lives of the heathen world, lives of gormandizing, guzzling and drunkenness. Peter admonishes Christians to endeavor to be "sober unto prayer." The epistle was written chiefly to the Greeks, the masses of which people were very social, and inclined to carouse and gormandize. And we Germans are accused of the same excess; not without some reason either.

3. With intent to turn Christians from these vices unto temperance and sobriety, Peter reminds them, as all the apostles are wont to do, of the obligations particularly incident to the Christian calling, to the only true, divine service, the things for the sake of which they have become Christians and which distinguish them from the remainder of the world. His meaning is: It is not for Christians to lead lives heathenish, profligate and riotous; to indulge in gormandizing, guzzling, carousing and demoralizing of themselves. They have something nobler to do. First, in that they are to become different beings, and be occupied with the Word of God wherefrom they derive their new birth and whereby they preserve it. Second, being born anew, they have enemies to fight; so long as they live on earth, they must combat the devil, also their own flesh, which is corrupted by the devil until it is full of evil lusts. Having, then, to assume the obligations of this calling and contest, they must not give way to drowsy indolence; much less may they become foolish, drunken sots, indifferent to all issues and heedless of their obligations. Rather, they have need to be watchful and sober, ever ready with the Word of God and with prayer.

4. These are the two kinds of armor, two weapons of defense, whereby the devil is vanquished and of which he is afraid: First, diligence in hearing, learning and practicing the Word of God, that instruction, comfort and strength may be received; second, sincere petitioning upon the authority of that Word, a crying and calling to God for help when temptations and conflicts arise. One or the other of these weapons of defense must continually be in active exercise, effecting perpetual intercourse between God and man—

either God speaking to us while we quietly listen, or God hearing our utterances to him and our petitions concerning our needs.

Whichever the weapon we wield, it is unendurable to the devil; he cannot abide it. Christians need both equipments, that their hearts may ever turn to God, cleave to his Word, and continually, with ceaseless longing, pray a perpetual Lord's Prayer. Truly, the Christian should learn from the temptations and straits wherewith the devil, the world and the flesh constantly oppress him, to be ever on his guard, watching for the enemy's point of attack; for the enemy sleeps not nor rests a single moment.

5. Here is applicable Peter's injunction for the Christian to keep within the bounds of physical temperance and sobriety; not to overload the body and injure it by excessive eating and drinking: so as to be watchful, intelligent, and in a mood, to pray. He who is not careful to discharge the obligations of his office or station with temperance and sobriety, but is daily in a sottish condition, is incapable of praying or performing any other Christian duty; he is unfit for any service.

6. Right here a special admonitory sermon might well be preached to us dissolute Germans, in warning for our excesses and drunkenness. But where would be forthcoming a sermon forcible enough to restrain the shameful sottishness and the drink devil among us? The evil of over-indulgence has, alas, swept in upon us like a torrent, overwhelming as a flood all classes. It daily spreads further and further throughout the nation, embracing every station from the lowest to the highest. All preaching, all admonition, seem far too weak—not vain and impotent, but despised and scorned—to meet the emergency. But the apostles, and even Christ himself, declared that in the end of the world such a state of affairs should obtain. For that very reason did Christ (Lk 21, 34) admonish Christians to take heed to themselves lest at any time their hearts be overcharged with surfeiting and drunkenness and the cares of this life, and so that day come upon them unawares.

7. Now, God having in his infinite goodness so richly shed upon us Germans in these latter times the Gospel light, we ought, in honor and gratitude to him, to try to reform ourselves in the matter of intemperance. We should fear lest through this evil besides committing other sins we draw upon us the wrath and punishment of God. For naught else can result from the pernicious life of intemperance but false security, and contempt of God. Individuals continually dead in drunkenness, buried in excesses, living like swine, cannot fear God, cannot be occupied with divine things.

8. Had we no other incentive to abandon our intemperate living, the scandalous reputation we have among the nations ought to move us to reform. Other countries, particularly those bordering on Germany, regard us with extreme contempt, calling us drunken Germans. For they have virtue enough to abstain from excessive drinking. The Turks are real monks and saints in this respect; so far are they from the evil of intemperance that in obedience to the teaching of their Mohammed they prohibit the drinking of wine or any other intoxicant, and punish the offense as the greatest evil in their midst. For this very reason are they better soldiers than our drunken masses. They are always awake and vigilant, alert concerning their own interests, planning attacks upon us and continually extending their dominion, while we lie sleeping in our excesses as if we could withstand the Turks by drunkenness and carousing.

9. But what is the use of multiplying words on the subject when the evil prevails to such extent as to be common custom in the land? No longer confined to the rude, illiterate rabble, to country villages and public taverns, it has penetrated all cities and entered nearly every house, being particularly prevalent among the nobility—in the courts of princes. I recall that when I was young drunkenness was regarded an inexpressibly shameful thing among the peerage, and that the dear lords and princes restrained it with serious prohibitions and punishments. But now it is more alarmingly prevalent among them than among farmers. It is generally the case that when the great and good begin to

go down, they sink to a lower level than others. Yes, intemperance has attained such prevalence that even princes and lords have learned the habit from their young noblemen and are no longer ashamed of it. Rather, they call it honorable, making it a civil virtue befitting princes and noblemen. Whosoever will not consent to be a drunken sot with them, must be discountenanced; while the knights who stand for beer and wine obtain high honors, and great favors and privileges, on account of their drinking. They desire fame in this respect, as if they had secured their nobility, their shield and helmet, by the very fact that they exceed others in the shamelessness of their tippling.

10. Yes, and have we not further reason for checking the evil when even the young practice it without fear or shame? They learn it from the aged, and unrestrained they disgracefully and wantonly injure themselves in the very bloom of life, destroying themselves as corn is cut down by hail and tempest. The majority of the finest, most promising young people, particularly the nobility, they of court circles, ruin their health, body and life, before arriving at maturity. How can it be otherwise when they who should restrain and punish commit the same sins themselves?

11. Hence Germany has always been a wretched country, chastised and plagued by the drink devil, and completely immersed in this vice, until the bodies and lives of her people, as well as their property and honor, are shamefully consumed and only a sordid existence remains. He who would paint the conditions must portray something swinish. Indeed, but a small proportion of the inhabitants of Germany are undebased by this evil. These are children, girls and women. Some sense of propriety in the matter remains to them, though occasionally we find even under the veil some intemperance; however, it is with restraint. Enough modesty remains to inspire the universal sentiment that so disgraceful a thing is it for a woman to be drunk, such a one deserves to be trampled upon in the streets.

12. In the light of their example, let us men learn to see our own shame and to blush for it. While noting how dis-

graceful is drunkenness for women, let us remember it is
much more so for ourselves. We ought to be saner and
more virtuous; for, according to Peter, the woman is the
weaker vessel. Because of the weakness of women, we
ought to have more patience with them. Man being endowed
with a broader mind, stronger faculties and firmer nature,
he should be the saner being, the farther removed from the
brute. It stands to reason that it is a much greater disgrace
for him to indulge in the vice of drunkenness. In proportion
to the nobility of his creation and the exalted nature wherewith God has endowed him, should be the disgrace of such
unreasoning, brutish conduct on his part.

13. What can be said for us? So complete is the perversion of all manly virtue and honor in our conduct in this
respect that it cannot be surpassed by any other possible
degradation of manhood. There remains to us but an atom
of good reputation, and that is to be found among the wom-
en. The occasional instance of drunkenness among them
but emphasizes our own disgrace. All countries look upon
us with scorn and contempt, regarding us as shameful and
sordid creatures, day and night bent upon making ourselves
surfeited and stupid, possessing neither reason nor intelligence.

The evil would be more tolerable, more excusable, if
drinking and carousing had any limit, if intoxication were
but an occasional thing—the case of a person inadvertently
taking one drink too much, or of taking a stimulant when
tired from excessive labor and worry. We excuse it in
women who may chance to drink a little more at wedding
parties than they are accustomed to at home. But this
excessive guzzling kept up unceasingly day and night,
emitting only to be filled again, is wholly inconsistent with
the character of a prince, a nobleman, a citizen, yes, of a
human being, not to mention the life of a Christian; it is
really more in keeping with the nature and work of swine.

14. Now, when God and all mankind permit you to eat
and to drink, to enjoy good things, not merely what is necessary for actual subsistence, but in a measure calculated to

afford gratification and pleasure, and you are yet not satisfied with that privilege—when such is the case, your sordid and gluttonous tendencies are worthy one born solely to consume beer and wine. But such are the excesses now to be seen in the courts of princes—the banqueting and the drinking—that one would think they meant to devour the resources of the country in a single hour. Lords, princes, noblemen—the entire country, in fact—are ruined, reduced to beggary, for the particular reason that God's gifts are so inhumanly wasted and destroyed.

15. As I said before, the evil of drunkenness has, alas, gained such ascendency as to be past restraint unless the Word of God may exert some controlling influence among the few, the individuals who are still human and who would be Christians. The masses will remain as they are, particularly as the civil government makes no effort to restrain the evil. It is my opinion that if God does not sometime check the vice by a special judgment—and until he does it will never be punished and restrained—even women and children will become inebriate, and when the last day arrives no Christian will be found but all souls will descend drunken into the abyss of hell.

16. Let all who desire to be Christians know that it is incumbent upon them to manifest the virtue of temperance; that drunken sots have no place among Christians, and cannot be saved until they amend their ways, until they reform from their evil habits. Concerning them Paul says plainly (Gal 5, 19-21): "Now the works of the flesh are manifest, which are these: fornication, uncleanness, lasciviousness, idolatry, sorcery, enmities, strife, jealousies, wraths, factions, divisions, parties, envyings, drunkenness, revellings, and such like; of which I forewarn you, even as I did forewarn you, that they who practice such things shall not inherit the kingdom of God."

Here you see that he who lies day and night in drunkenness has no more inheritance in the kingdom of God than the whoremonger, adulterer, and such like. Know then, just as idolatry, adultery and so on, are sins excluding you from heaven, so too, drunkenness is a sin which bars you from the blessings of baptism, and from remission of sins, faith in Christ and your personal salvation. Hence, if you would be a Christian and saved, you must be careful to lead a sober and temperate life. But if you disregard this admonition and yet hope to be saved—well, then continue to be an infidel and a brute so long as God permits.

17. Were you a Christian, even if you could permit yourself to be unmoved by the physical injury wherein, by drunkenness, you plunge yourself, not only wasting your money and property, but injuring your health and shortening your life; and if you could permit yourself to be unmoved by the stigma justly recognized by men and angels as attaching to you, a filthy sot—even then you ought to be moved by God's command, by the peril of incurring eternal damnation—of losing God's grace and eternal salvation—to refrain from such unchristian conduct. O God, how shameless and ungrateful we are, we so highly blessed of God in having his Word and in being liberated from the tyranny of the Pope, who desired our sweat and blood and tortured our consciences with his laws—how ungrateful we are in the face of these things not to amend our lives in some measure in honor to the Gospel, and in praise and gratitude to God!

18. Where peradventure there are still pious parents or godfearing Christian rulers, they ought, for the sake of lessening the evil of intemperance, to restrain their children and domestics with serious chastisements. Pastors and preachers are under obligation to admonish the people frequently and faithfully, holding up to them God's displeasure and wrath and the injuries to soul, body and property resultant from this evil, to the intent that at least some might be moved and profited. And they who wantonly and openly persist in the vice, being not disposed to amend their conduct but at the same time boast of the Gospel, should not be allowed to participate in the sacrament of the Lord's Supper nor to act as sponsors at baptism. Preachers and pastors should hold such as openly antichristian, and should make a distinction against them the same as with manifest adulter-

ers, extortioners and idolaters. Such is Paul's command (1 Cor 5, 11): "I wrote unto you not to keep company, if any man that is named a brother be a fornicator, or covetous, or an idolater, or a reviler, or a drunkard, or an extortioner; with such a one no, not to eat."

NECESSITY FOR PRAYER.

19. But we will not now remark further upon this subject. To return to Peter: He admonishes us to be sober so that we may give ourselves to prayer, as becometh those who are Christians and have turned from the vile, heathenish conduct of the world. Just preceding our text, in verse 3, he says: "For the time past may suffice to have wrought the desire of the Gentiles, and to have walked in lasciviousness, lusts, winebibbings, revellings, carousings, and abominable idolatries." He admonishes us as being now called and ordained to contend against the devil by faith and prayer. Later on (ch. 5, 8) he brings in the same warning in clearer phrase, exhorting Christians to be sober and watchful. Do you ask, What is the great necessity therefor? he says: "Your adversary the devil, as a roaring lion [in the midst of a flock of sheep], walketh about, seeking whom he may devour."

Peter's meaning is this: Since you are a people called to contend with this powerful spirit which is more intent on seizing your souls than is the wolf on seizing the sheep, it is essential you should take thought how to withstand him. Resistance is effected only through faith and prayer. But soberness and vigilance are necessary to enable one to pray. With gormandizers and drunkards, reason is dethroned and they are rendered incapable of respecting anything, or of performing any good work. Therefore, the ability to pray and call upon God has been taken from them and the devil overcomes and devours them at his will.

20. The diligence in prayer which characterized Christians of the primitive Church, even while undergoing great persecution, is apparent to us. They were more than willing to assemble daily for prayer together, not only morning and evening, but also at certain other appointed hours; and fre-

quently they watched and prayed entire nights. Some of
them, according to St. Augustine, carried their vigils to such
extent as at times to abstain from food for four days. True,
this was going to somewhat of an extreme, particularly
when later the practice came to be an example and a commandment. Yet their habit of perfect sobriety morning,
evening and at all times is commendable. With the cessation of this practice in the congregations, there succeeded
the wretched order of monks, who pretend to do the praying
for others. They, it is true, observed the same appointed
hours, the same seasons of prayer, in their matins, vespers,
and so on, but they did not really pray; they merely kept
up an incessant sound, muttering and howling.

We still retain from the ancient custom the observance of
morning and evening prayers in schools for children. But
the same practice should obtain in every Christian family.
Every father is under obligation to train up his children to
pray at least at the beginning and the close of day, commending to God every exigency of this earthly life, that
God's wrath may be averted, and deserved punishment withheld.

21. Under such conditions, we would be properly instructed and not have to be subjected to intolerable oppression and to prohibitions relative to eating, drinking and
dressing, being guided by nature's demands and our own
honor and pleasure. Yet we would not be inordinate and
brutish in these things nor shamefully dethrone reason.
Drunkenness is a sin and a shame to any man, and would
be even were there neither God nor commandment; much
less can it be tolerated among Christians. There is more
virtue in this respect among the very heathen and Turks.
They put us to shame, while it is our place to set an example shaming them. Our characters ought to be so noble
as to give no chance for offense at our conduct, that the
name of God be not defamed but glorified, as Peter admonishes in the conclusion of this epistle lesson.

TEMPERANCE IN ALL THINGS.

22. What we have said in regard to sobriety, we must

also say relative to that other virtue—temperance,* to which Peter gives first place. They are mutually related, but temperance respects not only eating and drinking, but is opposed to all immoderation in outward life—in clothing, ornament, and so on; to whatever is superfluous, or excessive; to any extravagant attempt to be greater and better than others. To such extent has immoderation gained the upper hand in the world, there is nowhere any limit to expense in the way of household demands, dress, wedding parties and banquets, in the way of architecture, and so on, whereby citizens, rulers and the country itself are impoverished, because no individual longer keeps within proper bounds. Almost invariably the farmer aspires to equal the nobleman, while the nobleman would excel the prince. As with sobriety, so with the virtue of temperance—there is scarce to be found an example of it in our midst, so completely has self-control, sincerity and discipline given way.

23. At the same time the apostle does not forbid appropriate and respectable recognition of the things of physical well-being, in keeping with each individual's station in life, even including things ministering pleasure and joy. For Peter would not have filthy, rusty, greasy monks nor sourfaced saints, with the hypocrisy and show of their simulated austere and peculiar lives, wherein they honor not their bodies, as Paul says (Col 2, 23), but are ever ready to judge and condemn other people—the maiden, for instance, who chances to join in a dance or wears a red dress. If you are a Christian in other respects, God will easily allow you to dress and to adorn yourself, and to live with comfort, even to enjoy honor and considerable pleasure, so long as you keep within proper bounds; you should, however, not go beyond the limits of temperance and moderation. In other words, do not overreach propriety and self-restraint, regardless of real pleasure, in the endeavor to show off in excessive and unprofitable squandering. Such conduct results in confusion and trouble—chastisement sent of God; in taxes, ex-

---

*The German text uses the two words "maszig" and "nichtern," which may be rendered "temperate" and "sober."

tortion, robbing and stealing, until finally lords and subjects
are ruined together.

> "Above all things being fervent in your love [have
> fervent charity] among yourselves; for love [charity]
> covereth a multitude of sins."

24. In the foregoing part of the text, Peter admonishes
Christians concerning their obligations to themselves; here
he tells what is to be their conduct toward others. He embraces all the good works named in the second table of the
commandments as obligations we owe to our neighbor, in
the little but forcible and comprehensive phrase—"fervent
in your love." This virtue, too, is incumbent on the Christian who must contend against the devil and pray. For
prayer is hindered where love and harmony are displaced by
wrath and ill-will. The Lord's Prayer teaches: "Forgive us
our debts as we forgive our debtors."

How can they pray one for another who feel no interest
in a neighbor's wants, who rather are enemies, entertaining
no good will toward one another? Where hearts are inflamed with hatred toward men, prayer has ceased; it is
extinguished. Hence, antichristians and all popedom, however holy their appearance, cannot pray while enemies to
the Word of God and persecutors of Christians. He who
repeats the Lord's Prayer while indulging wrath, envy and
hatred, censures his own lips; he condemns his own prayer
when he seeks forgiveness from God but does not think of
forgiving his neighbor.

25. With Christians there must be, not merely natural
human affection such as exists even among heathen, but ardent, fervent love; not the mere appearance of love, the
smoke—false, hypocritical love, as Paul calls it (Rom 12, 9)
—but real fervor and fire, which consent not to be easily
extinguished, but which endure like the love between husband and wife, or the love of parents for children. True
conjugal and parental love is not easily quenched, even
though the object of its affection be weak, diseased or dan-
gerously ill. Rather the greater the need and the danger of
one individual, the more is the heart of the other moved and
the brighter does love burn.

26. Such sincere love, as the apostle elsewhere styles it, must exist among Christians who are all children of one Father in heaven and brothers and sisters. Indeed, they are under obligation to love even their enemies—who are human beings of the same flesh and blood—and to wish no one evil but rather to serve all wherever possible. This love is the beautiful red robe for the adornment of Christians, supplementing the pure white garment of faith received in baptism. It is to be worn in obedience to the example of Christ, who for us, even while we were enemies, wore the same red garment of love when he was sprinkled with his own blood. It was then he burned with the intense fire of ineffable and most exalted love.

27. The apostles were moved to admonitions of this character because they clearly perceived the great weakness and imperfection bound to exist among Christians even in their outward lives. They knew that no one could, in his everyday life among men, live so discreetly as not at some time or other, by word, gesture or act, to give offense to someone, moving him to anger. Such perfection of life is found in no family, not even with husband and wife. The case is the same as in the human body: one member frequently comes in conflict with another; a man may inadvertently bite his tongue or scratch his face. He who would be a saint so stern and selfish as to endure no evil words or acts, and to excuse no imperfections, is unfit to dwell among men. He knows nothing of Christian love, and can neither believe nor put into practice the article of the Creed concerning the forgiveness of sins.

28. So the Christian's fire of love must be characterized, not by a dull, cold red, but by a warm scarlet—according to the Scriptures (Ex 26, 1), "Coccum bis tinctam" (rose-red). This love retains its fire and is really true, having which the Christian is not easily disheartened and overcome by wrath, impatience and revenge, but to a certain extent is able to endure and tolerate attacks upon himself calculated to distress. It manifests itself more strongly in suffering and enduring than in action.

29. Therefore, Peter extols such love, declaring it to be a virtue potent not only to bear but to cover "a multitude of sins." This statement he introduces from the Proverbs of Solomon (ch 10, 12). The Papists, however, pervert its meaning, explaining it in a way at variance with the doctrine of faith; they make of love to one's neighbor a work or virtue having merit with God. It is their desire to draw the conclusion that for the sake of our love our sins are covered; that is, forgiven and exterminated. But we shall not notice the dolts. It is clear enough from the text that reference is to hatred and love received from men; our own sins are not intended here, but the transgressions of others. To cover our sins in the sight of God, yet other love is requisite—the love of the Son of God, who alone is the bearer of sins in God's sight, and who, as John the Baptist says, takes away, bearing them upon his own shoulders, the sins of the whole world, including our own. And the example of his love teaches that we, too, should in love cheerfully bear and freely forgive the sins of others against us.

30. Solomon contrasts the two opposing principles of envious hatred and love, and shows the effect of each. "Hatred," he says, "stirreth up strifes; but love covereth all transgressions." Where hatred and enmity dwell in the heart, they must inevitably stir up strife and bring misfortune. Animosity cannot restrain itself. It either bursts out in pernicious language clandestinely uttered against the object of enmity, or it openly demeans itself in a manner indicating its ill will. Hence follow reveling, cursing, quarreling and fighting, and, when wholly unrestrained, cruelty and murder.

These things are due to the fact that the eyes of Younker Hate are so blinded by scorn and venom that he can see only evil in every man with whom he comes in contact; and when he actually finds it he will not let it alone, but stirs it, roots and frets in it, as the hog roots with defiled snout in offensive filth. "You must have viewed your neighbor from behind," we say when one can speak and think only the worst of a neighbor though he may have many good traits. Hate really desires only that everyone be an enemy to his neighbor and speak the worst about him, and if he hears aught in his neighbor's favor, he puts upon it the very worst construction, with the result that the other party is embittered and in turn comes to hate, curse and revile. Thus the fire burns until only discord and mischief can obtain.

31. But on the other hand, as Solomon tells us, Love is a virtue pure and precious. It neither utters nor thinks any evil of its neighbor. Rather, it covers sin; not one sin, nor two, but "a multitude of sins"—great masses of them, forests and seas of sin, as it were. That is, love has no desire to reflect itself in a neighbor's sins and maliciously rejoice in them. It conducts itself as having neither seen nor heard them. Or, if they cannot be overlooked, it readily forgives, and so far as possible mends matters. Where nothing else can be done, it endures the sins of a neighbor without stirring up strife and making a bad matter worse.

32. The apostle, upon authority of observation and experience, acknowledges that where people dwell together there must be mutual transgressions; it cannot be otherwise. No one will always do what is pleasing to others, and each is liable to commit open wrong. Peter would teach that since men must live together in their respective stations in life—for the Scriptures make no recognition of singular and intolerant saints who would promptly run out of the world when some little thing takes place at variance with their opinions —he who would live peaceably must so control himself as to be able to bear with others, to overlook their imperfections, and to cover their transgressions and thus avert further resulting evil.

Where no toleration is exercised, where no wrong is forgiven and forgotten, hate and envy must find place. The sole office of these is to stir up strife and contention. No peace and rest is to be had where they exist; wrangling and fighting, oppression and bitterness, must obtain. The unbounded ill-will, the innumerable strifes and wars, having place on earth, all result from the abominable evil of the lack of love among us and from the prevalence of pernicious

hate, which leads to anger and revenge when opposition
offers. Thus we become enemies to one another instead of
to evil, when it is our duty to love our fellow-men.

33. Now, if you would live as a Christian and enjoy
peace in the world, you must make every effort to restrain
your anger and not to give way to revenge as do others.
Rather you must suppress these passions, subduing your
hatred by love, and be able to overlook and bear, even
though you have to suffer great pain and injustice. So doing
you will develop a noble character fitted to accomplish much
good through patience and humility, to allay and abolish
enmity, and strife, and thereby to reform and convert others.
If you are unwilling to be patient under injustice, then go
on hating and envying, impatiently blustering about and
seeking revenge. But from such a proceeding only strife
and disquietude can be your portion, though your com-
plaints be long and your lamentations loud. You may run
hither and thither, and still you will not find the truth otherwise than as I have stated. This text would have to be done
away with first, and the Scriptures falsified.

34. Paul, having in mind Solomon's saying about love, in
extolling the same virtue amplifies the latter's statement
with various expressions, in the thirteenth of First Corinthians. Among other things he says there (verses 5-8): "Love
seeketh not its own, is not provoked, taketh not account of
evil; rejoiceth not in unrighteousness, but rejoiceth with the
truth; beareth all things, believeth all things, hopeth all
things, endureth all things. Love never faileth," etc. This,
mark you, is "being fervent in love," as Peter calls it. Here
is the heat, the fire, effective to consume all evil and to re-
place it with only good. This fire will not permit itself to
be quenched; it surmounts all checking. Whatever of evil
is heaped upon it, it remains in itself good, and works only
good.

35. The essential property, the "differentia essentialis,"
of genuine love, as its nature requires fervency, is the fact
that it cannot be embittered. He who has it, will not cease
to love, to do good and to endure evil. In a word love can-

not hate; it cannot be at enmity with anyone. No evil can be wrought too great for love to endure. No one can commit against it more sins than it can cover. It cannot be enraged to the point of refusing to forgive. Its attitude is not unlike that of the mother toward her child. The child may be imperfect and impure, even filthy, but the mother notes it not, even if she sees it. Her love blinds her. The eyes wherewith she looks upon her child as the beautiful and God-given fruit of her own body are so pure that she overlooks all imperfections, regarding them as nothing. Indeed, she excuses, even glorifies, them. Although the child squints, it must not be called squint-eyed, but love-eyed, and even a wart must be thought to become it.

36. Behold, this is covering sins with love—a virtue peculiar to Christians. The world does not possess that virtue. Such love is impossible to it, whatever its pretensions and ostentations in that respect. However precious the world's love may be, it is subject to delusion, vanity and hypocrisy; for the world is false in appearance and pretension. No worldling likes to be regarded hateful and envious toward his neighbor, but succeeds in conducting himself, so far as word and gesture are concerned, in an affable manner to all. This attitude he maintains so long as we show him favors and obey his pleasure. But when our love for him becomes a little disaffected and we happen to offer a word he regards insulting, he promptly withdraws his affections and begins to complain and to rage as if he had been done a great wrong. He makes out he is under no obligation to endure the injustice; and he boastingly plumes himself on having shown great faithfulness and love to the offender, such fidelity as would have led him readily to share with that one the very heart in his body, and now he is so ill repaid that henceforth he will leave such people to be served by the devil.

Such is the world's love. The world loves not "m deed," but "in word," as John expresses it. 1 Jn 3, 18. It has no sincerity of heart. Its love is a mere ignis-fatuus, shining but having no fire; a love which endures not, but is blown

out by a breath—extinguished with a word. The reason of
it all is, the world seeks only its own. It would be served,
would receive from others, and not make any return, particularly if response must entail any suffering and forbearance on its part.

37. "But," you may say, "shall evil go unpunished?
What would be the result were all evil to be tolerated and
covered up? Would not that be giving the wicked opportunity to carry out their evil designs? Would it not encourage them in their wickedness until life would not be safe to
anyone?" I reply: We have often stated what individuals
properly merit our anger, and the extent and manner of
punishment to be awarded them. It is truly the office of
civil government and also of the father of every family to
visit anger upon evil, and to punish and restrain it. Again,
every pastor and preacher is commissioned—yes, every
godly Christian—to admonish and censure when he sees a
neighbor committing sin, just as one brother in a family
admonishes another. But to be angry with evil and to inflict official punishment—punishment by virtue of office—is
a different thing from being filled with hatred and revenge,
or holding ill-will and being unforgiving.

38. It is not inconsistent with the character of love to be
angry and to reprove when a neighbor is observed to sin.
But true love feels no inclination to behold the sin and disgrace of a neighbor; rather, much rather, it desires his improvement. Just as parents correct with a rod a disobedient
and obstinate child but do not cast it out and become enemies to it because of that disobedience, their object being
only to reform the child, while the rod is cast away after
chastisement; so, too, according to Christ's words (Mt 18,
15-17), you may censure your brother when he sins, and
manifest your displeasure and indignation, that he may perceive and confess his wrong-doing, and if he does not then
amend his conduct, you may inform the congregation. At
the same time, his obstinacy does not justify you in becoming his enemy, or in entertaining ill-will toward him. As
said before, love to be true must not be dull and cold, too

indifferent to perceive a neighbor's sins; it must endeavor to relieve him thereof. It must have the red fire of fervor. He who truly loves will be distressed that a beloved neighbor wickedly trespasses against God and himself. Again, true love does not pale with hatred and revenge. It continues to glow red when the possessor's heart is moved with sympathy, is filled with compassion, for its neighbor. True, when fervor and admonition fail to effect any reform, the sincere-hearted Christian must separate himself from his obstinate neighbor and regard him as a heathen; nevertheless, he must not become his neighbor's enemy nor wish him evil.

39. Anger and censure prompted by sincere love are very different from the wrath, hatred and revengefulness of the world, which seeks only its own interests and is unwilling to tolerate any opposition to its pleasure. True love is moved to anger only when a neighbor's good demands. Though not insensible to evil and not approving evil, it is yet able to tolerate, to forgive and cover, all wrongs against itself, and it leaves untried no expedient that may make a neighbor better. Sincere love makes a clear distinction between the evil and the person; it is unfriendly to the former, but kind to the latter.

"Using hospitality one to another without murmuring: according as each hath received a gift, ministering it among yourselves, as good stewards of the manifold grace of God."

40. Having admonished all Christians to love one another generally, Peter mentions various instances where love should be externally manifested among Christians, and speaks particularly of those who have been favored above others with special gifts and special offices in the Church, whereby they are able to serve their fellows. Thus he teaches that the Christian's whole external conduct should be regulated by that love which seeks not its own advantage, which aims not at profiting itself, but lives to serve its neighbor.

41. First, Peter says, "Using hospitality one to another."

The reference is to works of love relative to the various
physical needs of a neighbor.   Christians are to serve one
another by ministering temporal blessings.   Especially are
the poor and the wretched to be remembered, they who are
strangers or pilgrims among us, or come to us houseless and
homeless.   These should receive the willing ministrations of
Christians, and none be allowed to suffer want.

42.   In the apostles' time, the primitive days of the
Church, Christians were everywhere persecuted, driven from
their possessions and forced to wander hither and thither in
poverty and exile.   It was necessary then to admonish Christians in general, and particularly those who had something
of their own, not to permit these destitute ones to suffer
want, but to provide for them.   So, too, is it today incumbent upon Christians to provide for the really poor—not lazy
beggars, or vagabonds—the outdoor pensioners, so called;
and to maintain those who, because of old age or other infirmity, are unable to support themselves.   The churches
should establish common treasuries for the purpose of providing alms for cases of this kind.   It was so ordained of
the apostles in Acts 6, 3.   Paul, also, in many places admonishes to such works of love; for instance (Rom 12, 13):
"Communicating to the necessities of the saints."

43.   Moreover, as Peter says, hospitality is to be extended
"without murmuring"—not with reluctance and aversion, as
the way of the world is.   The world is particularly reluctant
when called upon to give to Christ the Lord, in other words
to his poor servants the pastors and preachers, or to their
children, into whose mouths they must count every bit of
bread.   It regards oppressive and burdensome the contributing of even a dime for that purpose.   At the same time, it
lavishly bestows its gifts upon the devil; as, for instance,
under popedom it gave liberally and willingly to indolent,
useless monks and shameless, wicked knaves, impostors and
seducers.   Such is the inconsistence of the world; and it is
a just punishment from God that it is made unworthy to
contribute where it well might toward the preservation of
God's Word and his poor Church; and that it must give to

other and ungrateful purposes. Christian love must be sincere enough to do good "without murmuring." Paul says (Rom 12, 8) to "let him that showeth mercy do so with cheerfulness," or willingly, without restraint. Again (2 Cor 9, 7), "God loveth a cheerful giver," etc.

STEWARDS OF GOD'S GIFTS.

44. Peter speaks also of love's work in relation to the gifts of the Holy Spirit, which are bestowed for the good of the entire Church and particularly for its spiritual offices or government. He would have the Spirit's gifts used in the service of others, and admonishes Christians to consider all they have as given of God. The heathen have no such thought, but live as if life and all they possess were of their own attaining. But let Christians know they are under obligation to serve God with their gifts; and God is served when they employ them for the advantage and service of the people—reforming them, briging them to a knowledge of God, and thus building up, strengthening and perpetuating the Church. Of such love the world knows nothing at all.

45. So then, Peter says, we are to use the gifts called spiritual—gifts of the Holy Spirit—in the Christian Church "as good stewards of the manifold grace of God." He would have us know they are conferred upon us of grace. They are not given us to exalt ourselves therewith, but to make us stewards of the house of God—of his Church. They are manifold and variously distributed; for no one may possess all. Some may have certain gifts and offices, and other individuals certain others. But the mutual way in which these gifts are united and related makes one individual serve another.

46. Peter would remind especially each individual to take heed to the duties of his particular office. In the pursuance of his own occupation, each is to attend faithfully to whatever is committed to his charge; to do whatever he is commanded to do. As the Scriptures teach in many places, there is no work nobler than being obedient to the particular calling and work assigned of God, and satisfied therein; faithfully serving one's neighbor and not gazing after what is

committed to, or enjoined upon, another, nor presuming to transcend the limits of one's own commission. Many fickle, unstable spirits, however, especially the presumptuous, proud and self-sufficient, imagine themselves to have such measure of the Spirit and of skill that their own calling is not sufficient for them; they must control all things, must superintend and criticise the work of others. They are malignant souls, doing nothing but to stir up mischief, and having not the grace to perform any good work, even though they have noble gifts. For they do not make use of the gifts of their office to serve their neighbors; they only minister therewith to their own glory and advantage.

47. The apostle goes on to show how God distributes his gifts in various ways; he speaks of "manifold gifts." Paul likewise (1 Cor 12, 4-5) teaches that each one is given a special gift, and a particular office wherein he is to exercise his gift, continuing in his own sphere until called to another. Again, Paul says (Rom 12, 6-7): "Whether prophecy, let us prophesy. . . . or ministry, let us give ourselves to our ministry." It is not enough to have numerous special gifts; grace is also requisite—"manifold grace of God," Peter says. We must so use our gifts that God may be pleased to add his blessing, if we would successfully and profitably serve the Church and accomplish good. God's grace will not be given to those who do not, in faith and in obedience to his command, fulfill the obligations of their calling. Now Peter proceeds to illustrate, giving a rule of how we are to use our individual gifts. He says:

"If any man speaketh, speaking as it were oracles of God; if any man ministereth, ministering as of the strength which God supplieth."

48. It is highly essential that the Church observe this doctrine. Had it been regarded heretofore, the world would not have been filled with anti-christian errors and deceptions. For it fixes the bounds, it sets the mark, for all aspiring church members, however exalted their office and gifts; the limits of these they must not transcend.

49. The apostle classifies Church government in two divi-

sions: teaching, or "ministering" the Word; and holding office and fulfilling its duties in accordance with the teachings of the Word. In both cases, he tells us, we are to take heed that we are not actuated by our own ideas and pleasures; our teaching and ruling must ever be God's Word and work or office.

50. The workings of the Christian Church are not the same as the processes of civil government. They are unlike the operations that have to do with outward things, with temporal possessions. In the latter case men are guided by their own understanding. At the dictates of their own reason do they rule, instituting laws and regulations, and prohibiting, receiving and distributing according to those regulations. In the Christian Church we have a spiritual government of the conscience, an effecting of obedience in God's sight. Whatever is spoken or taught, promised or done, we may be assured, will avail and stand before God; indeed, we may know it has origin with him, whereby we are justified in declaring: "God himself uttered the command or performed the work; for in us, his tabernacles where he lives and rules, essentially he, as rightful Master in the house, commands and performs all, though employing the instrumentality of men's lips and hands."

ASSURANCE OF PURE DOCTRINE ESSENTIAL.

51. In the first place, therefore, it is necessary that both preachers and hearers take heed to doctrine and have clear, unmistakable evidence that what they embrace is really the true Word of God revealed from heaven; the doctrine given to the holy and primitive fathers, prophets and apostles; the doctrine Christ himself confirmed and commanded to be taught. We are not permitted to employ the teaching dictated by any man's pleasure or fancy. We may not adapt the Word to mere human knowledge and reason. We are not to trifle with the Scriptures, to juggle with the Word of God, as if it would admit of being explained to suit the people; of being twisted, distended and patched to effect peace and agreement among men. Otherwise, there would be no sure, permanent foundation whereon the conscience might rely.

52. Nor is it any more admissible for one who chances to have an office of greater influence than others, who is peculiarly holy, or who is of exalted spirit and intellect—even though he were an apostle—to presume upon his gifts and the office and take authority to teach according to his own inclinations, requiring his hearers to accept unquestioningly his word and rely upon it because what he teaches must be right. But thus the Pope in time past persuaded the world that because he occupied the seat of the apostles, the highest office, and assembled the councils, the latter could not err, and that therefore all men are obliged to believe and obey what they resolve and confirm.

53. This theory is opposed by Peter's teaching, and all the Scriptures forbid men, at the peril of losing eternal salvation, to rely on or respect anyone or anyone's gifts, in the things pertaining to faith. The Scriptures teach rather that we are to prove and judge all doctrine by the clear and sure Word of God given us from heaven and supported by the reliable, concurrent testimony of the apostles and the Church from the beginning. Paul, by way of denouncing the false teachers who boasted of being disciples of eminent apostles and relied upon the latter and their reputation, pronounced this sentence (Gal 1, 8): "Though we, or an angel from heaven, should preach unto you any gospel other than that which we preached unto you, let him be anathema."

54. Similarly, in the offices or government of the Church, there must first be convincing evidence that command and office are instituted of God. No one may be permitted to institute, promise or do anything of his own power or pleasure and compel men to regard it as divine authority or as essential to salvation, simply because of his appointment to office. Nevertheless, the Pope, by virtue of his ecclesiastical office, undertook to domineer over all men, to issue commands and institute laws and religious services binding upon everyone.

He who holds and would exercise office in the Church must first give clear Scripture proof of having derived his office from the authority of God. He must be able to say:

"I did not institute such and such a proceeding; it is of God." Then they who comply may be assured they are obeying, not the individual, but God.

55. For instance, if in obedience to Christ's command I, as a carer of souls, or servant of the Church, administer the holy sacrament or pronounce absolution; if I admonish, comfort, reprove; I can say: "That which I do, I do not; Christ performs it." For I act not of my own design, but in obedience to the command of Christ—to his injunction. The Pope and his adherents cannot make the above assertion. For they pervert the order and commandment of Christ the Lord when, in the sacrament, they withhold the cup from the laity, and when they change the use of the sacrament or mass, making it a sacrifice for the living and the dead. And thus they do also by innumerable other abominations in their false worship, things established without God's command, indeed contrary thereto; for instance, the invocation of dead saints, and similar idolatries, introduced by the Pope under cover of his office, as if he had the power from Christ to institute and command such things.

ASSURANCE OF DIVINE EFFICIENCY ESSENTIAL.

56. In the second place, it is not enough that office and commandment be God-appointed. We his ministers should be conscious—and the people should so be taught—that efficacy of office is not of human effort, but is God's power and work. In other words, that which the office was designed to accomplish is not effective by virtue of our speech or action, but by virtue of God's commandment and appointment. He it is who orders; and himself will effectively operate through that office which is obedient to God's command. For instance, in baptism, the Lord's Supper and absolution, we are not to be concerned about the person administering the sacraments or pronouncing absolution—who he is, how righteous, how holy, how worthy. Worthiness or unworthiness of either administering or receiving hand effects nothing; all the virtue lies in God's command and ordinance.

57. This is the explanation of Peter's phrase, "the strength or ability which God supplieth." Effect is pro-

duced, not through man's power, not in obedience to man's will; but through the "strength" of God and because of his ordering. No man has a right presumptuously to boast his own power and ability effective, as the Pope does in his pretensions about keys and ecclesiastical power. Know that it is necessary to the efficacy of your office and the salutary character of your work or authority in the Church that God himself give and exert the influence. And that influence is exerted when, as before said, God's Word and testimony are present that the ministry in question is commanded, or authorized, of God.

58. Therefore it is earnestly enjoined that in the Church no attempt should be made by any individual to institute any order or perform any work, much or little, great or small, merely at the prompting of his own inclinations or in obedience to the advice of any man. Let him who would teach and work be sure that his words and acts are really of God—commanded by him. Until he is certain in this respect, let him abandon his office—suspend his ministry; let him engage in something else for a time. Nor should we hear or believe anything presented to us that does not bear indisputable evidence of being the divine Word, or command. For God will not permit mockery of himself in the things of his own prerogative and on which depends the salvation of souls; for souls will be led to eternal ruin where this rule and command are disregarded.

"That in all things God may be glorified through Jesus Christ."

59. Here is named the motive for all effort in the Christian community. No one may seek for nor ascribe to himself power and honor because of his office and gifts. Power and glory belong only to God. He himself calls his Church, and rules, sanctifies and preserves it through his Word and his Spirit. To this end he bestows upon us his gifts. And all is done purely of grace, wholly for the sake of his beloved Son, Christ the Lord. Therefore, in return for the favor and ineffable goodness bestowed upon us regardless of our merits, we ought to thank and praise God, directing all our efforts to the recognition and glory of his name.

Pentecost

Text: Acts 2, 1-13.

1 And when the day of Pentecost was now come, they were all together in one place. 2 And suddenly there came from heaven a sound as of the rushing of a mighty wind, and it filled all the house where they were sitting. 3 And there appeared unto them tongues parting asunder, like as of fire; and it sat upon each one of them. 4 And they were all filled with the Holy Spirit, and began to speak with other tongues, as the Spirit gave them utterance. 5 Now there were dwelling at Jerusalem Jews, devout men, from every nation under heaven. 6 And when this sound was heard, the multitude came together, and were confounded, because that every man heard them speaking in his own language. 7 And they were all amazed and marvelled, saying, Behold, are not all these that speak Galilæans? 8 And how hear we, every man in our own language wherein we were born? 9 Parthians and Medes and Elamites, and the dwellers in Mesopotamia, in Judæa and Capadocia, in Pontus and Asia, 10 in Phrygia and Pamphylia, in Egypt and the parts of Libya about Cyrene, and sojourners from Rome, both Jews and proselytes, 11 Cretans and Arabians, we hear them speaking in our tongues the mighty works of God. 12 And they were all amazed, and were perplexed, saying one to another, What meaneth this? 13 But others mocking said, They are filled with new wine.

THE GIFT OF THE HOLY SPIRIT.

1. The historical facts of this day, as well as the beautiful sermon the Holy Spirit delivered through the apostle Peter, which might appropriately be fully treated at this time, we

shall leave for the special sermons on the various festivals of the year. For the present we will but briefly speak of the occasion of this festival, and of the office of the Holy Spirit.

2. The festival we call "Pentecost" had origin as follows: When God was about to lead the children of Israel out of Egypt, he permitted them to celebrate the Feast of the Passover on the night of their departure; and commanded them on every annual recurrence of the season to observe the same feast in commemoration of their liberation from bondage and their departure from Egypt. Fifty days later, in their journey through the wilderness, they arrived at Mount Sinai. There God gave them the Law, through Moses; and there they were commanded to observe annually, in commemoration of that giving of the Law, the fiftieth day after the Feast of the Passover. Hence the name "Feast of Pentecost," the word "Pentecost" coming from the Greek "Pentecoste," or "fiftieth day." Our Saxons, rather more in conformity to the Greek, use the word "Pfingsten." So we have it here of Luke: "When the day of Pentecost was now come," or "fully come"—when the Jews had properly commemorated the giving of the Law of God on Mount Sinai— the Holy Spirit came, in accordance with Christ's promise, and gave them a new law. We now celebrate this feast, not because of the old historical event, but because of the new one—the sending of the Holy Spirit. It is in order, then, to give a little instruction concerning the difference between our Pentecost and that of the Jews.

LITERAL LAW AND SPIRITUAL LAW.

3. The occasion of the Jews' observance was the giving of the literal law; but it is ours to celebrate the giving of the spiritual law. To present the point more clearly, we cite Paul's distinction of the two covenants. 2 Cor 3, 6. And these two covenants respectively relate to two kinds of people.

4. First, there is the written law commanded of God and composed of written words. It is styled "written" or "literal" because it goes no farther and does not enter the heart, nor are there any resulting works other than hypocritical

and extorted ones. Consisting only of letters—a written law—it is wholly dead. Its province being to kill, it ruled a dead people. With dead hearts men could not sincerely observe the commandments of God. Were every individual left to do as he pleased, being uninfluenced by fear, not one would be found choosing to be controlled by the Law.

Unquestionably, human nature is conscious of the fact that while it prefers to follow its own inclinations it is impelled to do otherwise; for it reasons: "If I observe not God's commandments, he will punish me, casting me into hell." Thus our nature is conscious of obeying unwillingly and contrary to desire. Because of the punishment men fear, they soon become enemies to God; they feel themselves sinners, unable to stand before God, and consequently not acceptable to him. Indeed, they would rather there were no God. Such enmity to God remains persistently in the heart, however beautifully nature may adorn itself outwardly. We see, therefore, how the Law, so long as it consists merely of written words, can make no one righteous, can enter no heart. Upon this topic we have elsewhere preached and written at length.

5. The other law is spiritual; not written with ink and pen, nor uttered by lips as Moses read from the tables of stone. We learn from the historical record of the event that the Holy Spirit descended from heaven and filled all the assembled multitude, and they appeared with parting, fiery tongues and preached so unlike they were wont to do that all men were filled with amazement. The Spirit came pouring into their hearts, making them different beings, making them creatures who loved and willingly obeyed God. This change was simply the manifestation of the Spirit himself, his work in the heart. He wrote in those hearts his pure and fiery flame restoring them to life and causing them to respond with fiery tongues and efficient hands. They became new creatures, aware of possessing altogether different minds and different tendencies. Then all was life and light; understanding, will and heart burned and delighted in whatever was acceptable to God. Such is the true dis-

tinction between the written law of God and the spiritual.
Herein we perceive what is the work of the Holy Spirit.

THE OFFICE OF THE HOLY SPIRIT.

6. From this we should learn what is the office of the
Holy Spirit in the Church, and how or by what means he
is received in the heart and works there. In time past it
was preached that he merely endorses what the councils
conclude and the Pope establishes in the Spiritless papal
Church. The fact is, however, the doings of Pope and
councils are mere outward matters; they relate to external
commands and government. The above theory is, therefore,
wholly inconsistent and perverse. Of the work of the
Holy Spirit, the Papists make a dead, written law, when
it is really a living, spiritual law. Thus they render the
Holy Spirit a Moses, and his words mere human prattle.
It is all due to ignorance of the character of the Holy
Spirit, of the purpose of his coming and the nature of his
office. Therefore, let us learn and firmly grasp those things
and be able rightly to distinguish the Spirit's office.

7. Observe here, the Holy Spirit descends and fills the
hearts of the disciples sitting in fear and sorrow. He renders their tongues fiery and cloven, and inflames them with
love unto boldness in preaching Christ—unto free and
fearless utterance. Plainly, then, it is not the office of the
Spirit to write books or to institute laws. He writes in
the hearts of men, creating a new heart, so that man may
rejoice before God, filled with love for him and ready, in
consequence, to serve his fellows gladly.

8. What are the means and process the Spirit employs to
change and renew the heart? It is through preaching
Jesus Christ the Lord, as Christ himself says (Jn 15, 26):
"When the Comforter is come, whom I will send unto you
from the Father, even the Spirit of truth, which proceedeth
from the Father, he shall bear witness of me." As we have
often heard, the Gospel is the message God would have
preached world-wide, declaring to every individual that
since no man can through the Law be made righteous, but
must rather become more unrighteous, God sent his own

beloved Son to shed his blood and die for our sins, from which sins we could not be released by our own effort.

9. It is not enough simply that Christ be preached; the Word must be believed. Therefore, God sends the Holy Spirit to impress the preaching upon the heart—to make it inhere and live therein. Unquestionably, Christ accomplished all—took away our sins and overcame every obstacle, enabling us to become, through him, lords over all things. But the treasure lies in a heap; it is not everywhere distributed and applied. Before we can enjoy it, the Holy Spirit come and communicate it to the heart, enabling us to believe and say, "I too, am one who shall have the blessing." To everyone who hears is grace offered through the Gospel; to grace is he called, as Christ says (Mt 11, 28), "Come unto me, all ye that labor and are heavy laden," etc.

10. Now, with the belief that God has come to our rescue and given us this priceless blessing, inevitably the human heart must be filled with joy and with gratitude to God, and must exultingly cry: "Dear Father, since it is thy will to manifest toward me inexpressible love and fidelity, I will love thee sincerely, and willingly do what is pleasing to thee."

The believing heart never sees God with jealous eye. It does not fear being cast into hell as it did before the Holy Spirit came, when it was conscious of no love, no goodness, no faithfulness, on God's part, but only wrath and displeasure. But once let the Holy Spirit impress the heart with the fact of God's good will and graciousness towards it, and the resulting joy and confidence will impel it to do and suffer for God's sake whatever necessity demands.

11. Let us, then, learn to recognize the Holy Spirit—to know that his mission is to present to us the priceless Christ and all his blessings; to reveal them to us through the Gospel and apply them to the heart, making them ours. When our hearts are sensible of this work of the Spirit, naturally we are compelled to say: "If our works avail naught, and the Holy Spirit alone must accomplish our salvation, then why burden ourselves with works and laws?"

By the doctrine of the Spirit, all human works and laws
are excluded, even the laws of Moses. The Holy Spirit's
instruction is superior to that of all books. The Spirit-
taught individual understands the Scriptures better than
does he who is occupied solely with the Law.

12. Hence, our only use for books is to strengthen our
faith and to show others written testimony to the Spirit's
teaching. For we may not keep our faith to ourselves, but
must let it shine out; and to establish it the Scriptures are
necessary. Be careful, therefore, not to regard the Holy
Spirit as a Law-maker, but as proclaiming to your heart the
Gospel of Christ and setting you so free from the literal
law that not a letter of it remains, except as a medium for
preaching the Gospel.

BELIEVERS MUST YET RESIST SIN.

13. Here we should be intelligent and know that in one
sense all is not accomplished when the Holy Spirit is received. The possessor of the Spirit is not at once entirely
perfect, pure in all respects, no more sensible of the Law and
of sin. We do not preach the doctrine that the Spirit's
office is one of complete accomplishment, but rather that it
is progressive; he operates continuously and increasingly.
Hence, there is not to be found an individual perfect in
righteousness and happiness, devoid of sin and sorrow, ever
serving all men with pleasure.

The Scriptures make plain the Holy Spirit's office—to
liberate from sin and terror. But the work is not then complete. The Christian must, in some measure, still feel sin
in his heart and experience the terrors of death; he is affected by whatever disturbs other sinners. While unbelievers are so deep in their sins as to be indifferent, believers
are keenly conscious of theirs; but Christians are supported
by the Holy Spirit, who consoles and strengthens till his
work is fully accomplished. It is terminated when they no
longer feel their sins.

14. So I say we must be prudent; we must take heed
we do not arrogantly and presumptuously boast possession

of the Holy Spirit, as do certain proud fanatics. The danger is in becoming too secure, in imagining ourselves perfect in all respects. The pious Christian is still flesh and blood like other men; he but strives to resist evil lusts and other sins, and is unwillingly sensible of evil desires. But he who is not a Christian is carelessly secure, wholly unconcerned about his sins.

15. It is of no significance that we feel evil lusts, provided we endeavor to resist them. One must not go by his feelings and consider himself lost if he have sinful desires. At the same time he must, so long as life lasts, contend with the sins he perceives in himself. He must unceasingly groan to be relieved of them, and must permit the Holy Spirit to operate in him. There is in believers continual groaning after holiness—groaning too deep for expression, as Paul says in Romans 8, 26. But Christians have a blessed listener—the Holy Spirit himself. He readily perceives sincere longing after purity, and sends the conscience divine comfort.

There will ever be in us mingled purity and imperfection; we must be conscious both of the Holy Spirit's presence and of our own sins—our imperfections. We are like the sick man in the hands of the physician who is to restore him to health. Let no one think: "Here is a man who possesses the Holy Spirit; consequently he must be perfectly strong, having no imperfections and performing only worthy works." No, think not so; for so long as we live in the flesh here on earth, we cannot attain such a degree of perfection as to be wholly free from weakness and faults. The holy apostles themselves often lamented their temptations and sorrows. Their feelings concealed from them the Holy Spirit's presence, though they were aware of his strengthening and sustaining power in their temptations, a power conveyed through the Word and through faith.

16. The Holy Spirit is given only to the anxious and distressed heart. Only therein can the Gospel profit us and produce fruit. The gift is too sublime and noble for God to

cast it before dogs and swine, who, when by chance they hear the preached message, devour it without knowing to what they do violence. The heart must recognize and feel its wretchedness and its inability to extricate itself. Before the Holy Spirit can come to the rescue, there must be a struggle in the heart. Let no one imagine he will receive the Spirit in any other way.

17. We see this truth illustrated in the narrative here. The beloved disciples were filled with fear and terror. They were disconsolate and discouraged, and sunk in unbelief and despair. Only with great difficulty and effort did Christ raise them again. Yet their only failing was their faint-heartedness; they feared the heavens would fall upon them. Even the Lord himself could scarce comfort them until he said: "The Holy Spirit shall descend upon you from heaven, impressing myself upon your hearts until you shall know me and, through me, the Father. Then will your hearts be comforted, strengthened and filled with joy. And so was the promise fulfilled to them on this day of Pentecost.

Luther's Church Postil contains no sermons on the epistle selections for Whit-Monday and Whit-Tuesday.

Pentecost Monday

Text: Acts 2, 14-28.

Only the text, without a sermon, is printed in the edition of 1559 of Luther's works. This and the following epistle text are too long to consider here, as they contain so many beautiful quotations from the Old Testament, which should not be passed over too briefly. Hence their discussion is reserved for their proper place.

Pentecost Tuesday

Text: Acts 2, 29-36.

FROM "THE MINNEAPOLIS JOUR-
NAL," Feb. 8, 1909.

LUTHER FIRST IN MISSIONARY WORK

Dr. J. N. Lenker Tells of the Evangelical Power of the Lutheran Church.

By J. N. Lenker, D.D.

The Christian religion being pre-eminently missionary, the reformation of the Christian church would necessarily be missionary. Protestant missions began with Protestantism. Luther's interest in the work of evangelism is seen in the name he designedly chose for the church of his followers. He did not call it Protestant nor Lutheran, but conscientiously insisted upon it being called the evangelical or gospel church, the evangelizing church. Because of Luther's emphasis on the word evangelical, there are, properly speaking, no Lutheran, but only Evangelical-Lutheran churches. That Europe is evangelized is due more to his labors and writings than those of any other. What those writings did for Europe they may do, and we believe, will do for the world in time in a greater or less degree.

In the modern and narrower sense of systematized machinery and organized methods of local and general societies or boards to collect funds, to send beyond the seas missionaries and to hold annual conventions and send out annual reports, there was very little of that in Luther's writings. Wittenberg was too far from the sea border. The sea powers in those days were Spain and Portugal, where even the reformation itself could not enter, much less could it make use of their ships. Moreover the heathenism in the Christian church claimed all the energy of young Protestantism.

All who retain the good old custom of the fathers in reading Luther's postil sermons on the gospel and epistle texts for each Sunday know what deep missionary thoughts are found in the sermons for Epiphany, Ascension day and Pentecost.

Luther on the Great Commission.

In one sermon for Ascension day on "Go ye into all the world and preach the Gospel to the whole creation," we read these words of the Sovereign Ruler commission these poor beggars to go forth and proclaim this new message, not in one city or country only, but in all the world."

Had the apostles depended upon their own power, they would have miserably failed before crossing their own thresholds. Afraid of their own people, the Jews, they hid themselves behind bolted doors. Whence did they receive such courage and strength? Surely not from any king of Persia nor emperor of Rome, Turkey, or Tartary. No, it was from the Lord alone, who ascended into heaven and commanded them to go and preach to the whole creation. And as Christ began to set up his kingdom, so it will continue to the end of the world. He is the one to whom all authority is given in heaven and on earth. Christ looks far into the future. He does not want his message hidden in a corner. He does not want his disciples to have any fear concerning it, neither to go about it secretly nor deceitfully. He wants it proclaimed so publicly that even the sun in the heavens, yea, the forests and stones might hear it; if they had ears. Christ thus sends forth, not a decree to stir up rebellion in the world, or to overthrow the legal power of kings, princes or other temporal authority, but he simply puts his word and command into the mouths of the disciples that they may carry into effect his own power by their speech and ministry.

Not a Worldly Message.

They shall speak not of worldly institutions, worldly authority or earthly riches, nor of the glory of the Jewish people, their laws, religious rites and priesthood, but the import of the message shall be to teach nobler things, how we may be reconciled to God, how he redeemed from sin, death and all evil, and be saved; how to obtain everlasting righteousness, life and glory. All the world is here sent to school, to hear and learn of Christ's kingdom and confess it knew nothing about it. Christ gives it a worthy name, calling it gospel preaching—evangelizing preaching. No doubt he gives it this peculiar new name for a special reason, to distinguish it from all other teaching and preaching. It is something different from the law of Moses and the teachings of men. A new name would impress itself upon the minds of the disciples. For the word "gospel" means a new message —a good message

The great contribution of Luther's homiletical, exegetical and catechetical writings to the problem of giving the gospel to the world, consists in making clear what the gospel is, so that we do not try to give something else to the world under the name of the gospel—that we evangelize the the world, nothing more and nothing less.

Showing Lutheran Work.

To show the work of the Lutheran church in the missionary field, the following table has been prepared for presentation to the Lutheran missionary conference that meets in Minneapolis March 14 to 15:

Society—	Organized.	Missionaries.	Members.	Receipts. 1907.
Leipzig	1705	134	23,528	$142,898
Hermannsburg	1849	123	68,891	105,362
Berlin	1824	259	60,390	275,000
Gossner	1836	131	86,556	95,000
*Rhenish	1828	362	142,745	266,752
*Basel	1815	390	59,166	464,970
North German	1836	50	5,541	50,000
Schleswig-Holstein	1876	35	12,055	52,000
East Africa	1886	34	1,109	23,176
Hanover Free Ch.	1892	12	4,546	10,000
Gen. Protestant	1884	10	1,000	33,000
Neuendettelsau	1886	23	1,477	22,234
German Orient	1900	8	500	14,000
Kaisersw. Deac.	1851	124	1,200	40,000
Jerusalem	1852	10	900	36,000
Liebenzeller	1899	9	200	24,000
Kill-China	1897	6	100	7,000
Micronesia	1906	8	4,945	8,000
Soudan	1900	4	200	5,000
China Alliance	1891	9	422	10,000
Women's China	1850	4	151	8,000
Women's Orient	1842	18	400	7,000
*China's Inland	1895	5	100	1,800
China's Blind	1890	3	62	5,000
Medical Mission	1906	....	....	20,000
25 in Germany		1,771	476,184	$1,925,692
Norwegian Society	1842	150	86,000	195,000
Norwegian church.	1877	18	1,500	6,000
Norwegian China..	1891	20	250	35,000
Norwegian Santal.	1888	17	16,000	9,000
Four in Norway		205	103,750	$245,000
Church of Sweden	1874	32	4,500	5,000
Fatherland	1856	95	2,600	170,000
Mission Union	1879	70	2,500	75,000
China Mission	1887	10	1,000	30,000
Lapp Mission	1880	4	250	2,500
Five in Sweden.		211	10,850	$282,500
Danish church	1705	25	15,000	25,000
Danish Society	1872	35	3,000	60,000
Danish Santal	1877	4	....	9,000
Loventhal	1872	2	100	6,000
Four in Denmark		66	18,100	$100,000
18 in Scandinavia		482	132,700	627,500
General Synod	1837	33	44,508	60,000
General Council	1869	18	17,500	85,871
Un. Synod of So.	1900	6	330	7,000
Three English		57	62,838	$102,371
Missouri Synod	1896	10	-225	-7,000
Ohio Synod		4	....	8,000
Iowa Synod		4	....	8,000
Wis., etc., Synod.	1893	8	300	5,282
*Evangel. Synod	1867	16	7,212	28,183
Five German		42	7,737	$56,445
Hauge Synod	1891	18	750	23,000
United Church	1895	29	1,756	46,143
Free Church	1885	7	700	12,025
Norwegian Synod.		5	500	13,835
Norw. Brethren	1895	8	200	8,099
Five Norwegian		67	3,906	$98,102
Sw. Augustana	1902	22	1,100	24,910
Sw. Mis. Friends	1887	31	1,000	43,389
Two Swedish		53	2,100	$68,299
United Danish	1892	3	320	5,050
Danish Church		2	100	2,000
Two Danish		5	420	$7,050
Scandinav. in U.S		125	6,426	163,451
Santal Mission	1891	2	....	7,000
19 in U. S....		224	76,501	$322,267
*Paris, France	1824	125	130,000	200,000
Madagascar	1895	2	1,000	5,000
Two in France.		127	131,000	$205,000
Finland	1859	30	3,500	50,000
Finland China	1890	4	100	5,025
Two in Finland		34	3,600	$55,025
Russia	1882	4	....	30,000
Poland		2	....	4,500
Holland	1880	5	300	5,000
Austria-Hungary.		....	......	8,000
Australia		6	700	4,000
South America		2	....	2,500
Asia	1867	17	16,000	120,000
Africa		....	......	200,000
Total for world		2,674	856,985	$3,454,984

*Lutheran and Reformed.

The $3,454,984 (13,819,936 marks or crowns in German or Scandinavian money) is a larger amount than many thought we were giving to this noble cause. The small sum of $322,267 from 13,000,000 Lutherans in the United States compared with the $245,000 from the 2373,000 Lutherans in Norway, makes us blush with shame. We may have had a little excuse for not doing better in the past, but not so in the future. Whether we realize it or not, the Lutherans of America are in a critical period just now in this matter. Think, the Reformed churches of America give more for heathen missions than all the Reformed churches of Europe. Lutherans in rich, prosperous America give about one tenth as much as their brethren in Europe. Let us all work together for a change.

Lutherans And The Reformed.

At present the Lutherans are stronger than the Reformed in Europe, Africa, South America and Northern Asia. The Reformed church leads in North America, Australia and Southern Asia. The Reformed churches are practically monoglot, all speaking English except 10,000,000, and are not very aggressive in other languages than English,

utherans First in Missionary Work.

THERANS AND THE EVANGEL-
IZATION OF THE WORLD.

epared by Prof. J. N. Lenker, D. D.,
t the request of the Minnesota Luth-
ran Missionary Conference.

r Share In Evangelizing the World.
ince one half of all the Protestants
the world and 68 per cent of the Pro-
tants of Minnesota are Lutherans,
becomes a question of conscience,
ll we do our part in the Evangel-
tion of the 600,000,000 heathen, who
ver heard of Christ.

Dr. Christlieb, the German author-
on missions, wrote in his book
out 25 years ago these words: 'The
rman Lutheran church in the last
tury (if we include the Moravians,
o had not really separated in doc-
ne), surpassed all other evangelical
urches in foreign and Jewish mis-
ns, and, although not under colonial
ligations, was the pioneer of the
spel in the East and West Indies;
t within the last 80 years she has
en outstripped in spreading the gos-
l by her Reformed sister and has
en roused again to new missionary
ivity within the last 10 years by
se lands in which once she set the
ample in mission work, namely,
gland and Holland."

t is well known that during the Six-
nth, Seventeenth and Eighteenth
turies the Lutheran church far sur-
ssed the Reformed churches in mis-
nary work among the heathen. The
son the Reformed churches sur-
ssed her in the Nineteenth century
s because of the ruin and poverty
used by the Napoleonic wars on the
tinent and the exceptional pros-
rity of English Reformed countries.
ce 1870, however, Germany and
andinavia have developed marvel-
sly in foreign missions.

ust a quarter of a century after
70 marks another epoch in recent
ssion history, when on Nov. 29, 1905,
therans in all lands and languages
ebrated the 200th anniversary of the
rman-Scandinavian mission at Tran-
ebar, India, founded by the Scandi-
vian King Frederick IV of Den-
rk and the two orphan mission-
ies, Ziegenbalg and Pluetschau, ed-
ated by Francke at Halle, Germany.
r new and increased interest in uni-
rsal missions during the 20th cen-
ry will doubtless be traced back in
large measure to these Ziegenbalg
lebrations.

here give the names and the num-
r of years the fifty-four illustrious
rman and Scandinavian missionaries
m Francke's orphanage labored in
dia during the eighteenth century,
rty-four of whom were on the field
fore Carey arrived in 1793. It was
egenbalg and the pietistic German
d Scandinavian Lutherans who
rted the modern missionary move-
nt in 1705 and not Carey and the
glish in 1793

Pioneers in Mission Field.

The list reads:
artholomew Ziegenbalg, 1705-1719;
nry Plutschau, 1705-1711; J. E.

Grundler, 1708-1720; A. J G. Bovingh,
1708-1711; B. Schultze, 1719-1743 (the
founder of the Protestant mission in
Madras); N. Dahl (a Dane), 1719-1747;
J. H. Kistenmacher, 1719-1722; M.
Bosse, 1725-1749; Charles F. Pressier,
1725-1738; Charles T. Walther, 1725-
1739; Andrew Worm, 1729-1735; S. G.
Richsteig, 1729-1735; J. A. Sartorius,
1730-1738 (he began the mission in
Cuddalore); J. E. Geister, 1732-1746; G.
W. Obuch, 1737-1745; J. C. Wiedebrock,
1737-1767 (nearly thirty years of service); J. Balthasar Kohlhoff, 1737-1790
(over fifty-three years of service); J.
Z. Kiernander, 1740-1799 (a Swede,
studied in Upsala and Halle, was the
founder of Protestant missions in
northern India and built the first Protestant church in Calcutta in 1770, in
which he preached for seventeen
years; he was 60 years in India; Carey
built on the foundations he laid); J.
P. Fabricius, 1740-1791 (fifty years in
India); Dan. Zeglin, 1740-1780 (labored
nearly forty years at Tranquebar);
Olof Maderup, 1741-1776 (a Dane and
labored at Tranquebar more than thir-
ty-four years); J. Klein, 1746-1790
(labored at Tranquebar nearly forty-
four years); J. C. Briethaupt, 1746-1782
(more than thirty-six years in India);
C. F. Schwartz, 1750-1798 (labored ele-
ven years in Tranquebar and began
the mission in Trichinopoly in 1762,
(forty-seven years in India); Dan.
Poltzenhagen, 1750-1756 (was the first
missionary to the Nicobar islands,
where the Moravians later labored);
G. H. Conrad Huttemann, 1750-1781;
Peter Dame, 1755-1766 (a Dane); W. F.
Gericke, 1766-1803; J. F. Konig, 1768-
1795; F. W. Leidemann, 1766-1774; W.
Jacob Muller, 1771 (died after in India
six months); C. S. John, 1766-1813
(forty-two years of labor at Tranquebar); J. C. Diemer, 1774-1792 (labored
at Calcutta); J. W. Gerlach, 1776-1791
(located at Calcutta); J. P. Rottler,
1776-1836 (sixty years in India); J. J.
Schollkopf, 1777 (died the same year);
C. Pohle, 1777-1818 (forty-one years in
India); L. Fred Rulfsen, 1780 (a Dane,
died the year he arrived); J. Dan. Men-
tel, 1781-1784; Peter Rubek Hagelund,
1786-1788 (a Dane); J. Caspar Kohlhoff,
reared by Missionary Schwartz, ordained by him in 1787 and labored at
Tanjore until his death in 1844); Jo-
seph D. Jaenicke, 1788-1800 (brother to
Pastor Jaenicke, who founded the mission school in Berlin, Germany); Au-
gust Fred Cammerer, 1791-1837 (was
shipwrecked on his way out at the
cape; for many years he was the only
missionary at Tranquebar); C W. Pa-
zold, 1793-1818; E. P. Stegmann, 1796-
1799; W. T. Ringeltaube, 1799-1820; I.
George Holzberg, 1797-1824; L. C.
Fruchtenicht, 1799-1802; C. H Horst,
1792-1810; Dan Schrevvogel, 1804-1840;
C. A. Jacobi, 1813-1814; J. G. P Sper-
schneider, 1819-1826; L. P. Haubroe,
1819-1830 (a Dane); David Rosen, 1819-
1838 (a Dane, was the head of the
Danish colonization experiment on the
Nicobar islands, 1831-1834).

Were All Lutherans.

The above fifty-four ordained missionaries were all Lutherans, and their faithful labors compose the first century of modern missions, during which century the Reformed churches did practically nothing for the heathen. In 1840, the Leipzig mission sent J. H. C. Cordes to Tranquebar, which came under English rule from 1808 to 1815, and for one reason or another many converts were transferred to various English societies, and others reaped where they never sowed. The above fifty-four missionaries laid the foundation, broad and deep, for the evangelization of India. Notwithstanding the Lutheran church in India lost thousands of converts to the English churches, she is today outnumbered there only by the Church of England, and all her missions are in a healthy and prosperous condition, numbering 353 missionaries, 1,752 churches, 234,-000 members and 1,639 schools The German and Scandinavian Lutherans laid the foundation for the modern world-evangelization movement, and it is our hope and prayer their interest and labors may increase until the work is finally accomplished We need, however, to watch and pray that we do our part.

All of these fifty-four missionaries died in the heathen mission field except eight, and eighteen were buried in the New Jerusalem church at Tranquebar the Roskilde or Westminster of India. Laymen occasionally accompanied the ordained missionaries and their wives. The first native pastor of modern missions in India and Asia, by name Aaron, was born of heathen parents at Cuddalore in 1699, baptized at Tranquebar in 1718, ordained by Pressier, Walther and others, Dec. 28, 1733, who died June 25, 1745. In all, fourteen natives were ordained from 1733 to 1817. Some like Ziegenbalg visited Europe, and others returned home who spread and deepened the foreign mission interest in the Protestant countries of Europe.

London Lutherans Contributed.

"When Ziegenbalg visited England he became intimate with the pastors and members of the Lutheran churches of London who contributed liberally to the mission. The pastors of these German churches, like Ziegenbalg and Muhlenberg the patriarch of the Lutheran church of America, were as a rule students from Halle and they kept in touch with Tranquebar, and translated many letters and reports from Tranquebar and Halle into English for the 'Society for Propagating Christian Knowledge,' of which they were as a rule members or warm friends In this way the heathen missionary work was semi-officially introduced into England during the eighteenth century by this Scandinavian-German mission Ziegenbalg had the honor of an audience with King George and the royal family in 1716. 'The Society for the

Propagation of Christian Knowled presented to him a congratulatory dress in Latin to which he replied Tamil. Encouraging letters were ceived by him from Dr. Wake, Ar bishop of Canterbury. A letter rece ed from him in India after Zieg balg's death bears testimony to apostolic spirit and work in th words:

"'I consider your lot is far hig than all church dignities. Let 9tl be prelates, patriarchs and popes; them be adorned with purple and sc let; let them desire bowings and ge flections, you have won a greater h or than all these and a far more m nificent recompense shall be gi you.'"

When it is said, England contribu to the Tranquebar mission, the G man and Scandinavian Lutherans England are meant.

Time for Action.

The English settlers in the Uni States are older and hence wealtl than the German and Scandinav settlers, who only of late ye have been in a condition to take this branch of church work ener tically. In every synod the fore missionary interest is growing and impression prevails that now is an portune time for a systematic uni sal advance. Those interested in F voking one another to good works uncertain which of the two equ divided Protestant armies will lag hind during the Twentieth century, German and Scandinavian Luther or the English Reformed. The reju nating of the Hanseatic German of the Viking Scandinavian life, 15,000,000 Lutherans who live in E lish Reformed countries and the that the Lutheran church in the Un States has so recently sprung fro little insignificant church in Ame to third place in the country as whole and the strongest church in Northern and Northwestern sta these and other considerations m the Lutherans quite hopeful.

Although our financial sho for the conversion of the heathen not as poor as we generally imag yet it is by no means as high as cause or our ability demands it sh be While the Lutherans have m advantages in this work over the formed yet in this one point of giv they are ahead, not because they so much wealthier but because are better developed to give syste tically.

The Lutherans of Minnesota last year 30 cents per member heathen missions, the Presbyterian cents This is largely due to our of systematic giving

"We know our weakest point. us come together and devise ways means to change it. The Catl church as a church is wealthy, her people are poor, while the L eran church as a church is poor her people are in comfortable circ stances all over the world. Why is this? Because of the teachings of Luther. The Lutheran church asks for money not to make herself rich but to give to lift up the people. The Lutherans will not forget what made them as they are. They will give that their fellow men everywhere may receive what was given to them. This is a matter of conscience for our people all over the world to consider.

A Layman and Missions in 1664.

Laymen in the Lutheran Church have always been encouraged to do Christian work. The work of laymen is not new among us. Laymen have been especially prominent in the missionary work for the conversion of the heathen. This may be due to the fact that the movement for the organization of the first heathen missionary society of Protestantism originated in the heart of a Lutheran layman, an Austrian nobleman, Justinian von Welz. In the year 1664 he published a little book in five chapters under the title: "A hearty Christian Exhortation to all true Christians of the Augsburg Confession to organize a Special Society for the Extension, with the Help of God, of the Evangelical Religion. Addressed (1) to all Evangelical Rulers, (2) to the Nobility, (3) to Doctors, Professors and Preachers, (4) especially to Students of Theology, (5) to Students of Law and Medicine, (6) to Merchants and all who sincerely love Jesus." In the first chapter he raises three pointed questions, which reveal his true missionary spirit: 1st, "Is it right for us Evangelical Christians to keep the Gospel to ourselves and never seek to spread it abroad?" 2d, "Is it right that we everywhere encourage so many to study theology and never give them an opportunity to labor abroad in the spiritual vineyard of Jesus Christ, but rather keep them waiting three, six and more years until parishes become vacant, or they become German school teachers?" 3rd, "Is it right that we Evangelical Christians should expend so much in the pride of dress, inexcessive eating and drinking, in useless amusements and costly fashions, and never think of providing means to spread the Gospel?" Opposed by the theologians, possessing means of his own, he planned for the founding of a "College for the Propagation of the Faith," in which three Professors were to teach (1) the Oriental languages, (2) the best methods for the conversion of the heathen, and (3) geography and the missionary journeys of Paul, Ansgar and others. Unable to carry out these plans he gave 36,000 marks to the cause went to Holland, sailed to Dutch Guiana, South America, and founded a mission on the Surinam river, where the Moravians have since had their most fruitful mission. Few laymen did more for the cause of missions to the heathen than Justinan von Welz. His book and life are worthy of study

Luther And Missions.

Herzog's Encyclopaedia says: "Luther himself already seizes every o portunity offered by a text of the vine Word in order to remind believe of the distress of the heathen a Turks and earnestly urges them pray in their behalf and to send o missionaries to them. In accord wi him all the prominent theologians a preachers of his day, and of the su ceeding period inculcated the missio ary duty of the church. Many also the Evangelical princes cherished t work with Christian love and zeal."

Of the 110 volumes Luther wrote treat of the pure evangelical teac ings of the Bible in commentaries, s mons and catechetical writings. popularized the word "evangelic and labored incessantly for the eva gelization of Europe.

Lutheran Missionary Conferences

not new. Twenty exist in Germa some dating from 1879. They working organizations essentially d ferent from the 25 missionary societi While the latter gather at home t necessary means and men for car ing on mission work among t heathen and Mohammedans, the m sionary conferences stimulate and courage the missionary spirit at ho They carry on an agitation in beh of missions in ever widening circl trying to increase existing knowled of missions and to deepen the int est in the missionary enterprise. Th literary work, year-book and supply the daily press with missionary ne have added greatly to the marvel growth of missions in the Germ empire during the last 20 years. From "Minneapolis Journal," Feb. 8,

PRAYER AND MISSIONS.

Dr. Warneck, the German author in Foreign Missions, in his pamph on "Prayer for Missions," says, "Pr er is a great power in the Kingdom God. In missions in particular, need the strengthening that is prayer. It is much more difficult pray for missions than to give to th The best school for the prayer life to carefully study the prayer life Jesus Christ and St Paul as far as insight into them is possible for ....As far as I can see there are principal points to be included in content of prayer for missions: m sionary workers; converts; those authority in mission fields; oppone of missions, and thanksgiving"

"The promise of the Father, "Ask me and I will give thee the heathen thine inheritance and the utterm parts of the earth for thy possessi (Ps 2, 8), was doubtless a dominat thought of our Lord when his disci asked him to teach them how to p and he taught them to say, "Our Fa er who art in heaven, Hallowed by name, Thy kingdom come. Thy be done, as in heaven, so on earth.

The Lutheran Part in Evangelizing the World

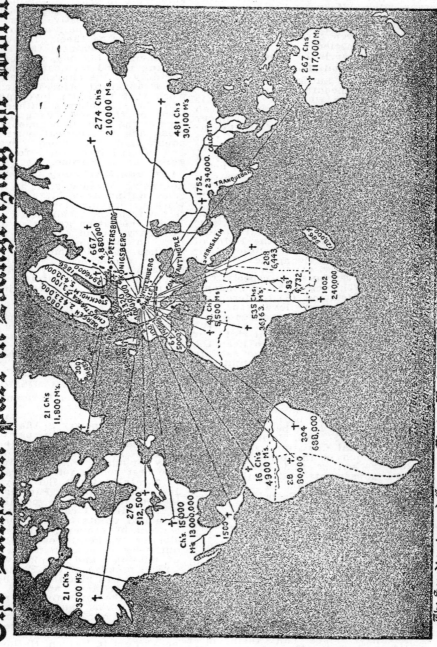

The Scandinavian and German Mission Work in the Old World. What will be Our Work in the New World?

The Unity of God's Teachings.

Right Faith in God and True Love to Our Neighbor.
As set forth in the Catechism and in this volume.

Ten Words of God to Man.

GOD'S COMMANDMENTS.[1]

First Table of the Law.

Our Love and Duty to God.

1. I am Jehovah thy God. Thou shalt have no other gods before me.

2. Thou shalt not take the name of Jehovah thy God in vain; for Jehovah will not hold him guiltless that taketh his name in vain.

3. Remember the Sabbath day to keep it holy. (Thou shalt sanctify the holy-day or rest-day.)

Second Table of the Law.

Our Love and Duty to Man.

4. Honor thy father and thy mother.

5. Thou shalt not kill.

6. Thou shalt not commit adultery.

7. Thou shalt not steal.

8. Thou shalt not bear false witness against thy neighbor.

9. Thou shalt not covet thy neighbor's house.

10. Thou shalt not covet anything that is thy neighbor's.

For I Jehovah thy God am a jealous God, visiting the iniquity of the fathers (etc).

Ten Words of Man in Reply.

THE APOSTLES' CREED.[2]

True Faith in the Triune God; Father, Son and Holy Spirit.

1. I believe in God the Father Almighty, maker of heaven and earth.

2. I believe in Jesus Christ my Lord (etc.), who came from heaven to reveal God's name to me by his teachings, death and resurrection.

3. I believe in the Holy Spirit (etc.), for whose work of applying Christ's redemption the holy-day has been set apart.

THE LORD'S PRAYER.[3]

Seven Petitions Christ Taught.

4. Our Father who art in heaven, hallowed be thy name.

5. Thy Kingdom (of grace and life) come.

6. Thy will (and not the will of the flesh) be done (in me).

7. Give us this day our daily bread. (Then we need not steal.)

8. And forgive us our debts, as we forgive our debtors.

9. And lead us not into temptation.

10. But deliver us from evil.

For thine is the kingdom and the power and the glory for ever and ever. Amen.

[1]"The Word of the Lord abideth for ever." 1 Peter 1, 25.

[2]"Thou art the Christ, the Son of the living God." Matt 16, 16.

[3]"God is a Spirit: and they that worship him must worship in spirit and truth." John 4, 24.

Meditate upon the relations of these words of God and of man to each other. God commands, man believes and prays. Luther says, "The Ten Commandments are the doctrine of doctrines, the Apostles' Creed the creed of creeds, and the Lord's Prayer the prayer of prayers. God the Father gave the Ten Commandments; Christ dictated the very words of the Lord's Prayer; and I believe the words of the Apostles' Creed to be inspired by the Holy Spirit." The Trinitarian is the only true conception of God. Here we have the will of the Father, the redemption of the Son and the work of the Holy Spirit. The Lord's Prayer repeats and includes the Commandments and the Creed in prayer. "Wherever the Holy Spirit is there is nothing but prayer." The first part of the Catechism awakens fear, the second love, the third trust. Try to obey, try to believe, try to pray.

WORLD-WIDE INFLUENCE OF LUTHER'S WRITINGS.
The Methodists and Presbyterians give their communicants, and the others rite he baptized members or adherents.

Country	Lutherans	Episcopalians	Methodists	Baptists	Presb'rians
Germany	37,800,000	11,139	15,450	30,669	....
Denmark ...	2,570,000	298	3,205	3,928	....
Norway	2,373,000	518	5,396	2,709	....
Sweden	5,340,000	340	15,646	42,011	....
Iceland	78,489	....	....	....	....
Faroe Isles...	15,230	....	....	....	....
Scandinavia ..	10,376,719	1,156	25,247	48,648	....
Russia	4,190,000	....	....	29,925	....
Finland	2,850,000	....	....	2,133	....
Poland	460,000	....	....	....	....
Europ'n Russia	7,500,000	....	....	32,058	....
Austria	420,000	2,169	....	8,549	....
Hungary	1,300,000	....	....	....	....
Roumania	20,000	416	....	317	....
Bulgaria	2,100	....	271	101	....
Turkey	3,000	1,518	....	....	....
Italy	25,000	7,230	3,602	1,481	....
Switzerland ...	150,000	2,812	7,912	834	....
Spain	5,000	4,771	339	265	....
Portugal	2,000	1,798	424	....	....
France	105,000	36,447	1,667	2,409	....
Belgium	25,000	3,789	....	....	....
Holland	100,000	480	....	1,182	....
British Isles....	272,500	16,000,000	886,083	377,747	1,498,947
Europe	58,106,319	16,071,725	937,995	504,260	1,498,947
Palestine	3,000	2,122	....	129	2,591
Asia Minor	4,000	....	....	....	....
Persia	2,980	296	....	....	2,844
Caucasia	46,000	....	....	....	....
Cent. Asia ..	7,100	....	....	....	....
Siberia	48,000	....	....	....	....
Asiatic Russia.	101,000	....	....	....	....
India	221,000	305,917	44,040	115,622	53,829
China	21,000	20,230	14,312	10,453	17,284
Japan	2,500	8,165	4,506	2,327	7,236
Asia	355,580	336,730	62,858	128,531	83,784
Algeria	5,000	....	....	....	....
Egypt	1,400	400	....	....	....
East Africa ...	2,245	2,290	62	....	710
South Africa..	221,644	110,234	95,162	3,897	11,323
West Africa ..	25,403	29,921	21,886	3,552	1,851
Cent. Africa...	3,874	38,844	236	3,391	....
Madagascar ...	125,000	19,500	....	....	....
Africa	384,566	211,189	117,346	10,840	13,884
Australia	117,000	1,221,366	131,225	17,240	55,000
Tasmania	1,000	76,300	....	772	....
New Zealand ..	12,757	253,331	....	3,721	26,000
Borneo	2,061	3,750	183	....	....
Sumatra	67,253	....	....	....	....
Phillipines	300	....	795	121	1,070
Oceanica	200,371	1,554,747	132,203	21,854	82,070
North'n S. Am.	7,000	20,000	....	....	....
Brazil, etc. ...	470,000	1,548	2,334	1,932	3,676
Argentine Rep.	85,000	....	....	100	....
West'n S. Am..	60,000	....	1,052	....	522
South America	622,000	21,548	3,386	2,032	4,198
Cent. America	1,000	3,000	1,737	846	41
Greenland	10,816	....	....	....	....
Canada	310,000	680,346	293,597	99,593	219,670
United States..	11,400,000	2,225,000	6,084,755	4,330,462	1,635,016
Mexico	1,000	17,000	2,879	1,314	3,902
West Indies ..	5,200	74,185	32,820	38,406	12,000
Alaska	3,000	....	....	50	1,222
North America	11,730,016	2,996,531	6,414,051	4,469,825	1,871,810
World	71,399,852	21,195,470	7,669,576	5,138,188	3,554,734

Date Due

BR 330 .E5 1903 8

Luther, Martin, 1483-1546.

The precious and sacred
 writings of Martin Luther .

ND - #0087 - 060223 - C0 - 229/152/19 [21] - CB - 9780484792974 - Gloss Lamination